Dangerous Hoops

A Forensic Marketing Action Adventure

DANGEROUS HOOPS

D. LARRY CRUMBLEY,
FRED H. CAMPBELL, THOMAS J. KARAM,
AND PETER A. MARESCO

LOUISIANA STATE UNIVERSITY
BATON ROUGE

Published by Louisiana State University Press
Copyright © 2011 by Louisiana State University Press

DESIGNER: Michelle A. Neustrom
TYPEFACE: Whitman
PRINTER AND BINDER: IBT Global

LIBRARY OF CONGRESS CATALOGING-IN-PUBLICATION DATA

Dangerous hoops : a forensic marketing action adventure / D. Larry Crumbley . . .
[et al.].
    p. cm.
    ISBN 978-0-8071-3911-0 (pbk. : alk. paper) — ISBN 978-0-8071-3912-7 (pdf) —
ISBN 978-0-8071-3913-4 (epub) — ISBN 978-0-8071-3914-1 (mobi) 1. Marketing. 2.
Basketball. I. Crumbley, D. Larry.
    HF5415.D26 2011
    658.8—dc22

                                                                      2011015405

The songs "I'm Thinking about You" and "Daddy's Going Guitar Pickin'"
are copyrighted by Robert H. Kelly.

Dedication to our grandchildren
Caleb, Dane, Daniel, Davis, Jacob, Ryan, and Sloane

Thou shall not kill.

—DEUTERONOMY 5:17

Preface

angerous Hoops is a supplementary text to be used near the end of a marketing course, at the beginning of the second marketing course, or a sports-marketing course to add excitement and entertainment. This educational novel would be ideal for an MBA program that has a light coverage of marketing. The novel could be used in a company's in-house training program or sports-marketing course.

Through the use of an educational novel, technical information can be presented in a way that facilitates learning and infuses enthusiasm. The use of an imaginative novel is an extension of the scenario approach. Students tend to relate to fictional characters in action-packed adventures. Today's students are accustomed to television and movies, and the video generation likes mental stimulation and verbal pictures to jog their memories, rather than gray pages of technical material alone. Proven aids in learning include the element of surprise when a learner encounters an unexpected phenomenon and the retention of a new concept that appears in a dramatic, unusual context.

This instructional novel mixes basketball, marketing, serial killers, sarin, and scuba diving to help students learn many sports-marketing principles. A Celtics vice-president of sales and an FBI agent work together to hunt a mass murderer who strikes at basketball games. Along with the marketing humor, a reader follows the exciting life of a sales executive for a professional basketball team, who is also a part-time marketing professor at Boston College.

Since the purpose of marketing is to make sales and the resulting profit, basketball franchises are used to illustrate many marketing concepts. Marketing environments, sponsorships, the 4 Ps, promotional mix, forensic marketing, bait-and-switch, branding, ambush marketing, and market segmentation are some of the topics covered. Learn about careers in sports marketing, consulting activities, courtroom testifying, the Lanham Act, marketing channels, developing advertising campaigns, personal selling, and push-and-pull strategies.

Dangerous Hoops will do for marketing what *The Goal* did for manufacturing. Students will learn that marketing majors are not merely salespeople. As Mark Cuban, the owner of the Dallas Mavericks said: "The NBA (National Basketball Association) is never just a business. It's always business. It's always personal. All good businesses are personal. The best businesses are very personal." A marketing person should adopt Elvin Hayes's goal: "I take the floor for every game confident that I can beat any man and determined to do so."

Please note that this novel is written based upon one season, and players do move and retire. For example, Elvin Hayes is now (2011) a member of the Houston Cougars' Men's Basketball Radio Broadcast Crew. Piston owner William Davis passed away March 13, 2009.

D. Larry Crumbley
Louisiana State University

Fred H. Campbell
University of North Carolina at Charlotte, retired

Thomas J. Karam
Louisiana State University

Peter A. Maresco
Sacred Heart University

Dangerous Hoops

Marketing is typically seen as the task of creating, promoting, and delivering goods and services to consumers and businesses. In fact, marketing people are involved in marketing ten types of entities: *goods, services, experiences, events, persons, places, properties, organizations, information, and ideas.*

—PHILIP KOTLER

anice was mad. Baseball management had given Sandy and her only $300,000. Chicken feed. She wanted the $4 million worth of diamonds that they had demanded. That FBI agent had killed her partner, Sandy, in Yankee Stadium. Luckily she had become scared and had left the stadium early. She read that 57 people had died from the sarin mist.

Janice had not known Sandy's real name, but she was able to get back to Denver before the FBI found his apartment. She removed all of her clothes, money, equipment, and disguises before wiping down his entire apartment. She stored all of the deadly chemicals that Sandy had accumulated. Apparently, the FBI did not know who had helped Sandy terrorize Major League Baseball. She left Denver and went to New Orleans, where she deposited most of the loot in two banks before flying to Miami. She then took Cayman Airways to Grand Cayman, and on to Cayman Brac.

For at least one week she planned to stay at Brac Reef Beach Resort. Advertised as a resort of unforgettable adventure, Brac Reef had been one of Sandy's and her alternative destinations after the diamond drop. They had read about the resort in *Scuba Diver Magazine.* You can dive two islands in one Cayman Island vacation. She liked scuba diving. She was most interested in diving the Bloody Bay Wall and the Russian Frigate Wreck site. The plunging walls surrounding Cayman Brac and Little Cayman are some of the most beautiful dive sites in the Caribbean.

Columbus first sighted the Caymans on May 10, 1503. The three Cayman Islands are the tops of a submerged mountain range. The Caymans have a form of democracy like the British system, but women could not vote until 1959. Income taxes or land taxes do not exist; neither do corporate-profit taxes, capital-gain taxes, or estate or death taxes. There are many British, Swiss, U.S., and Canadian banks in Grand Cayman. Janice set up a small bank account in Grand Cayman with some of the extortion money.

Cayman Brac lies 86 miles northeast of Grand Cayman, 5 miles east of Little Cayman, 480 miles south of Florida, 90 miles south of Havana, Cuba, and 175 miles northeast of Jamaica. Cayman Brac itself is only twelve miles long and about one mile wide, surrounded by beautiful blue water. With a population of about 2,000, the island is pollution-free and has little crime.

On her first day on Brac, Janice was so upset that she merely explored the island in a rental car. She took a breathtaking view of the island from a fully functioning lighthouse at the end of a nine-mile dirt road. She even climbed up the stairs within the lighthouse. She explored several of the so-called bat caves tucked into the limestone bluffs. She saw no bats in the caves or any indication that bats actually lived in the caves. False advertising for sure, if not just "puffery."

Cayman Brac takes its name from the Gaelic word *brac*, which translates to "bluff." The bluff or brac is about 140 feet tall. Along the walls of Brac's huge cliffs are petrified remains of fossilized corals and sea creatures. Supposedly the caves were once hiding places for pirates' treasures.

Janice had not received her pirate's treasure from baseball management. What should she do? Clearly, baseball would not pay. They knew she was not a terrorist group. She needed another sports group. Basketball, football, or hockey were possibilities. Football was outdoors, so basketball and hockey were better. Janice decided to take on basketball. Inside an enclosed arena more people could be killed. Getting the extortion money was the problem. The authorities already knew two ways she and Sandy had used to get extortion money. Was another approach necessary?

While pondering her next move, Janice walked along the white sandy beaches, where lush coconut palms and seagrape trees grew. She could hear the wind rustle through the palm fronds. She would have difficulty getting a job there. A residence card was necessary to work on the island, and open jobs had to be advertised for any island citizen first.

She had no alternative but to enjoy the week and get to a new location. She would not be able to be a dive master on Brac or possibly anywhere else, even though she was certified as a dive master. For her certification, she had to pass an open water, advanced open water, and rescue test before preparing and passing the dive master test itself. On Tuesday morning, the Twin Sister dive boat took Janice and a group of divers over to the first dive site Janice had been anticipating, the Bloody Bay Wall on Little Cayman. This wall is so named because a massacre of pirates by the British took place at Bloody Bay. There have been more than 325 known shipwrecks around the Cayman Islands. After the hour boat ride, the group dove at a site called Marilyn's Cut. The dive master said the name came from the fact that a female photographer was taking photos at the spot but cut her fingers on some corals. Her blood drew three reef sharks, and she had to hide in some caves—hence Marilyn's Cut. She eventually escaped.

Janice thought that this site was one of her best dives ever. On this one dive she saw a puffer fish, a nurse shark, a barracuda, several white file-fish, two turtles, three large lobsters, several stingrays, a number of school-masters' fish, and some trumpetfish. She was able to pet a friendly Nassau grouper. Her favorite was the juvenile French angelfish—black with color-ful yellow stripes and some blue.

The Wall itself was underwater magic. Gorgonian fans and bright-orange antler sponges clung to the face of the Bloody Bay Wall. Looking over the wall was like looking into the abyss; Janice could not see the bot-tom of the ocean over the sheer wall.

These plunging walls start as shallow as 20 feet and plummet to 6,000 feet. Scuba divers should not dive deeper than 110 feet, however. Janice saw 98 feet on her dive computer on her 41 minutes dive. Janice really did not like deep dives. The deeper a diver goes, the less time she can spend on the dive. Besides, the fish are more plentiful and beautiful at shallower dive sites.

On Wednesday morning at 8:00, the Twin Sister dive boat carried Janice and the other divers to the Russian Frigate dive site. The Russians do not name this class of ship, so it was given a number, # 356. Now called m/v Capt. Keith Tibbetts, this retired Cuban frigate is the only diveable Russian-built warship in the Western Hemisphere. Built in 1984, the Brigadier Type II Class Frigate was accomplished through a joint marketing effort of the Sister Islands government.

Located at the west end of the island, the frigate sits on the bottom about 900 yards offshore on the north side. It is about 315 feet long and about 68 feet in height. On the dive, Janice could see most areas of the ship, including the missile launcher, machine-gun turrets, fore- and aft-deck cannons, living quarters, bridge, and some machinery spaces. Janice floated down onto the deck of the Cuban frigate and tried to walk on the deck with her fins. It's hard to walk underwater with fins. She saw an eagle ray foraging for food in a sand bed surrounding the wreck near the stern. Then the Twin Sister returned to shore.

The unique feature of the Brac Reef Beach Resort is the number of messages painted on rocks, driftwood, boards, tree trunks, coconuts, and brain coral by previous divers. Janice walked around the resort area that evening reading the messages. "The Diving Elvis." "Skinny Dippers." "We Dive, Surge, Purge, 3-10-98." "No worries, no hassles, no luggage." "Over there and thru the chum, look out sharks, here we come." "Shaved Ape Divers." Janice liked "Had enough Flack; Put your stuff in a sack; Get back to Brac." There was even a "TAM, Gig 'em Ags!" maroon sign on a board. These messages were an excellent marketing/sales promotion feature of the resort.

Later that evening, Janice's depression began to lift. Six feet tall and physically talented, she could have made an excellent guard for a professional basketball team. But there were no profitable female basketball teams when she had graduated. There was, of course, the now-defunct Women's Professional Basketball League from 1978–81. But the Women's National Basketball Association only began on June 21, 1997, with the full backing of the men's National Basketball Association. The NBA gives an annual $12 million subsidy to the WNBA to cover operating costs, since the women's teams have only about half the attendance of the men's teams. There have been 17 professional women teams, and four of them no longer exist.

The real difference came down to salaries. A rookie female player's minimum salary was $5,880 (2011), whereas the men's minimum salary was $473,604 (2010–11). A WNBA player with three years of experience had her salary capped at $42,000. The WNBA players have to supplement their meager income by playing in the European and Australian leagues in the off-season. Janice knew it was tough running up and down a hardwood floor week after week for chicken feed. In contrast, the maximum WNBA salary was $103,500 (2010–11). In the 2006–07 season, the Minnesota

Timberwolves' Kevin Garnett's annual salary was $21 million and the Miami Heat's Shaquille O'Neal's annual salary was $20 million.

Plus there was outside income. Kevin Durant signed with the former Seattle Supersonics (now the Oklahoma City Thunder) in 2007 after one year at the University of Texas for a $4.17 million salary. But he immediately received a $60 million contract with Nike, to be spread over 7 years. The Cleveland Cavaliers' 18-year-old LeBron James had earlier received a $90 million, 7-year contract with Nike before he even set foot on a professional basketball court. Signing the unproven high-school senior was a risky endorsement deal for the $10 billion sneaker company. Reebok had offered $75 million.

Janice got really mad when she read a story in *Forbes* about the enormous salaries paid to the world's top-earning athletes. They were all males. She had read that the top earner, Tiger Woods, was paid $30 million annually by Nike. The top ten were as follows:

RANK	ATHLETE	AGE	EARNINGS
1	Tiger Woods (golf)	35	$105,000,000
2	Floyd Mayweather (boxing)	33	$65,000,000
3	Kobe Bryant (basketball)	32	$48,000,000
4	Phil Mickelson (golf)	40	$46,000,000
5	David Beckham (soccer)	35	$43,700,000
6	Roger Federer (tennis)	29	$43,000,000
7	LeBron James (basketball)	26	$42,800,000
8	Manny Pacquiao (boxing)	32	$42,000,000
9	Eli Manning (football)	29	$39,900,000
10	Terrell Suggs (football)	28	$38,300,000

She had decided what to do. She would go after professional basketball. She picked up Sandy's guitar and sung a corny song.

> Scuba Aruba, because you cannot live in Brac.
> After the full court press, she split because she's a brat.
> She left me with a mess;
> just like Michael Jordan,
> the judge gave her the full net.

Janice had been a part-time member of a five-person band during high school and some of her college days at the University of Georgia. Her group had even won a round on the Ed McMahon's *Star Search*. Her group, called the Divers, traveled around the southern states singing for high-school dances, fraternities, sororities, and several nightclubs in Athens, Georgia. They traveled around from city to city with a van and truck. The times were hard, and they made little money. As she became more successful on the basketball court, she had to curtail her singing activities. Her twin sister replaced her on many gigs. Janice was taller and a better singer than her sister.

On Thursday morning at a dive site called Cemetery Reef, one of the woman divers freaked out as she entered the water. She began to shout, "I can't see!" Her mask was fogged, and apparently she had put no air into her BCV vest. Putting sunscreen on your face is bad. The sunscreen will find its way to the lens, causing it to fog. Sunscreen can also cause the mask to leak. After someone cleaned her mask, the woman still panicked, shouting, "I can't see!" One of the dive masters jumped into the water and swam her back to the Little Sister.

At the end of the same dive, one of the older male divers swam to the wrong boat. Twin Sister and Little Sister had to move side by side, and they tossed his equipment to the proper boat. The diver then jumped into the water and swam to the proper boat.

Later that afternoon Janice put on her old green-and-purple Charlotte Hornets' ball cap and walked the beach, where she found a board and took it to the painting table at the resort. In the Channel Lounge she left a $15 deposit and received some red and white paint and paintbrushes. Janice painted the board red and then painted in white the following message, "N.Y. Knicks, the first!"

Janice finally had a good night's sleep, the best she had had since the FBI and baseball management cheated her out of the $4 million in diamonds. Janice dreamed about the Boston Celtics during the night. She was standing inside the Celtic's Fleet Center with a sign, "Basketball will pay; the Bulldog will get you."

On Friday morning the Twin Sister boat again went back to Little Cayman to dive the Bloody Bay Wall. The first dive, at Mixing Bowl, was a Viagra dive, bottoming out at 89 feet. On the second dive, at Joy's Joy, Janice noticed one diver using the secondary octopus of his buddy. She and her buddy followed them for some time, since apparently the diver had forgotten to check the amount of air in his tank before jumping into the water.

Since the diver had a used tank with little air, he was using his buddy's air. A diver is trained never to dive alone—always dive with a buddy.

After about 20 minutes into the dive, the partner gave up the secondary octopus to go back to his own air. Janice thought that the diver had lost the secondary life line, so she swam over immediately to offer the diver her secondary octopus. The diver shook her off, so Janice swam back to her partner. Moments later she saw the diver make a controlled but hasty ascent from about 35 feet. Later the diver told Janice that he could not find his main octopus, and when he went to his secondary yellow octopus, it would not work. Diving can be hazardous. If during the controlled ascent, the diver had not let air out as he went up, his lungs might have ruptured. Air expands inside your body as you move to the surface. Janice was reminded of some graffiti she had read in Utila, Honduras: "Remember when sex was safe and scuba diving was dangerous?"

The hour-long boat ride back to Brac was extremely bumpy, like a long bull ride. Janice tried to trade her Hornet's hat to Jason, the dive master, for his hat which said, H_2 Outrageous. He wouldn't trade.

Janice's dive master for most of her dives was excellent. Jason would always give a description of the dive area beforehand, and then he would say, "The pool's open, kids." Apples and oranges were available after each dive. On one occasion Jason had cut a cantaloupe for the divers. He said, "Eat some cantaloupe to get rid of your scuba mouth." After a long dive or two, there is a funny taste in your mouth.

Later that night Janice read in the *Caymanian Compass* that smallpox and anthrax are considered among the biggest potential biological weapons threats in the U.S. Both diseases incubate for several days to a week, which makes it hard to spot an outbreak even if doctors recognize early symptoms. Both can mimic the flu. Anthrax is treatable only if caught early, and only the military has a vaccine now. Americans are no longer vaccinated against smallpox, but about 8 million vaccine doses are stockpiled.

The only other single woman at the small resort was a young, chubby girl named Terri. Janice spent some time with Terri and helped her study for the advanced diving course. Talking to her about the Miami area brought Janice's divorced sister to mind. She lived in Key Largo, Florida, on a houseboat. Key Largo is known as the diving capital of the world. The city is sandwiched between the watery wilderness of the Everglades National Park to the west and the fish-covered coral formation of North America's only coral reef to the east. Janice now knew how to safely get the extortion diamonds from the National Basketball Association. Key Largo was important, for the drop would require excellent navigational skills. She needed a partner. Would her twin sister, Wanda W. Wallace, help her? Janice nicknamed her twin sister W cubed—W^3. Wanda, also a diver, owned a dive shop. After her week's stay in Cayman Brac, Janice flew back to Miami, bought a used car, and drove to see her sister.

For a month Janice helped her sister with her scuba-diving shop, but she also spent some time exploring the Everglades. Janice basically took over as the shop's marketing manager. She had majored in marketing at the University of Georgia, and upon graduating had been a sales representative and purchasing agent for two employers. She could sell anything. A lot of scuba business is now done over the Internet. Her sister had a primitive website, but Janice knew that in the future a strong Internet site was necessary for a scuba shop. Web sites are a 24-hour-a-day public-relations and advertising agent. If a business becomes a Yahoo! "Daily Pick," thousands of visitors come to the site. A scuba shop also has to worry about complaints on the Internet and correct them fast. Often it is far cheaper and generally less time-consuming to complain online than to write a letter. Negative goodwill is deadly for a business. Janice hoped to give the NBA some horrendous negative goodwill. In her spare time she was able to research the history of the NBA, especially an old player called "Big E," Elvin Hayes. Big E, the basketball power forward, had been named after the Navy's aircraft carrier, the U.S.S. *Enterprise* (also called the Big E).

Janice needed a scuba C-card with a name other than her own. One cannot dive without a C-card, which has a photo of the diver. There are several agencies that certify scuba divers. The Professional Association of Diving Instructors (PADI) is the largest certifying agency, with more than 5,300 PADI Dive Centers and Resorts in approximately 180 countries. The National Association of Underwater Instructors (NAUI) and Scuba School International (SSI) are two other certifying agencies. Janice spent three weeks passing the open-water tests. She had to be careful to pretend that she knew little about diving. She got a new PADI C-card under the name of Shirlee Ann Kelly. That had been her performing name with the Divers.

As she was driving back from getting her new Florida driver's license under the same name, she began to hum one of Sandy's old songs:

The girl in the band's named Shirlee Ann . . . and she's a tall pretty girl singer.
She sings the best of the country songs . . . with a voice that's sweet and tender.
The country sounds are still around . . . and tonight nothing will be missing.
Mama, get ready. You're gonna have fun while daddy's going guitar pickin'.

Mama don't fix no supper tonight . . . 'cause daddy's going guitar pickin'.
We'll grab a bite at the corner café . . . 'cause I'm tired of sitting and listening.
We'll sing and dance and have a lotta fun . . . and tonight nothing will be missing.
Mama don't fix no supper tonight . . . 'cause daddy's going guitar pickin'.

But would her sister help her with the extortion plan? She still needed to get the rebreather that Sandy had stored after the last failed extortion drop. A rebreather allows you to dive without making a lot of bubbles. For her schemes, there could be no telltale bubbles. After working with her sister for several months in Key Largo, Janice decided not to ask her to help go after basketball. Her sister was too happy with her new boyfriend. Besides, the fewer people who knew about her plot, the better. She would do it alone.

She used some of the money that Sandy had gotten from baseball and bought a used RV without telling her sister. She parked the RV in Homestead, Florida. Her plans would require her to move around the U.S. without planes or trains.

One morning she left her sister's house leaving a cute note that said, "Goodbye, sister. I love you." She drove north to Denver and retrieved Sandy's RV and motorcycle. She moved the stored items into the RV and sold her car, but kept the motorcycle with saddlebags on the back. She drove back toward the Keys. In Homestead, Florida, she transferred her equipment to the newer RV and sold Sandy's RV. The retrieved equipment included diving guns, underwater scooter, boxes of disguises, an underwater GPS device, base stations, a diving computer, rubber hoses, and some bottles of poison. She was very careful with the poison.

Next she drove slowly south to Marathon, Florida, checking out the various bridges and mile markers along the U.S. Route 1. Marathon is a 10-mile city at the midpoint of the Florida Keys island chain. Along the way she noticed some oleander bushes. Sandy had taught her that both the leaves and branches of the oleander bush were extremely poisonous.

In Marathon she parked her RV at a RV park to begin a new life close to the beach. For about three weeks she practiced with the rebreather, the underwater scooter, and the GPS device. In the typical open-circuit scuba, her entire breath was expelled into the surrounding water, thus using only about 25 percent of the oxygen. A rebreather does not discharge the waste, but recovers it for use by adding oxygen to replace that which was used. The rebreather made fewer bubbles and made less noise than an open-circuit scuba.

She found that the GPS device did not work underwater, since the radio signals upon which it depends cannot pass through water. So she had to tether a base station at a certain depth.

Shirlee Ann was slowly getting used to her new name. In the evening while she was studying she would repeat her new name, Shirlee Ann, over and over. She studied the history of basketball and the various stadiums where the professional teams played. She read the book *Basketball Arenas* by Thomas S. Owens and checked out the ballparks.com Internet site. It was not fun studying, but she had to be prepared.

She was trying to become an expert in poisons and diamonds. The poisons were the problem. She really did not wish to kill anyone; she only wanted to make them sick. But Sandy had not labeled the poisons in the fingernail polish–remover bottles well. She was flying by the seat of her pants. Before Sandy had died, he had explained to her why diamonds were important. Think about how large a package of $4 million in $100 bills would be. Plus the victim will keep the serial numbers on all the bills, so you cannot pass them. A package of $4 million in diamonds is much smaller. There are no serial numbers. They cannot put an ink bomb in it. You can sell a few diamonds at any time in any country in the world.

Early in the morning and before the sun set, she made some trips on her motorcycle up and down U.S. Route 1. She had to practice slowly on the motorcycle. She had read that former Chicago Bulls guard Jay Williams, Pittsburgh Steelers quarterback Ben Roethlisberger, and Cleveland Browns tight end Kellen Winslow had had bad accidents on motorcycles. She always wore a helmet, non-slip durable gloves, protective leather pants, a long-sleeved leather jacket, and leather boots.

One-sized motorcycles do not fit all, but surprisingly she could reach the ground with both feet when sitting on the motorcycle. She could reach the controls as well. She tried to drive defensively at all times, because she felt that a biker has little protection against a two-ton pickup truck.

To the north of Marathon is Duck Key, which is on the ocean side of U.S. Route 1 at mile marker 61. The two mile–long island is connected to the highway by a causeway built in 1953. About 450 people live on the low, rocky island between Conch Key and Grassey Key. When she read that salt was mined there at one time, Shirlee Ann began to scuba around the island. One afternoon around 4:00 she discovered an underwater cave on the Route 1 side of Duck Key. The underwater cave went for about 20 feet and opened into a small, underground cavern. The air was fresh in the cavern, and from the appearance of it no one had found the cavern before. Perhaps over the years the ocean water had slowly eaten out a vein of salt. In any case, she now knew how to safely get the extortion payment from professional basketball.

She was smiling as the Sea Doo Seascooter propelled her 14 feet underwater back to her RV home at Marathon. The dive-propulsion vehicle could reach a maximum speed of 3 MPH, down to 100 feet. The rechargeable battery had a life of one and a half hours and weighed only 18 pounds in its Cordura carry bag.

For the next two days she tethered several base stations at an appropriate depth along the route that she would take from U.S. Route 1 to the underground cavern. She practiced, practiced, and practiced. What was the saying about valuable real estate? Location, location, and location. She was equipped with a device that emitted a sonar request pulse to the base station. When the base station picked up the pulse, the station replied with its own signal giving the diver's device information, which allowed the diver to pinpoint his or her exact location. Sometimes she made the run only with her dive-computer compass, just in case the GPS device did not work.

Her wristwatch dive computer was essential each time she went diving. Since a person cannot breathe underwater, she had to take breathing gas with her. Without oxygen, one dies. With too much oxygen, serious physiological problems occur. So oxygen is mixed with nitrogen and helium. But underwater there is pressure that causes some of the gases to dissolve in her tissues. The dive computer measured the depth and time of her dive and calculated the safe ascent rate and displayed it. Otherwise she would get decompression sickness if she ascended too quickly because of the nitrogen bubbles in her blood and body tissues. She did not wish to get the bends.

She wanted to buy a new Aeris Elite T3 dive computer. This wrist-watch scuba computer did it all. A wireless, air-integrated computer, it could track three different gas mixes. The digits were bigger, the bar graphs bolder, and everything she needed was displayed on the main screen. A fine product.

On the third day she went to Duck Key and got a job as a waitress at the Hawk Cay Resort. She would work in the Palm Terrace during the day and the Water's Edge restaurant in the evenings. Duck Key is comprised of five islands joined by Venetian-style bridges. Hawk Cay Resort makes up one of five islands on about 60 acres. Shirlee Ann learned that Arnold Schwarzenegger stayed there when filming *True Lies*. Ironic, she thought.

The Evolution of Marketing

During the twentieth century, marketing evolved to where it is now the driving force in the business organization. This evolution of the role of the marketing function within the firm is shown below.

Production Orientation: This philosophy emphasized the role of production or operations within the firm. With excess demand, companies had a ready market for their product and as a result were oriented toward quality and efficiency of production. A classic example is Henry Ford's production of the automobile. His assembly lines produced any Ford the market wanted as long as it was a black Model T.

Sales Orientation: As companies began to get more efficient in their production and as competitors began to enter the market, there arose a surplus of supply. No longer was it sufficient to "produce, produce, produce." The firm became sales or personal selling oriented. "Get out there and sell as much as you can to as many customers as you can." Selling, rather than production, became the driving force.

Marketing Orientation: After World War II, military veterans began returning home and taking advantage of the GI Bill. The marketplace became better informed through better education and the advent of mass-media advertising, particularly in the form of television. The customer, with better information, demanded more from the seller. As a result, firms began to focus on the wants and needs of the customer. This orientation, which says the firm's social and economic reason for being is to satisfy the customer's wants and needs while meeting organizational objectives, has become known as the *Marketing Concept.*

Societal Marketing Orientation: This philosophy takes the firm's orientation beyond merely satisfying the wants and needs of the customer and the economic needs of the firm. It offers the idea that the firm exists to enhance the long-term best interests of individuals and society. It furthers the concepts of recycling, corporate philanthropy, safer products, and generally combining the environmental interests of society with that of the firm.

N o one noticed the nondescript woman wearing a baseball hat and sunglasses standing near the bathroom, watching people entering and exiting. She was pretending to be reading a *Slam Magazine,* which had been given free to attendees. After observing for a while she entered the restroom to check out the killing site.

The restroom was currently empty, so she entered two separate stalls. In each stall she shook out a basketball card from a sandwich bag, being careful not to touch the cards. She was wearing thin medical gloves. She entered the third stall and carefully removed her gloves and placed them inside another plastic bag. She placed the plastic bag inside her gym bag. She exited the bathroom and went back to the basketball celebration.

* * * *

The Trenton YMCA, just off of Trenton Freeway, was celebrating the 150th anniversary of the Greater Trenton area YMCA. There was live entertainment and a historical reenactment of the first professional basketball game. The gym was decked out with 30-foot rope netting walls around the basketball court, similar to the first known professional basketball game in 1896 in a Masonic Hall in Trenton, N.J. Although the then-Trenton basketball team normally played at the YMCA, another sporting event had forced them to the alternate Masonic Hall. So the Trenton players rented the hall, charged admission, and agreed to share the profits.

The turnout was sizeable, and the gate receipts exceeded the rent. So at the first known professional basketball game, each player received $15. The one dollar left over after the split went to Fred Cooper, the team captain. Thus, Fred Cooper became the highest paid professional player at $16.

Before the game, the organizer of the reenactment game, George Duncan, walked into the middle of the gym floor. He welcomed the crowd and introduced the main speaker, Ben Osborne, the online editor of *Slam Magazine*, a basketball magazine launched in 1994 with a hip-hop flavor.

Ben Osborne began his speech first by rolling a funny looking ball down the gym floor toward the Trenton team. The court for today's match was only 65 feet long and 35 feet wide, or roughly two-thirds the size of a regulation NBA court. As instructed beforehand, the captain of the Trenton basketball team picked up the primitive, brownish-color leather ball with laces along one side. The ball was larger than today's molded basketball and looked like a round football. The captain was dressed in long tights and velvet shorts.

"Welcome, everyone, to our celebration of the 150th anniversary of the YMCA in Trenton." Osborne moved the microphone closer. "For some of the visitors from outside Trenton, let me relay some historical facts that I found about Trenton on the Internet. Trenton was chartered as a city in 1792, and it had an ordinance that authorized the hiring of one marshal. According to the Trenton Police Museum online, this ordinance required the marshal to carry in his hand a small staff, or wand, similar to those usually carried by a sheriff. He was to walk through the different parts of the city at least once a week hunting for idle and disorderly persons. Also, he had to enforce the laws relative to the prevention of swine running at large, which was against the dignity and peace of the community.

"Did you know that Trenton served briefly as the United States capitol in 1784 and 1799?" Osborne raised his right arm, "O.K., enough about Trenton. Most of you are here to see our Trenton basketball team take on this fine team from Herkimer, New York.

"You may be asking, 'Why Herkimer?' Herkimer is a small village of about 7,500 people located halfway between Syracuse and Albany. This year is Herkimer's bicentennial, and we have a strong basketball team from Herkimer County Community College to take on your Trenton squad. Stand up, fellows." Osborne pointed to the Herkimer team.

Nine young students stood up. They were wearing black, long-sleeved wool jerseys and long gray trousers.

"Give them a hand. They are wearing uniforms like those worn in the late 1800s and early 1900s. Of course, we could find no shoes like those worn back then." There was some applause.

"Now stand up, Murphy Cuneo. Professor Cuneo teaches marketing at the community college, and he recruited the Herkimer team. He is also the chairman of the trustees of the Frank J. Basloe Free Library in Herkimer. There is an Irving M. Basloe Genealogy Room in the library. Frank Basloe, 1887–1966, was a professional player and coach of the Herkimer team, which toured the U.S. from 1903 to 1923. *The History of Jews in Basketball* says that basketball 'was ideally suited to the crowded urban areas where most of the nation's Jewish population lived. Jewish settlement houses on New York's East Side and Chicago's West Side gave Jewish youth their first opportunity to play the game and set many players on their way to stardom. Paul "Twister" Steinberg was an early Jewish professional player.'

"But I digress. Your organizers of this reenactment game picked Herkimer because there is some indication that the first professional basketball game might have been played at an 1893 event in Herkimer. Apparently, a group of basketball enthusiasts rented the Fox Opera House and played a team from Utica, sharing the proceeds. But the official *NBA Basketball Encyclopedia* states that the first game here in Trenton is better documented.

"Now, just as there were no swine running around outside when you arrived, there are a few other differences between tonight's game and the one played in the late 1880s. To help explain these differences, it is an extraordinary pleasure for me to introduce Ian Naismith, the grandson of the inventor of basketball, James Sherman Naismith. He will show us the 13 original rules of basketball as written by his grandfather. Come on out here, Ian.

"While he is walking out here, let me remind you that you can purchase a high-quality, embossed color copy of the history of these 13 rules in a sturdy basketball grain folder with Ian Naismith's signature for $25 plus shipping, with all proceeds going to Ian's nonprofit Naismith International Basketball Foundation. Ian's purpose for the NIBF is to restore sportsmanship to basketball, especially in regard to his grandfather's fifth rule: 'No shouldering, holding, pushing, tripping, or striking. . . .'

Ian Naismith took the microphone. "Thank you very much, Mr. Osborne. I am very happy to be here and help restore sportsmanship to professional basketball. I did not get to meet my grandfather, Dr. James A. Naismith, because I was only a year old when he died.

"My grandfather was born in 1861 in Almonte, Ontario, Canada. He went to work at a lumberyard and in surrounding farms at age 10. He dropped out of high school at age 15, but went back and got his college diploma at age 22. My grandfather had been a captain of the McGill University rugby team. Upon graduating from McGill after studying to be a Presbyterian minister, he accepted a position as an instructor at the YMCA Training School in Springfield, Massachusetts. His job was to train instructors for YMCAs.

"When he was 30, his boss, Superintendent Luther H. Gulick, challenged him to invent a winter sport that could be played indoors. He later said that boys would not play 'Drop the Handkerchief.' During the next two weeks he invented basketball, based upon the childhood game 'Duck on a Rock.' This game requires each person to rush and find a rock. The last person to find a rock must place his rock on a larger rock or stump, becoming a guard. The other kids then throw their rocks, trying to knock off the guard's rock. If they throw their rock and miss, they must retrieve their rock without being tagged. If a player is tagged, he becomes the guard.

"Mrs. Lyons typed up his 13 rules, and he asked the YMCA janitor to find two 18-inch boxes to put at both ends of the gym floor. The janitor could not find two boxes but gave him two peach baskets. He nailed them 10 feet up on a balcony railing on opposite ends of the gym and posted two copies of his 13 typed rules on the bulletin board. At 11:30 on Friday, December 21, 1891, he divided 18 students into two teams of nine, and they played basketball with a soccer ball for the first time. Their goal was to toss the soccer ball into the opposite peach basket. A William R. Chase made the only basket.

"Apparently after this first game the rules disappeared from the bulletin board. One of the players, Frank Mahn, a southerner, later told my grandfather that he removed the rules as a souvenir because the game was going to be a success. After the Christmas break, my grandfather joked to his students that the name Naismith ball would ruin the game. Mahn suggested Basket Ball—two words. My grandfather loved the name and wrote on top of his rules 'Basket Ball.' But can you imagine the game if the janitor, Mr. Stebbins, had found two boxes? Box ball or Naismith ball?" There was some laughter from the audience.

"The game did spread around the world through the global YMCA network—to China by 1893. The University of Chicago played its first college basketball game in 1894, defeating the Chicago YMCA Training School, 19–11. Within two years a Rhode Island company, Narragansett Machine, began producing a strong, iron, indoor basketball hoop. My granddad introduced the game of basketball to the 1936 Olympics in Berlin. In 1939, the University of Oregon beat Ohio State University, 46–33, in the first Men's College Basketball Championship.

"My grandfather kept a copy of the rules folded in his desk for the next 35 years. In 1939, he gave the original rules to his son, James Sherman Naismith, who kept them in a safe-deposit box for much of the next 41 years. By the way, these original rules were loaned to the Naismith Memorial Basketball Hall of Fame in Springfield in 1969, but they remained in storage, never to be displayed. I reclaimed the rules from the museum. I sold the original rules to the Smithsonian for $5 million, and they plan to put the rules on permanent display. The proceeds went to my nonprofit NIBF.

"Would you please dim the lights? Now, don't leave on me. The first couple of slides are copies of his handwritten manuscript, detailing the first basketball game. You probably cannot read his notes. But a handwritten copy of his manuscript was sold by Heritage Auction Galleries on December 7, 2006, for $71,700.

"The next slide shows the 13 rules. They were published in 1892 in the Springfield College newspaper, *The Triangle*.

"Oh, sorry, these are the original players. Notice that only one basket was made, by William R. Chase."

THE ORIGINAL PLAYERS

William H. Davis
Eugene S. Libby

John G. Thompson

George R. Weller

Wilbert F. Carey

Ernest O. Hildner

Lyman W. Archibald

T. Duncan Patton

Finley G. MacDonald

Raymond P. Kaighn

Genezabaro Z. Ishilkawo

Franklyn E. Barnes

Edwin P. Ruggles

Frank Mahn

William R. Chase*

Benjamin S. French

George E. Day

Henri Gelan

Made the only basket.

"OK, here are the 13 rules."

DR. JAMES NAISMITH'S ORIGINAL 13 RULES

The object of the game is to put the ball into your opponent's goal. This may be done by throwing the ball from any part of the grounds, with one or both hands, under the following conditions and rules.

1. The ball may be thrown in any direction with one or both hands.

2. The ball may be batted in any direction with one or both hands (never with the fist).

3. A player cannot run with the ball. The player must throw it from the spot on which he catches it. Allowances will be made for a man who catches the ball while running if he tries to stop.

4. The ball must be held by the hands. The arms or body must not be used for holding the ball.

5. No shouldering, holding, pushing, tripping, or striking in any way the person of an opponent shall be allowed; the first infringement of this

rule by any player shall count as a foul, the second shall disqualify him until the next goal is made. If there was evident intent to injure the person, for the whole game, no substitution allowed.

6. A foul is striking the ball with the fist, violation of Rules 3, 4, and such as described in Rule 5.

7. If either side makes three consecutive fouls it shall count as a goal for the opponent (consecutive means without the opponent making a basket in the meantime).

8. A goal shall be made when the ball is thrown or batted from the grounds into the basket and stays there, providing those defending the goal do not touch or disturb the goal. If the ball rests on the edges, and the opponent moves the basket, it shall count as a goal.

9. When the ball goes out of bounds, it shall be thrown into the field of play by the person first touching it. He has the right to hold it unmolested for 5 seconds. In case of a dispute the umpire shall throw it straight into the field. The thrower-in is allowed 5 seconds; if he holds it longer it shall go to the opponent. If any side persists in delaying the game, the umpire shall call a foul on that side.

10. The umpire shall be the judge of the men and shall note the fouls and notify the referee when three consecutive fouls have been committed. He shall have the power to disqualify men according to Rule 5.

11. The referee shall be judge of the ball, and shall decide when the ball is in play, in bounds, to which side the ball belongs, and shall keep the time. He shall decide when a goal has been made and keep account of the goals with any other duties that are permitted by the referee.

12. The time shall be two 15-minute halves with 5 minutes' rest between.

13. The side making the most goals in that time shall be declared the winner. In case of a draw game the game may, by agreement of the captains, be continued until another goal is made.

"Please read Rules 3 and 5 closely. My granddad believed in sportsmanship at all times. Does anyone know why the University of Kansas is noted for their successful basketball teams? In 1898, he became a combination school pastor and athletic director at KU, staying there 41 years. He was a lifetime student, however, obtaining four doctorate degrees.

"On October 10, 1961, the post office issued a 4¢ stamp honoring basketball and my grandfather. On September 3, 1991, another stamp was issued honoring basketball's 100th anniversary, a 29¢ Basketball Centennial. Another basketball stamp was issued on May 10, 2000, honoring basketball and Youth Team Sports, a 33¢ one.

"Now before we turn the lights back up, let me show you a Canadian 60-second television vignette about my grandfather's first game. During the vignette, one of the students says 'Is this some kind of Canadian joke?' In order to retrieve the soccer ball, the janitor saws a hole in the bottom of the wooden half-bushel peach basket and a broom handle is used to knock out the soccer ball.

"You'll notice that there is rope netting around the court, which is about two-thirds the size of a normal court. Let me read from a September 28, 1997, article on Hooptown, USA. The title of the article is 'On a Wintery WMass Night, Basketball Was Born.' I quote:

> Those early contests were brutal and often bloody. Players slammed into one another with reckless abandon, often causing brawls. These games were so intense that wire cages were built around the court to prevent the violence from spilling into the crowd.
>
> The wire cages also protected the players from the fans, some of whom were known to throw bottles and nails to the court. The atmosphere was so raucous that the refs often carried guns to keep the game and the crowd under control. Hitting a player with a technical foul just didn't do the trick in basketball's early days. End of quote.

"Some people still call basketball players 'cagers.'

"So my grandfather invented a game to be played in Young Men Christian Organizations. Yet its early history is not pretty. Wire backboards were added in 1893 to keep spectators from interfering with the flight of the ball. Wooden backboards became mandatory in 1904.

"The cage did speed up the game because the ball would deflect off the chicken wire, metal, or rope netting onto the court. Let me read another paragraph from the *Official NBA Basketball Encyclopedia*. I quote:

> Meanwhile, some "fans" amused themselves by jabbing hatpins and lighted cigarettes through the cages at the players' legs. In tough Pennsyl-

vania coal towns, miners favored nails, which they would heat with mining lamps and throw in the direction of the referee or the opposing free-throw shooter. As if that wasn't enough, players frequently had to contend with floors that had been highly waxed—in anticipation of the social dances often held in conjunction with the games. End of quote.

"Let me give one more illustration of the early years provided by Robert W. Peterson in his book entitled *Cages to Jump Shots: Pro Basketball's Early Years*. I quote:

> In the cage, it was common practice if the man with the ball was near the net, you would grab the net on both sides of him and press him into the net so he couldn't pass the ball, and they'd have a jump ball. Otherwise, the cage didn't make much difference in how the game was played.
>
> We only had one official. There was an awful lot of picking off—blocking. The official couldn't cover everything, and when he had his back to you there were a lot of pick-offs—that kind of roughness. And when your man went in to the basket, you'd take him into the net pretty hard. End of quote.

"As you can see, we do not have a chicken-wire cage and no peach baskets. Our players will not be tossed against the wire, and hopefully there will not be blood all over the floor. Remember there is no dribbling, no boundary lines, and no free throws. If a team commits three consecutive fouls, the other team gets one point. There will be two fifteen-minute halves with five minutes' rest between. For safety reasons, we will use six players per team rather than my grandfather's nine per team. We have two referees rather than one. So, audience, please behave, and let us begin the game of Basket Ball—two words, of course."

The subsequent game was mostly a comedy of errors as the players would forget and dribble the strange ball, or else start to dribble, stop themselves, and fall. There was much laughter as the players tried to pass or bat the ball with an open hand. The players could not figure out how the ball would rebound off the rope cage.

There was so much pushing and pulling on the floor that Murphy Cuneo thought about the push-and-pull strategies affecting a company's promotional mix. The promotional mix is the developed part of the promotion piece of the marketing mix. It involves several techniques: advertising, personal selling, public relations, and sales promotion.

Under the push strategy a wholesaler tries to push merchandise forward by persuading a retailer to handle the goods. Consumers will see the merchandise and purchase it. In contrast, under a pull strategy, a company focuses its promotional efforts on the end consumers. As demand for the goods confronts the retailer, the retailer will pull the goods from the manufacturer.

One of the Trenton players ran down the court, tapping the ball over his head. Initially one referee called this player with a foul, but after conferring with the other referee and umpire, the foul was removed. Other players tried this technique without success because of their lack of practice beforehand. There were more fouls than points, and two players were ejected. Trenton beat Herkimer 11 to 9. Three of the total points were from fouls. Will Simmen, the overhead dribbler, had four points and was the Most Valuable Player. He admitted to researching the history of the game.

* * * *

At the end of the game, Murphy Cuneo had to go to the bathroom before driving back to his hotel. When he got close to the bathrooms he noticed yellow crime scene tape with the words "Do Not Cross" around the bathrooms. "Horsefeathers," he mumbled. He needed to use the bathroom. He saw three uniformed policemen standing around. One of them said, "Sorry sir, you'll have to use the restroom downstairs. These are closed."

"What's the problem?" Cuneo asked.

"There's been an accident, sir."

Rather than leaving completely, Cuneo moved down the hall a short distance and waited. Several other people were directed by the policeman to go to the other restroom. Eventually he saw a gurney with a body on it being rolled out of the women's restroom. The individual was not moving. Then he saw an empty gurney being pushed into the same bathroom. After about three minutes, a second gurney with another inert body was pushed out of the restroom. Following the gurney was a man dressed in a suit. The man talked briefly to one of the policemen, glanced around and saw Cuneo, but turned back toward the bathroom door as a photographer exited it, followed by a female CSI personnel. The CSI person was carrying several brown paper bags.

Cuneo took out his Blackberry and emailed the head librarian in Herkimer and asked her to collect any newspaper items about the recent deaths at the Herkimer bicentennial celebration. The CSI person spoke to the suited man. "Detective Wales, the photographing and sketching is complete. They are both dead. Funny, I found two basketball cards near the bodies, which I have taken to be processed. I'll get you the results of the autopsies tomorrow. There did not appear to be foul play. No cuts. No bruises."

"Wait a minute," Detective Wales said. "Two dead bodies in one women's bathroom. Give me a break. Rush this. By noon."

"I'll try. How's your wife and kids?"

"Same as usual. Spending me to the poor house."

"Hey, you married her." The CSI woman winked at the detective and walked away.

The detective followed her with his eyes and then spoke softly to the nearest policeman. The policeman immediately turned and walked quickly toward Cuneo. She had her right hand resting on her gun.

"Sir," pointing at Cuneo, "Would you walk this way? Detective Wales wants to talk to you."

"Sure." Cuneo put his hands in front of his body, palms up, and walked toward the detective.

"Do you know these people?" Detective Wales asked.

"No, if you are referring to the two bodies I saw rolled out of the restroom. I'm in town by myself."

"Why are you here? Did the officer not tell you to go to the other bathrooms?"

"Yes, she did. But I was curious about the police tape," Cuneo said.

"Why? Why are you in town by yourself?"

"The reenactment basketball game just finished, and I recruited the visiting team who played tonight. I teach at Herkimer County Community College," Cuneo responded quickly. "We lost."

"Why are you hanging around here? What do you teach?"

"Marketing. I also own a sports business in Herkimer."

"Hey, I like that *Numb3rs* show. Can't understand some of it. So?" The detective raised his voice.

Cuneo shrugged and said, "So what?"

"Why are you hanging around?"

"Probabilities," Cuneo answered.

"Probabilities?" Detective Wales looked confused. "What do you mean? What do you know about these accidents?"

"Well, two months ago we—uh, Herkimer—celebrated our bicentennial. Although many people believe that the first known professional basketball game was played in Trenton, some historians believe the first professional basketball game was played in Herkimer."

The detective broke in, "What's the connection? Please."

"Well, that evening at the celebration three people died. The newspaper blamed it on food poisoning. Too much of a coincidence, I believe. Suspect all coincidences. Was this food poisoning?" Cuneo asked.

"I don't know. Were the three people in Hicker female?"

"Herkimer. Yes. I emailed someone at our library for newspaper reports about the deaths. But the library is closed now."

"Probabilities. Coincidences. Food poison." The detective scratched his mustache. "Where is Herkimer?"

"Central New York," Cuneo answered. "Equal distance between Albany and Syracuse."

"I'm Detective Mel Wales. Here is my card. I need your name, address. Everything. Do you have a business card?"

"Sure." Professor Cuneo reached into his shirt pocket and handed the detective his card.

"Will you be in town tomorrow?"

"No. I leave to go back to Herkimer early in the morning. I'll fax you information about our similar deaths."

"Thanks, Professor." The detective turned and walked back to the other officers.

Cuneo just nodded. There was nothing else to say. He hurried to find another bathroom.

Detective Wales told an officer to follow the professor to his hotel room. "Check with the hotel desk and get his address. Make sure he is a professor from Herkimer."

No mention was made of the two deaths in the Sunday *Trenton Times*'s write-up about the reenactment basketball game on Saturday night. Instead the reporter talked about the difficulty the players had with the old rules.

Before the reenactment basketball game Saturday, at the Trenton YMCA, Ian Naismith spoke to the group about bringing civility back to the sport of basketball. Mr. Naismith, of course, is the grandson of the inventor of basketball, Dr. James A. Naismith. Dr. Naismith, a Canadian, invented the sport in 1891 at a YMCA Training School in Springfield, Massachusetts, to occupy students during the cold winter months.

The grandson showed the crowd outside the roped cage the 13 original rules his grandfather developed. In basketball's early days, the smaller court was surrounded by chicken wire to keep the audience from hurting the players.

In a low-scoring game with no dribbling allowed, a group of Trenton players beat a team from Herkimer, N.Y., by the football score of 11 to 9. Many historians believe that the first professional basketball game was played in Trenton in 1896. Some argue that the first game was played at an event in Herkimer in 1893.

Whichever historian is believed, last night's game was a comedy of errors as the players tried to advance the ball down the court without dribbling. They could never get the hang of the ball bouncing off the rope netting around the court, which kept the ball on the court at all times. The audience had a great time, and they did not throw hot nails or other objects at the players. Will Simmen, an overhead dribbler, scored 4 points and was voted the Most Valuable Player. I do not believe this will be an annual event. Maybe 100 years from now.

Push-Pull Strategies

To encourage channel intermediaries (middlemen), such as wholesalers or retailers, to carry products and/or promote products, producers *push* the product down the marketing channel to the ultimate customer. This process can be in the form of personal selling, sales promotion activities, or even trade advertising. In contrast, producers often advertise directly to the intermediary's customer. The purpose is to get the customer to ask for the product from the middleman, thus "pulling" the product through the channel. A great example of *pull* strategy is the TV and magazine advertising for drugs that can only be prescribed by physicians. The pharmaceutical companies employing this strategy are hoping the patient (the ultimate customer) will ask the doctor if that product is appropriate for his or her illness.

Make your product easier to buy than your competition, or you will find your customers buying from them, not you.

—MARK CUBAN

On Sunday, Detective Mel Wales checked with the police officer who followed the professor to his hotel room. The fellow had used the name "Murphy Cuneo" at his hotel.

Detective Wales plugged the name into Google and found that Murphy Cuneo was a trustee for the Herkimer Library, a professor at Herkimer County Community College, and owner of the Herkimer Sporting Goods store. He looked legitimate. "But why did he hang around the bathroom?"

Next Wales surfed on the Internet for any news about the "sickness" at Herkimer's bicentennial. The village of Herkimer was the county seat of Herkimer County, named after General Nicholas Herkimer, who died from battle wounds in 1777 after taking part in the Battle of Oriskany. This battle was one of the decisive battles in the Revolutionary War. Thank goodness for Wikipedia, the free encyclopedia, Wales mused. He wished he could solve crimes by merely searching the Internet. Wales laughed out loud when he read that Herkimer's police department was beginning to use cast-aluminum wheel boots to catch people with multiple parking tickets. "Wow, this really is a village."

Aside from the original Mighty Mohawks of the Iroquois Nations, the county was first settled by Palatine Germans in 1708. The county is known for producing unusual clear, doubly terminated quartz crystals, called Herkimer diamonds. There are several commercial mines that cater to tourists.

Sure enough, the *Evening Telegram* ran several stories about the deaths of the two women and one girl around the time of the bicentennial celebration. The newspaper reports blamed it on food poisoning or some type of virus. Several other people had gotten sick but had survived. There was no mention of any basketball cards at the scene.

From the news reports, Wales obtained the name of one of the investigating officers. He found the telephone number of the Herkimer police station, called the station, and asked for Detective Sarah Stamp.

"She's not here, Detective. Do you want to leave a message on her voice mail?"

"Yeah, but could you give me her cell phone number and email address?"

"We generally don't give out that information, Detective."

"This may be important. It may involve the three murders at your bicentennial several months ago," Wales pleaded.

"I do not believe we had three murders at that time."

"But you did have three people die from food poisoning," Wales said.

"Oh." The voice paused. "I remember that. One of our officers got sick at that time. O.K., here's the info."

As he hung up, his phone rang. The female CSI officer was on the other line. "We got a problem, Detective. A big problem."

"What's the problem? You can't get my work done. It's 11:00," Wales said.

"Worse than that. The two women last night were killed by a mixture of poisons. Sarin. Nicotine. Dimethyl sulfoxide. The last item is called DSMO. This DSMO is an excellent medium for carrying stuff into your body even when applied topically. It's quickly absorbed through the skin, carrying the poison."

Wales was silent.

"Are you still there, Wales?"

"Yeah," Wales responded. "Where have I heard about sarin?"

"March 20, 1995. The Tokyo subway system. A group now called Aleph. Five men carried liquid sarin in plastic bags into the subway system and punched holes in the bags with the tips of their umbrellas. Now, a single drop of sarin the size of the head of a pin can kill a person. Sarin is a colorless and odorless liquid with a short shelf-life of several weeks. So it is not a good inhalation weapon."

"How many people died?" Wales asked.

"At least twelve. The hospitals saw at least 5,500 people."

"You said nicotine, right?" Wales asked.

"Yes, nicotine was mixed with sarin and dimethyl sulfoxide. You and I are lucky to be alive. The DSMO crap was smeared onto the basketball cards. If we had picked them up, we would be dead."

"What about the photographer that was with you?" Wales asked.

"Oh, he's OK."

"Nicotine. Do you think this is some type of anti-smoking campaign?" Wales asked, almost as a joke.

"It certainly would be effective." There was no laughter. "About four cigarettes, if you eat them, can kill an adult. Whoever did this must have let cigarettes stand in water for a long time and used the water on the cards. I sent everything to the FBI's National Center for Analysis of Violent Crime (NCAVC) in Quantico, Virginia and requested any indication of another similar incident. I'm worried."

Established by President Ronald Reagan on June 21, 1984, to identify and track repeat killers, NCAVC is located 60 feet underground in a former nuclear bunker below the FBI Academy on the U.S. Marine Corps base at Quantico, Virginia. The FBI Academy covers a 600-acre guarded enclave in the Virginia countryside.

"Good idea," Wales said. "Last night the professor from Herkimer said three women died at an event there several months ago. Blamed on food poisoning."

"I remember. That's why I contacted VICAP."

VICAP, or the Violent Criminal Apprehension Program, is the FBI's multimillion dollar computer system, which has a serial crime databank housed in the Washington, D.C., headquarters of the FBI. The purpose of VICAP is to store, collate, and analyze all unsolved homicide crimes reported to NCAVC by law-enforcement agencies.

"Do you think terrorists are behind this?" Wales asked.

"Could be, but we still need to check out their husbands or boyfriends. Maybe a trial run for terrorists."

"Wait, don't hang up. What is this DSMO? Explain it again." Wales asked.

"That's why we're lucky. DSMO is absorbed through the skin and mucous membranes. Of course, it's not good for you either. It's highly toxic. It smells like onions. By the way, there was a trace of fingernail-polish remover."

"I'd better call Herkimer. I have the cell phone number of a detective there. Let me know what you hear from the FBI. Also, get more information about the basketball cards."

Wales immediately called the cell phone number of Sarah Stamp. She answered on the fourth ring.

"Hello," said the pleasant voice.

"Detective Stamp, I'm Mel Wales, a police officer from Trenton. I would like to chat with you if possible."

"How did you get my cell phone number? I gave at the office last week."

Wales chuckled. "I have ways of talking people into doing things for me. But I believe it is important for me to talk to you today. I do apologize for calling you on your day off."

"No problem, Mel. What can you do for me this fine day? I'm broke, however."

"I'm interested in the three deaths that you had around your bicentennial. Three women supposedly died from food poisoning."

"What do you mean by 'supposedly'?" Stamp asked.

"Well, Detective Stamp, those people may have been murdered. Last night at a Trenton YMCA 150th anniversary celebration, two women were killed in a bathroom during a so-called re-creation basketball game. It was played like basketball was played in the 1880s."

Stamp broke in, "I don't get the point. We did not have a basketball game at our bicentennial. Our people died of food poisoning."

"Please give me a moment. Apparently, there is some minor dispute as to whether the first professional basketball game was played in Trenton or Herkimer. Were your deaths in or near a bathroom?" Wales asked.

"Yes, they were. Give me more," Stamp asked.

"Were there any basketball cards in the bathroom?"

"I recall there were some cards, but I don't know if they were basketball cards. I still don't get a connection."

"I heard that one of your police officers also got extremely sick. Was he at the scene of the crime?"

"Crime? Yes, I believe he was there, but he only got food poisoning. He just got sick."

"I'll bet you two boxes of doughnuts to one that he picked up one of the basketball cards."

"What kind of doughnuts?"

Wales immediately liked Stamp. "Your choice."

"Do they sell poisonous basketball cards now? Were they from China?" Stamp asked. "I like chocolate-filled doughnuts. No poison. You're on."

"OK. Yesterday evening two women were killed in a bathroom when they picked up basketball cards. The cards were smeared with sarin, nicotine, and something called dimethyl sulfoxide."

"Gee, that's overkill. So you think my women were killed by the same creep who poisoned your people?"

"Good possibility," Wales said. "They cover the basketball cards with the poison, throw them down in a woman's bathroom, and leave. Someone picks up the card and is somehow poisoned," Wales explained. "The DSMO sucks the poison into the body."

"So we're talking about a female killer," Stamp said.

There was a short pause.

"Looks like it. Can you call your police officer and see if he picked up the card? Find out what kind of cards they were. We need to get them to the FBI for testing."

"I'll get back with you shortly. You really made my day. A mass murderer in our little village. How did you know to call up here? How did you connect the dots? ESP? Like you got my cell phone number?"

"I got lucky. A professor from your community college there in Herkimer had to go to the bathroom after the re-creation game. He saw the police tape and hung around. I spotted him and talked to him. Somehow he connected the dots. A Murphy Cuneo. You need to check him out to make sure he isn't somehow a part of this."

"Murphy Cuneo." Stamp repeated the name. "Anything else?"

"Call your officer. Put a tail on Cuneo. Find out about the basketball cards. We may have to dig up your victims. How will you get me the doughnuts? I like cherry-filled doughnuts."

"That's lovely. See you." Stamp broke the connection.

On Monday morning, Sarah Stamp called Wales and said, "Yes, basketball cards were dropped in the bathroom. I owe you a box of doughnuts, cherry-filled. But you'll have to come and get them. The police officer did pick up the card, but he was wearing latex gloves. He may have touched the gloves when he took them off, though. He doesn't remember being careful."

"Who was on the cards?" Wales asked.

"Some team called the Seattle SuperSonics. It was the 1977–78 season. Players were . . ." she stopped to look at her notes. "Mike Green, Bruce Seals, Paul Silas. I've never heard of them."

"We had the same type of cards down here. The Seattle SuperSonics. The 1977–78 season. So there is truly a connection. Have you started the process to examine the bodies?"

"Not yet. I was waiting to hear from you. I guess I better talk to my supervisors." Stamp did not seem too enthusiastic.

"When are you going to bring me the doughnuts?" Wales asked.

She laughed and hung up.

At 6'2", Wales had played some basketball both in high school and during his freshman year at Pfeiffer University in North Carolina until he blew out his knee. He was too short for basketball anyway. The Pfeiffer Falcons, he mused. A number of students from New Jersey still go to Pfeiffer University, a small Methodist university in Misenheimer. He had graduated in 1988 and had moved back to Trenton, where he had been a cop for the last nineteen years. His knee still sometimes hurt in cold weather. "Why basketball cards?" Wales thought. "Why Seattle SuperSonics, 1977–78 season?" He had collected baseball cards as a kid, not basketball cards. He decided to go to the local library.

In *Basketball: Sports Team Historics*, by M. C. LaBlanc, he read that the Sonics began playing in 1967–68. In their eleventh year of existence, 1977–78, they lost to the Washington Bullets in the seventh game of the NBA Championship. But in the next season (1978–79), the Sonics beat the Bullets in five games.

In the *Official NBA Basketball Encyclopedia*, he read that there were two violent incidents during that season, but neither of them dealt with the Sonics. The Los Angeles Lakers' Kareem Abdul-Jabbar had punched the Milwaukee Bucks' rookie center, Kent Benson, breaking his hand. Abdul-Jabbar received a $5,000 fine. Later in December 1978, the powerfully built Lakers' Kermit Washington got in a fight with Houston center Kevin Kunnert. Houston's forward, Rudy Tomjanovich, rushed forward to help Kunnert. Washington turned around and swung his fist, inflicting massive injuries to Rudy's eye, jaw, and cheek. Washington was fined $50,000.

He found and jotted down the players on the Sonics' team during the

1977–78 season, and from a basketball price list he placed the low-end cost of their basketball card beside their name:

Fred Brown, G	15¢
Al Fleming, F	50¢
Mike Green, C-F	10¢
Joe Hassett, G	?
Dennis Johnson, G	25¢
Bruce Seals, F	18–25¢
Paul Silas, F-C	20¢
Byron Dean Tolson, F	?
Slick Earl Watts, G	?
Marvin Webster, C	15–45¢
Gus Williams, G	19¢
Willie M. Wise, F	?

Finding nothing more of interest, he left the library and stopped at a Wendy's. Hamburger. Chili. Coke. His favorite fast food.

Back at the station, he had a message to call William Douglass. Who is William Douglass? He needed to go to the bathroom, so he stuck the message into his shirt pocket. Inside the bathroom he looked around to make sure there were no basketball cards.

When he got back to his desk, he called his wife and left a message. "Make sure you warn the kids not to pick up any basketball, baseball, or any kind of cards. I'm serious."

As he hung up the phone, it began to ring. Probably his wife. "Hello, dear."

There was silence. Finally a voice asked, "Is this Mel Wales?"

"Yeah. Sorry. I thought you were my wife. I just left a message on her phone."

"No problem. You're the officer in charge of the Trenton YMCA deaths, right?"

"Uh-huh, who are you?"

"Sorry, I'm Special Agent William Douglass with the FBI."

"That's fast," Wales said.

"Well, we may have a small problem on our hands. What kind of sports cards were left at your YMCA bathroom scene?" Douglass asked.

"Basketball cards from the 1977–78 season. Players on the Seattle SuperSonics professional basketball team."

"Yes, that's what your VICAP questionnaire stated. Was there anything written on the cards?" Douglass asked.

"Well, you know those cards—photos, statistics, and. . . ."

Douglass broke in, "What I meant, was there anything written on the cards, say in ink? Anything other than what is printed on the card?"

Wales paused for a moment. "I don't know. I'll have to go to the evidence room to check on that. Is it important?"

"Maybe." Douglass replied. "But don't touch the cards."

"Mr. Douglass, I believe we have a mass murderer involved. Or maybe a group of terrorists."

"Why do you say that?" Douglass shot back.

"The event at the Trenton YMCA was a re-creation of the first professional basketball played. But some experts believe that the first game was played in Herkimer, N.Y."

"So?" Douglass asked.

"Several months ago Herkimer celebrated their bicentennial. There wasn't a basketball game, but three people died and a number of people became ill, supposedly from food poisoning."

"Go on," Douglass said.

"Basketball cards, Seattle SuperSonics cards, 1977–78 season, were found in the bathroom up there. A police officer became ill who was at the crime scene. He may have touched one of the basketball cards. Oh, I forget, my cards down here were covered with sarin, nicotine, and something called DSMO."

"How did you find out about the Herkimer incident?" Douglass asked.

Wales told Douglass about the marketing professor from the Herkimer County Community College.

"Who is in charge of the Herkimer problem?"

"An officer by the name of Sarah Stamp. Funny name. She owes me a box of cherry-filled doughnuts."

"Why?"

"I bet her that the sick police officer had been at the crime scene."

"Swell. Is there anything else that might be important?"

"Not really. Most of it was in the report," Wales said.

"That's true. Can you give me Sarah Stamp's phone number?"

"Sure." Wales gave Douglass all of her phone numbers. "Don't tell her I gave you her cell phone number."

"I won't. Can you go check on anything written on the basketball cards? Here's my cell phone number. Call me as soon as you know. Thanks." The line went dead.

* * * * *

"We've got more than a small problem." Wales was thinking as he went down to the evidence room. He put on some latex gloves. He did not want to get near those cards again.

Fifteen minutes later, he was shaking his head as he walked back to his cluttered desk. How had the FBI agent known? On both of the cards, a small "SK" had been written on the back side. "So this crazy woman has hit somewhere other than Trenton and Herkimer," Wales said out loud.

He pulled out the list of players on the Seattle team. None of them had the initials SK. "Swell." Wales repeated what the FBI agent had said.

His phone rang. "Hello."

"You told him my cell phone number," a female voice said. "Forget the doughnuts."

"But . . ."

Stamp started laughing. "No problem. What did you find written on your cards? There was a small 'SK' written on all three of the basketball cards found up here. Was there anything written on your two cards?"

"The same. 'SK' on the back. The FBI agent called you?" Wales asked.

"Yes, and he almost ordered me to start exhuming the bodies and getting autopsies. Do you know what is going on?"

"Not really. Since he knew to ask the question, the woman must have struck before," Wales suggested.

"Could be a man dressed as a woman," Stamp said.

"True. Let me know what you find about the bodies. I bet you two boxes of doughnuts to one box that they were poisoned. Is it a bet?" Wales asked.

"No way," Stamp responded.

"Let me go. I haven't called the FBI agent yet."

Wales called Douglass and told him that "SK" was written on the basketball cards.

Douglass did not say much or ask any questions.

Utility

Utility is a term used to describe the ability of a product to meet a customer's needs or wants. The business organization can create five types of utility. They are *time, place, possession, psychological,* and *form utility.*

Time Utility: A company provides time utility when it makes its product available when the customer wants it. For example, gas stations or restaurants open 24/7 provide exceptional time utility.

Place Utility: A company's products are high in place utility when they are where the customer wants them. Typically this is when the customer needs them. For example, home delivery of pizza during the Super Bowl.

Possession Utility: A company offers possession utility when it enhances the transfer of ownership or title to products, i.e., makes them easier to acquire. For example, a store selling expensive furniture or jewelry would provide possession utility by accepting credit cards or time-payment plans.

Psychological Utility: Products that provide positive experiences or psychological benefits of satisfaction provide psychological utility. For example, a football game provides psychological utility, especially if your team wins.

All of the above forms of utility are created by the marketing function in an organization. The last form of utility, form utility, is created by the operations/production function.

Form Utility: The way the product is constructed and the ability to easily use the product yields form utility. For example, if the product has an easy-to-open package, has knobs that are easy to turn, or in any way simplifies usage, it provides form utility.

4

The 4-M's of Retailing:

- Merchandising
- Markup
- Marketing
- Methodology

—A. L. SHAFFER

rofessor Murphy Cuneo was in front of his marketing class at Herkimer County Community College. "When you hear the words, 'You're Fired,' what comes to your mind?" Cuneo asked.

Five or six students raised their hands.

"Melissa," Cuneo asked, "what came to your mind?"

"Donald Trump," Melissa answered.

Pointing to another student, Cuneo asked, "Sam, what did you think?"

"*The Apprentice*," Sam smiled and answered.

"That's what I thought you would say. Most of you have never been fired, and most of you are too young to remember George Steinbrenner, owner of the Yankees, and manager Billy Martin. George hired and fired Billy a number of times. George and Billy made a Miller Lite commercial where they argue about 'less filling' and 'great taste.'

"There is also a BBC Apprentice series lead by Sir Alan Sugar.

"But back to the point. Donald Trump is that rich guy with the dopey hairstyle who created the reality-TV show, *The Apprentice*, which brings in 16 young people, divides them into two teams, and gives them marketing-related tasks. The team that loses the task on that episode generally has one of the team members fired by Trump. The eventual winner gets to work for Trump when he says, 'You're Hired.'

"By the way, Trump has put in a patent application to trademark the phrase 'You're Fired.' He probably should trademark his haircut. He has high negatives, but his techniques do enlist an emotional response. He is someone that a person can learn to hate."

There were a couple of laughs.

"On Saturday night I had the honor to attend a re-creation of the original game of basketball. Just as basketball has its history, marketing also has its history. A hundred years ago Henry Ford was mass-producing Ford automobiles. He was able to sell all the cars he could produce because there was greater demand than could be supplied. Thus, his focus and that of Ford Motor Company was produce, produce, produce. This production orientation meant that Ford concentrated on production efficiency and the ability to produce more cars as inexpensively as possible. If you were in the market for a new car, you had your choice of a black Model T or a black Model T. Ford was not interested in making different models or colors because that reduced production efficiency, and his company could sell all it produced.

"Soon, however, competition entered the market and supply began to catch up with demand. This situation meant that companies remained concerned about production efficiencies, but selling became more important because they had to convince people to buy their brand of automobiles rather than their competitors' cars.

"In the 1950s, television was entering its heyday and families were glued to their favorite TV shows. TV offered manufacturers the opportunity to tell the masses about their products and to distinguish them from the competition. Americans were thus becoming better informed about their choices for satisfying their needs and wants. This information meant that marketers of products had to do a better job of finding out what those wants and needs were and developing goods and services to satisfy them. This new orientation, which evolved from a production orientation to a selling orientation to a marketing orientation, became known as the 'marketing concept.' The adoption of this concept meant that producers developed and produced the goods and services that the marketplace wanted.

"Okay, enough history.

"Marketing and advertising are creative disciplines, and thinking outside the box can be helpful. Marketers tend to be right brain thinkers: visual, intuitive, holistic, and integrative. Regrettably, some experts argue that you can spot a liar by watching their eyes. If they are about to lie, they will look up to their right, your left, as if they are developing a story or fiction.

"Marketers should be ethical. Roger D. Blackwell, a former professor of marketing at Ohio State University's Fisher College of Business, was convicted of multiple counts of insider trading and two counts of making false statements. He received 72 months' imprisonment and a $1 million fine. Before his conviction, Professor Blackwell had been named marketing professor of the year for three consecutive years in a row by the Ohio State Chapter of the American Marketing Association (AMA). He was the founding father of Consumer Behavior and co-author of one of the leading textbooks about marketing. Each of you must be ethical. I do not wish to read about your imprisonment in the *Wall Street Journal* one day.

"Debbie LaChusa, founder of the 10-Step Marketing System, says that a person is hit by over 5,000 marketing messages a day. That's a lot, and I'm not sure it's that high. However, there's a lot of clutter out there, and LaChusa says that a marketer must be creative to capture the audience's attention. She calls it connecting with the customer rather than merely entertaining them. LaChusa believes advertising can become too creative, though, or too far removed from reality. For example, one of *The Apprentice* episodes involved both teams having to develop a 30-second television commercial for Dove Body Wash. Both teams prepared commercials so bizarre that they did not target women who buy the products. They became too creative and did not sell the product to the proper market. They did not connect, because both teams showed men using the Dove Body Wash.

"I like what Debbie LaChusa suggests. Identify and know your audience and then aim to connect with them in a relevant way. Your goal should be to jump into the conversation that they are having in their head about your product or service. If you, as a marketer, can do this technique with the advertising media, you will capture people's attention and sell your service or product.

"Another marketing expert, Ethan Hathaway, maintains that there are a lot of lessons to be learned from the Trump reality shows. The five major rules from the show are:

1. Give the client or customer what they want. In other words, ask the customer what they want and give it to them.
2. Sell and market what you know, and sell those products and services that you can truly stand behind.

3. Find different ways to create new revenue streams from existing businesses. For example, the NBA owns the Women's National Basketball Association (WNBA). They need to mine this revenue stream.

4. Price it right. There is psychology in pricing. If you price it too low or too high, you lose. A higher price may add prestige to a product such as perfume. A price much lower than the market expects may lead the customer to suspect a low quality or other problems with the product.

5. Concentrate on marketing and generating more revenues from customers, clients, and prospects with whom you already have relationships.

"The product Rogaine is trying to expand its target audience by at least a decade." Cuneo rubbed his balding spot. "Hopefully, everyone knows what Rogaine is for." He laughed.

"Johnson & Johnson bought the hair product from Pfizer in 2006 and created a mousse-like version. The new foam version is dispensed by pressing a nozzle. J&J has an ad campaign trying to encourage younger guys to start using the product before hair loss is evident. Their slogan is, 'Use It or Lose It.' Their commercials show young men in the morning shaving, showering, brushing their teeth, and putting Rogaine into the crown of their head."

Cuneo touched his crown again. "If I had only used Rogaine when I was younger I could have run for President or Vice-President.

"Under Pfizer, sales of Rogaine had been falling, down to $31 million in 2006. J&J is trying to move their product into the realm of everyday bathroom essentials, like toothpaste and deodorant. J&J is putting ads on dry-cleaner hangers now. In 2007, under J&J, sales for the product jumped 25 percent to $42 million. I could not find anything in their 2010 financial report about Rogaine.

"Before we start utilizing our marketing mix, we must first ask ourselves, 'What business are we in?' This brings to mind a famous article written in the *Harvard Business Review* years ago by Professor Theodore Levitt. The gist of the article was about what Levitt called 'marketing myopia.' Can anyone tell me what myopia is?" Cuneo asked.

One student responded, "It means 'nearsighted.'"

"Correct. But in marketing terms, Levitt was saying, know what business you are in and who your market is. For example, in the middle of the twentieth century, television was becoming a commercial success and the motion-picture industry was concerned about this threat to their industry.

Before long, the motion-picture companies were in financial trouble. They began selling off assets and seeking to merge with other motion-picture production companies. Had they viewed themselves as being in the *entertainment* business, they would have seen television as an opportunity.

"What does this mean to us today?"

Gary responded, "It means we need to set some guidelines to assist us in making good business decisions."

"Great answer, Gary! We call these guidelines a *mission statement*. A company needs to develop a mission statement that explains why they exist, what business they are in, and who their market is. This statement guides them in making decisions for the long-term viability of the company.

"Let me give you an example. Who is the Oracle of Omaha?"

Jim was quick to respond: "Warren Buffet!"

"Correct. As I understand the story, Buffet was attending a board meeting of Coca Cola in Atlanta. The management team was discussing an opportunity to buy the Quaker Oats Company. It is alleged that one of the executives said, 'That would be a great acquisition for us since we sell soft drinks. By adding salty snack foods to our product mix, we could market them to our existing customers very efficiently.'

"Buffet is said to have responded by asking the senior management team, 'What business are we in?' and before they could respond, he said, 'Our mission statement says we are in the beverage business, and Quaker Oats is not in the beverage business.'

"Class, this means you do what you do best and what you know how to do. Coke's expertise is in the beverage business.

"Let me tell you another short story. Some years ago, the H. Daroff firm had long been a premier manufacturer of men's suits and related apparel. They had great brand names, and they decided to vertically integrate and open their own retail stores, cutting out the profits of the intermediaries.

"Guess what happened?"

Sue answered, "They went broke?"

"Exactly. You see, their expertise and competitive advantage was in manufacturing and not in retailing. They were in the apparel manufacturing business and not in the retailing business." Cuneo gave a thumbs-down sign.

"This rule means that you need to know your competitive advantage.

Michael Porter says you need four things for competitive advantage. They are 'superior quality, superior innovation, superior technology, and superior efficiency.'" Cuneo handed out a sheet with his Marketing Key to the Universe.

"Likewise, as you view the diagram I have just given you, remember: you need to know what business you are in, who your customer is, and where you have a competitive advantage. This approach means you need to know your target market.

"We learn about market opportunities by first conducting marketing research. We look for people who have a need for what we sell. Once we have done that research, we begin to sort people into groups of potential buyers based upon some identifying characteristics. This research can be done in a number of ways, such as by demographics, ethnicity, gender, age, income, and, in the case of sports marketing, fan experience. We may also profile them by lifestyles: activities, interests, and opinions. Once we have sorted the potential market into segments, we then must decide for which segments we have competitive advantage. In other words, which segments do we want to target?"

Jim spoke up. "Are you saying that just because we can identify potential segments, we only go after those segments we feel match up with our offerings and ability to market to them effectively?"

"Jim, I could not have said it better myself. Thank you.

"After we select our target segment or segments, we need to develop our marketing mix in a way that will lead to success. Remember, the marketing mix is the four P's—product, price, place, and promotion.

"Promotion also has its own mix, which includes advertising, personal selling, sales promotion, and public relations along with publicity. And, with the Internet and email, we have added direct marketing as another promotional tool.

"As we go along this semester, we will talk in detail about these individual items. But let me give you an example of sales promotion. At least one movie theater chain has frequent moviegoers rewards cards. Under the Royal Crown Club card, a user earns credits when buying tickets or concession-stand snacks. As credits mount up, the customer gets a free drink, popcorn, or movie. The potential rewards encourage the person to pick that movie chain rather than another movie house."

Marketing Keys to the Universe
(Goal: Make Profits/Avoid Major Risks)

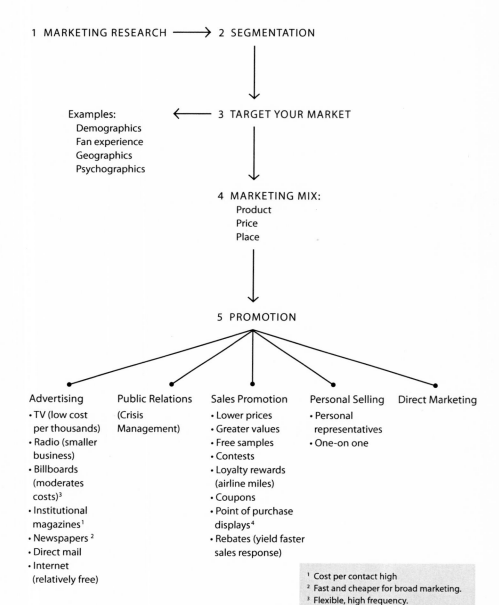

1 MARKETING RESEARCH ⟶ 2 SEGMENTATION

Examples: ⟵ 3 TARGET YOUR MARKET
 Demographics
 Fan experience
 Geographics
 Psychographics

4 MARKETING MIX:
 Product
 Price
 Place

5 PROMOTION

Advertising
- TV (low cost per thousands)
- Radio (smaller business)
- Billboards (moderates costs)[3]
- Institutional magazines[1]
- Newspapers[2]
- Direct mail
- Internet (relatively free)

Public Relations
(Crisis Management)

Sales Promotion
- Lower prices
- Greater values
- Free samples
- Contests
- Loyalty rewards (airline miles)
- Coupons
- Point of purchase displays[4]
- Rebates (yield faster sales response)

Personal Selling
- Personal representatives
- One-on one

Direct Marketing

[1] Cost per contact high
[2] Fast and cheaper for broad marketing.
[3] Flexible, high frequency.
[4] Dump bins, aisle interrupters, wobblers, and lipstick board.

Cuneo then handed out a copy of *Advertising Age*'s annual pie chart of how money was spent by advertisers in 2009. "Please note that the majority of advertising monies are spent in magazines and newspapers, and on network TV. Next on the list are cable-TV networks, spot TV, Internet, and radio.

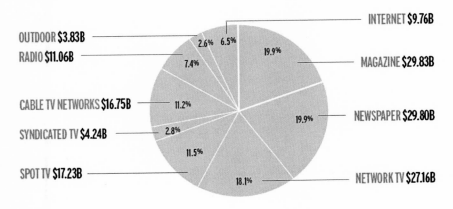

"Advertising can be expensive. Almost 106.5 viewers watched the New Orleans Saints' 31–17 win over the Indianapolis Colts in 2010. Advertisers had to pay around $2.5 million for a thirty-second commercial. That is about $84,000 per second. Ads must appeal to a broad market to be effective.

"Stuart Elliott in the *Wall Street Journal* says advertisers want their commercials to be amusing or intriguing. They want viewers to watch them again after the game on Internet sites such as AOL, MySpace, Yahoo!, YouTube, and Facebook.

"Let me talk about this area of sales promotion, which you normally don't hear from a marketing person. I'm talking about the fourth-quarter games that some companies play with working capital. Accountants call it cooking the books. Playing these games can be as careless as turnovers in a basketball game. They can be addictive and very destructive to a business. Companies try to reduce working capital and increase cash flow near the end of the fourth quarter.

"These games played by sales, accounting, collection, and operation staff can be destructive. I'm saying:

- Discounts and rebates reduce margins and produce distorted views of demand, making forecasting more difficult.
- Customers begin to expect fourth-quarter discounts and rebates.
- Trying to hurry up collection from customers annoys them.
- Delaying payments to vendors strains relationships.
- Shipping back inventory makes vendors mad.

"Stephen Payne, president of REL Consultancy Group, indicates that in the last fiscal quarter of 2006, America's top 1,000 businesses increased their working capital by $100 billion. He says this dash for cash is a short-run solution because the first quarter of the next year will be hurt. Mr. Payne says that 'for those who care about effective supply-chain processes, healthy customer and supplier relationships, fatter margins, and just plain old integrity, renouncing year-end gamesmanship is required.'

"AOL capitalized the costs of making and distributing its CDs. They viewed this marketing campaign as a long-term investment and capitalized expenses, thereby transferring the marketing costs from the income statement to the balance sheet. When you get out into the real world, do not engage in 'cooking-the-book' schemes. Marketing people, just like CEOs and accountants, can go to prison.

"Crisis management is a part of marketing, falling under the category of public relations, especially after the Sarbanes-Oxley Act of 2002. Enron disappeared because they cooked the books. Don't do it. A material weakness at a company can cause stock to plunge. Three new terms are important." Cuneo handed out two more pages and talked about letting the public know about your material weaknesses early and correcting them before the annual statements are released.

He went over the handout:

Control deficiency—one that might allow a bad number to get into the financial reports (e.g., the likelihood that a company misstates reports)—is remote: 1 out of 20. Example: company does *not* check changes made by a salesman in a *minor* contract.

Significant deficiency— a more serious flaw or a number of flaws that increase the chances that wrong numbers will significantly distort financial statements (e.g., more than remote). Need only to report to Board of Directors, but some companies are making them public. Example: company not checking for changes made by salespersons to terms of several key contracts.

Material weakness—deficiencies are so bad that there is more than a remote chance of a *material* misstatement in financial statements. They must be reported to the general public. Example: a bank does not regularly check for errors in estimating loan-loss expenses (i.e., Fannie Mae reported a $1.3 billion error from its computer model, many errors in an uncontrolled environment).

Cuneo continued, "For example, executives may reduce advertising expenditures in order to achieve financial-reporting goals of avoiding earnings decreases and losses, or to meet analysts' expectations. Focusing on the short-run can impact the long-run future of a business.

"An example of both crisis management and the value of creative advertising is Cadbury's United Kingdom chocolate business. A salmonella recall in 2006 wiped 30 million pounds off sales and provoked a 1 million–pound fine. Cadbury's U.K. marketing director Phil Rumbol and the advertising agency Fallon dressed up an actor in a gorilla suit and had him play the drums along with Phil Collins' 1981 hit 'Coming in the Air Tonight.' This television and poster campaign boosted sales of Cadbury's Dairy Milk brand by 9 percent and helped Cadbury's U.K. market share in chocolate bounce back in 2007. The gorilla clip became one of the most watched commercials on YouTube.

"There is a reality television show called *Celebrity Rehab with Dr. Drew* where fallen stars try to overcome their addictions. I believe there is a need for a show that deals with company executives who have flunked their company crisis and destroyed their companies.

"Are there any questions?"

"Will anything from the pie chart be on the examination?" one student asked.

The most common question asked in the classroom in the U.S. today, thought Cuneo. "Maybe. Any other questions?" He had seen research reporting that students study an average of six hours a week—less than one hour a day.

"OK, let me discuss the written project due two classes from today. Some of you realize that the NBA owns the WNBA, the women's professional basketball teams. I want you to do some marketing research and segment the market for the WNBA. If you had to advise the NBA, what target markets would you select in order to increase the revenues from the WNBA? I assume you are aware of the huge success of TV poker in recent years. Try to use that situation as an analogy. Any questions about your assignment?" He paused and looked around. There were no hands. "Please do not be late with the project. See you."

Cuneo answered several questions from two students about the written project, and one student asked him about Pepsi. "I didn't want to bring it up in class, but Pepsi has been doing much better than Coke over the past years. Pepsi is around $64 per share, and Coke is around $53 per share. Pepsi has Frito-Lay, Tropicana, Quaker Oats, and Gatorade," Tony said.

"You're quite right, Tony. Please bring that fact up next class," Cuneo said. "There really are no absolute rules in marketing, and what will work in one country may not work in another country.

"For example, when I was in Taiwan last year I found that in most cities, except Taipei, there were so-called glass boxes on many street corners. There are scantily dressed, young girls sitting on stools inside these small buildings, many dressed in bikini bathing suits. They are called 'spicy girls.' They sell betel nuts, bottled water, and other small items to truckers and taxi drivers. When a customer drives up, the provocative girls come outside to take the order. Apparently, the betel nut gives the user a mild buzz when chewed. They turn the individual's gums and teeth a permanent red color, however."

Cuneo went to his office to work on an examination for the next class. The first question on the exam addressed the scientific method of problem solving.

1. What is the first step in marketing research (marketing problem-solving)?
    a. Gathering primary data.
    b. Conducting a situation analysis.
    c. Designing a survey instrument such as a questionnaire.
    d. Defining the problem.
    e. None of the above.

Cuneo had tried to instill the correct answer in his students' minds from the first day of class. The correct answer, "d," was so important. Too often he had seen companies trying to address a symptom rather than the problem itself. He had frequently used the example that if you have a headache and the doctor gives you some medicine to relieve the pain, the problem itself has not been solved if you have a brain tumor. He wanted his students to know the importance of accurately defining the problem so their efforts to find its solutions would not be misdirected. This principle is all too true in marketing. Companies see a sales decline as a problem when that may only be a symptom of an underlying issue, such as a wrong pricing strategy, a poorly performing sales force, or even some external factor, such as competitor actions.

The same can be said for solving crimes, Cuneo realized. First gather as much evidence as possible, and then define the crime or situation in terms of a problem that can be solved by a deliberate plan of action. Reading about a crime case in the newspaper would be using secondary data. Talking with witnesses to the crime would be gathering primary data.

Market Segmentation

Market Segmentation is the process of taking the entire potential market for a product and dividing it into groups of buyers with similar characteristics as buyers and who are likely to respond in a similar way to a given marketing message.

Market Targeting is the process of looking at the various segments in a market and deciding the one(s) to which the firm will direct its marketing activities. Each segment targeted may require a separate marketing strategy or marketing program.

The common bases for *market segmentation* are:

1. *Geographic:* spatial criteria that can be objectively determined, such as region, density of population, climate, city or Standard Metropolitan Statistical Area (SMSA) size, or physical features that impact marketing activities.
2. *Demographic:* objective variables such as age, income, marital status, stage in the family life cycle, religion, ethnicity, occupation, or gender.
3. *Psychographic:* criteria of lifestyle as influenced by people's activities, interests, and opinions.
4. *Behavioral:* differences in attitude, beliefs, knowledge and/or use of, or response to a product or marketing message. Examples are occasions, benefits, buyer readiness, and company or brand loyalty.

Marketing Concept

The Marketing Concept is a marketing philosophy that suggests the selling organization should first find out what the customer needs and then profitably provide the customer with the desired solution to that need. Accordingly, a firm should be structured to enable this process to occur in the most efficient manner.

Sensing the loyalty and heightened interest in sports entertainment, companies attach their products to events in the hopes of cultivating the same infectious loyalty for their products and services. The fundamental premise is that sports attract a captive audience.

—PHIL SCHAAF

On his drive home Monday afternoon Douglass called Fleet Walker, the internal auditor for the New York Yankees. He could not locate Walker initially so finally called his home, where his wife answered.

"Hello, Flo, is Fleet watching Jeopardy reruns? This is Bill Douglass."

"Hello to you, Bill. How is the FBI treating you? You're not going to arrest my Fleet for watching Alex Trebek, are you?"

"No, Flo. Just want to chat."

"Sure you do. I'll get him. Don't get him in trouble again."

"I won't, Flo. Promise."

Fleet Walker was the baseball historian who had helped Douglass solve the perfect-game riddle when a madman calling himself Sandy Kojak had terrorized Major League Baseball two years ago. Sandy had eventually died from his own poison in Yankee Stadium, but not before fifty-five people had died and many were hospitalized from the sarin.

"Hello Douglass," Fleet said. "Are you looking for a job?"

"You're a fine one to talk. How have you survived Steinbrenner? I thought you were history when Joe Torre escaped to the Dodgers," Douglas joked.

"Oh, you know, hard work and fine living. What can I do you out of, Douglass?"

"I believe one of our extortionists is back," Douglass said.

"Really. We always thought there was more than one. Where did they strike?" Fleet asked.

"Not baseball. Basketball, probably. She killed two people in Trenton at a re-creation basketball game, and maybe three more in a village called Herkimer in central New York."

"Close to me. How do you know it's a she?"

"She's hitting women's bathrooms," Douglass answered.

"You thought it was a woman accomplice also. How do you know it's not a copycat?" Fleet asked.

"She's printing 'SK' on the cards," Douglass said. "Only you, I, and a few other people knew about the signature Sandy Kojak left."

"Do I need an alibi?"

"Yes, you do." Douglass smiled.

"Where do you wish me to be, what day and what time, so you can solve this case quickly? Thus, you will not have to waterboard me."

"Fleet, Fleet, Fleet. You must be a Democrat," Douglass said.

"Not this season. I'm a Yankee. How can I help? I don't know much about basketball." Fleet turned serious.

"I need a basketball historian," Douglass said. "Fast."

Fleet paused. "I don't believe there is a formal group of basketball historians as in baseball. There is an Internet site, I believe, called the Association for Professional Basketball Research. But I do have a friend, Caleb Pehrson, who is the vice-president for sales with the Boston Celtics. He knows a great deal about basketball. Of course, most of the statistics can be found on the Internet now. No brainer."

"Would you email me all of his telephone and fax numbers, and addresses? Everything," Douglass asked.

"Will do it tonight. Anything else?"

"No, but I'll be in touch. This is, of course, confidential."

"I understand," Fleet said. "I'll keep my fingers and toes crossed."

"You take care of Flo."

* * * * *

That evening around 9:30, Wales's doorbell rang and his wife went to the front door. She came back to the den where Wales and his two sons were watching Monday Night Football and said, "A suit is at the door."

When Wales got to the front door, the suit was holding up an FBI badge in his left hand and a box of Krispy Kreme doughnuts in the other hand.

"Mel, I'm Bill Douglass. Is there any way that we can talk privately? Cherry-filled."

"Sure. Is Starbucks OK?" Wales asked.

"That's fine," Douglass replied.

"Let me tell my wife." Wales did so, picked up his gun, and then directed Douglass to a nearby Starbucks. They engaged in small talk on the way to the coffee shop. The doughnuts smelled good.

Douglass ordered a latte, and Wales asked for hot chocolate. Douglass directed Wales outside, where it was chilly. No one was outside.

"Are you stationed in Trenton?" Wales asked. "I've never seen you before."

"No, I'm out of D.C. this week, so the drive was only about 160 miles," Douglass explained. "Have a donut."

"Thanks. I didn't think your Chevy was a rental car," Wales said.

"Once I explain things, I believe you'll understand why I came to Trenton tonight. Do you remember two years ago when baseball was threatened by the baseball-card murderers?"

"You're kidding me." Wales remembered. "I thought he was killed in Yankee Stadium."

"Yes, one of the criminals was killed by his own poison, but I always felt that there were two or more participants. In fact, I always thought that his accomplice was a woman. She sent me a baseball card several weeks after the killings in Yankee Stadium. I've been dreading her return."

"How do you know it's the same group?" Wales asked. "The 'SK' initials?"

"Right. They left the initials 'SK' on most of the baseball cards. That fact was never released to the public." Douglass picked up a donut and took a bite. "Not bad."

"Have they sent an extortion note yet?" Wales asked.

"Not that we know. It's probably too early in the game. They played a cat-and-mouse game last time, giving us hints about perfect baseball games," Douglass said.

"That's right. They were hitting on the dates and the stadiums of the perfect games. There's no perfect game in basketball," Wales remarked.

"Is there anything close to a perfect game in basketball?" Douglass asked.

"Not really. Even in the re-creation game Saturday night both teams scored points."

"There may be a pattern, however. The first hit two years ago was at a re-creation baseball game. I need to find a basketball historian. Do you know one?" Douglass asked.

"Nope."

"They tried to set someone up last time. Maybe, just maybe, they'll try to do the same thing this time." Douglass was thinking out loud.

"What do you want to do here?" Wales asked.

"Go out to the scene. Poke around. See the basketball cards. So far she has left . . ." Douglass pulled out his Blackberry. "Mike Green, Bruce Seals, Paul Silas, Al Fleming, and Marvin Webster."

"The cards aren't worth much. I checked most of the players on the Sonics' team for that year. Under 50 cents," Wales said.

"Same as last time. Cheap, common cards. They aren't spending much money, except on travel costs. They have to move around," Douglass said.

"They have to buy the cards, too," Wales said.

"Hmmm," Douglass responded, contemplating almost long enough to grow a goatee. "I'll have to check that out."

* * * * *

Douglass spent some time in Trenton checking the scene of the crime, and then he traveled to Herkimer. He visited with the police in Herkimer and tried to hurry the exhumation and autopsies.

Douglass was a field-profile coordinator, a member of the elite A-team in Quantico. He was forty, with no gray in his short reddish-brown hair. He had a dark complexion and bright, hazel eyes. His 6-foot frame carried about 190 pounds.

On Sarah Stamp's office computer, Douglass went online and searched for the Association for Professional Basketball Research. Sure enough, there was a website by that name out of Phoenix. The group had been established in December 1997. They had a Frequently Asked Questions section, but none of the questions dealt with mass murders in basketball. There was a story about the shabby treatment of the pre-pension players, better known as the pre-1965 NBA Players' Association. Former player Bill

"Tosh" Tosheff was leading the battle to gain increased benefits for those forgotten pioneers.

A number of APBR member sites were listed, but most of them were other Internet sites, such as the *Journal of Basketball Studies* and sonicscentral.com. The latter was a private site for the Seattle team. He did not find any site for the Celtics or Caleb Pehrson.

He called and set up an appointment to talk to Pehrson.

* * * * *

Well, my darling, I love you so,
In my heart I'll always know,
Because I'm thinking, I'm thinking about you.

And, my dear, when I'm away,
I hope that you will know each day,
That I'm thinking, I'm thinking about you.

Because of joy in my heart, I can't hide anymore,
Since I've told all my friends you're the girl I adore.

And I know while I live, all my love to you I'll give,
Because I'm thinking, I'm thinking about you.

Yes, I'm thinking, I'm thinking about you.

Shirlee Ann was listening to a tape recording of Sandy singing and playing the guitar. Sandy had told her that he had written the song for her. She, of course, knew better, but she was still crying. Sandy had told her he had never been able to sell any of his music. "It's a tough business," he had said.

She sang along with some of the lines. She was wearing two sets of surgical gloves, not trusting the Derma Shield that Sandy had always used to cover his hands and arms while he worked with poison. She was carefully transferring oleander water into fingernail polish–remover bottles.

Shirlee Ann had stewed oleander leaves and branches in a bucket of water for a week. She was sad that people had died in Trenton and Herkimer; she had only wanted them to become ill. Since she had misjudged Sandy's poison, she was manufacturing a milder poison. Now she knew that DSMO worked so well, she had to mix the poison with something else that would be absorbed through the skin.

She picked up HeadOn, a topical product heavily advertised to reduce the discomfort of headaches. She had seen the annoying commercial showing someone applying the product directly to the forehead. Someone would say, "HeadOn, I hate your commercials, but I love your product." She used a pair of pliers to break the container and poured the liquid into the water. She dumped two more bottles of the liquid into the water. She hoped the liquid would absorb through the skin. Surely the product was not poisonous.

After seven bottles were filled, she poured the remainder down the sink. She wrapped six of the bottles with tissue paper and placed each one inside a Ziploc sandwich bag. She had labeled the bags "mine." Her entire kitchen table was covered with newspaper, with three bags of peanuts and packets of Heinz tomato ketchup, Kraft mustard, and pickle relish spread around on the table.

Next she began the tedious task of using a hypodermic needle to put the oleander mixture inside some of the peanuts. Each bag of peanuts was placed inside a sandwich bag.

Next she used the needle to place some of the toxic mixture into the little packages of Heinz ketchup, commonly found at fast-food restaurants. She had picked them up at various locations. She covered the tiny hole made by the needle with a small amount of glue. She repeated the process with the Kraft mustard and sweet pickle-relish packages. Each item was placed separately into a small sandwich bag.

Once finished, she used tissue paper to carefully remove her double set of gloves before disposing the gloves, tissue paper, bottle of glue, needle, and newspaper in a garbage bag. She then went to the bathroom and washed her hands carefully, drying them on paper towels. She removed the white surgical mask, similar to the ones Japanese people wear during the flu season, and threw it into the trash can. Glancing into her mirror, she saw that she had forgotten to take off her protective glasses. She carefully used tissue paper to remove the glasses and washed them thoroughly.

She noticed in the mirror that she was still crying. Although she was six feet tall, she had a slender build. Light-brown hair with blond highlights framed her hazel eyes. She felt that she was still reasonably attractive. As a young adult her height had frightened many boys, but she had dated a few sports jocks.

Was she crying because of Sandy or because of the pain she would cause at the basketball game? She did not know for sure. Sandy was so different than she. In the end, she knew that Sandy had enjoyed killing the baseball fans from afar.

* * * * *

The Boston Celtics had a 23,000-square-foot office suite at 226 Causeway Street, which was a former bakery for Stop & Shop Supermarket. The Boston developer Intercontinental converted the building into offices and luxury condominiums, and in the summer of 2007 the Celtics moved from 151 Merrimac Street to the newly remodeled offices.

About 50 employees work at the Celtics' Causeway office, which has state-of-the-art audio and video systems, including plasma and LCD screens and microphones for conference calls in the boardroom and two conference rooms. The microphones were built into the conference tables and ceilings. Douglass read an article by Steve Adams in *The Patriot Ledger* as he waited for Caleb Pehrson.

A 40-inch television screen, called the "plasma," hung on one wall of the sales office, displaying an area map of the 18,600-seat TD BankNorth Garden, where the Celtics played. Each employee's desktop has a smaller version of the clickable analytics interface called StratTix. Every seat was rendered in various shades of orange, red, yellow, or green that indicated which seats were sold or available on a real-time basis. There was a three-minute, fifteen-second delay from the time any ticket data from both internal and TicketMaster sales comes in until the updated seat status appeared on the screen.

Douglass read another article by Hannah Smalltree, which quoted Daryl Morey as saying that the Celtics were using sophisticated business tools to sell tickets. "I've never seen a business that shouldn't be more analytically driven than ticket sales. We have fantastic data on who the customers are, where they're sitting, and what they'll pay," Morey said. "We have a complex ticketing structure with over 100 different pricing levels for individuals, sections, packages, competitive games, students, and more.

"We have a complete data base that lists all of our ticket holders. We are able to develop from this data base a profile of individual customers and also a profile of the typical fan who buys Celtics tickets. Thus, we are able to segment our potential markets for ticket buyers.

"It really is quite amazing how we are able to identify more than just demographics about our fans including their lifestyles and activities other than basketball.

"By doing this we are also able to reach out to those who cannot get tickets but are potential buyers of licensed Celtics products. This information enables us to build relationships and develop a broader revenue base.

"Customer relationship marketing involves, as I just mentioned, finding out as much as marketers can about a customer and then directing the marketing activities toward establishing, developing, and maintaining successful customer relations. A company must develop long-term relationships and improve business performance through customer loyalty and customer retention. For example, the Green Bay Packers' Lambeau Field has been sold out since 1960. Fans go to Packers games for more than just football. They go for the experience and the total atmosphere created by the Packers organization. The Packers have done a great job of developing relationships with their customers.

"Customer-specific marketing is a concept found in Brian Woolf's book *Customer Specific Marketing,* in which a company gives different offers to different people. Customer-specific marketing is based upon two ideas:

1. Not all customers are equal, and
2. Behavior follows rewards.

"Woolf maintains that mass marketing is dead for a number of reasons. One is the cost of placing advertising in the mass media. A second reason is that through the use of information technology, marketers are now able to better identify our potential customers and utilize sophisticated targeting to reach them. For example, marketers can find out about their lifestyle, what programs they watch on TV, the magazines they read, and much more about what motivates them, which in turn enables us to develop integrated marketing communications to reach each segment and appeal to them effectively.

"Since the top 20 percent of customers over a year spends more than 50 times the amount of the bottom 20 percent, average pricing does not work well for the bottom-line profit."

"Mr. Douglass, Caleb will see you now," a nice-looking assistant said. She ushered him into Caleb Pehrson's office.

"Have a seat," Caleb said, pointing to a chair in front of his desk. "How many seats does the FBI wish to buy?"

Douglass smiled. "No seats today. Fleet Walker, the internal auditor for the Yankees, recommended you as an expert in the history of professional basketball. He also suggested that you would be quite discreet."

"I got to know Fleet at North Carolina A&T. He went into accounting, and I went into marketing. We keep in touch. And he's right, I do know my round ball history, and I will be discreet. Is one of my players in trouble?"

"Oh, no. Nothing like that. You can rest easy," Douglass said.

"Great. So what's the problem?"

"Do you recall the baseball murders?"

"Sure. How could anyone forget that media circus? A disaster for baseball."

"Are you a member of the Association for Professional Basketball Research?"

"Yes. Still fairly primitive," Caleb answered.

"I saw that you wrote an article in the *International Journal of Sports Finance* entitled 'Evaluating Ticket Pricing Models.'"

"Some time ago. Are we fencing? What's the problem?" Caleb asked politely, looking at his watch.

Douglass noticed the caricature of the Celtics' famous logo, a leprechaun with the words "Boston Celtics" arched around it in a circle, on Pehrson's desk. The figure's left eye is winking, his left hand rests on his shillelagh, his right index finger points straight upward with a brown basketball sitting atop it, and his left foot crosses over and to the side of his right foot. He smiles broadly, with a pipe projecting from the right corner of his mouth, and he is dressed in black buckle shoes, black pants, a gold front-button vest with a matching bow tie (with green three-leaf clovers displayed prominently on both), and a long-sleeved white shirt. The outfit is topped off with a black derby hat with the same matching three-leaf clovers.

Douglass spoke carefully, "I believe that one of the characters involved with the baseball murders is now active against professional basketball. There is not much evidence yet, but she struck at two basketball-related locations. Two people were fatally poisoned at a Trenton, N.J., re-creation game, and there is a strong possibility that three people died in Herkimer, N.Y., from the same poison."

"What do you mean by 'possibility'?"

"We have not yet performed autopsies on the three victims in Herkimer," Douglass said.

"So why do you believe that the same group is back?" Caleb asked.

"They are using the same type of delivery system and poisons, and they seem to be using the same type of timeline." Douglass omitted the use of the basketball cards.

"I'm certainly willing to help. All I need is some sick criminal going after basketball like they did baseball. How can I help?"

"I need someone with a deep knowledge of basketball history. They may follow a similar pattern as last time. Fleet was able to help me greatly with respect to the baseball stadiums they planned to attack. I hope you can provide similar input discreetly."

"Consider it done. To seal the deal, let me take you to The Harp, a famous Irish restaurant and pub on Causeway. And if any of my players get in trouble, you'll give me advance notice," Caleb said.

"I'll go with you to The Harp in case I have more questions," Douglass agreed. "I don't believe you have to worry about your players."

Before they left for lunch, Douglass told Caleb that he knew some things about sports cards. "I recall that the rookie card is the most important with respect to value over time. Older the better. Better condition. Scarcity. These items make sports cards increase in value. I understand that common cards are cheap. Tell me more about basketball sports cards."

"You are right about the items you mention creating value. A gem, minted first-year card, called a rookie card, of Michael Jordan may be worth around $40,000 today." He turned to his computer and typed in Kobe Bryant's name. "I follow basketball cards. Here is a top condition, PSA 10 Kobe Bryant 1996 Topps Chrome for $320." He points to the screen. "Here is one in slightly less condition, PSA 9, for $150. Condition 10 is the best and condition 1 is the worst, of course.

"This pricing is similar to almost anything in business," Caleb continued. "The elasticity of demand means that there is a scarcity of a product, and a lot of people want the product. Thus, the seller can raise the price to the optimum price the market is willing to pay.

"The two major basketball card companies today are Topps and Upper Deck. Topps first sold basketball cards in 1957, but they stopped after one season. They started again in 1969, but they again stopped in 1982. Luckily they started again in 1992, the rookie year of Shaquille O'Neal. Theoretically, 2007–08 is the 50th anniversary of Topps." Caleb paused for a moment.

"Upper Deck began in 1988, and I noticed in 2006 that baseball Iron Man Cal Ripken, Jr. joined Upper Deck as its exclusive spokesman. It's fairly common for the top basketball players entering the NBA to sign exclusive contracts with either Upper Deck or Topps. I believe that Topps signed Greg Oden out of Ohio State University, and Upper Deck signed a multiyear deal with SuperSonics Kevin Durant. The two companies slug it out each year." Caleb looked at his watch. "Shall we go?"

At lunch Douglass enjoyed a bowl of New England clam chowder and the Gateway Style fish and chips. He had a Coke, and Caleb had a Heineken with his California chicken club. Between bites, Caleb explained how the Celtics had to compete in the NBA world. "We have to manage profitability, balance cash flows, analyze statistics, communicate with fans, and maintain our reputation. We have a sophisticated statistical scouting database, which evaluates our own players' performances as well as our competitors' players' performances on a day-to-day basis," Caleb indicated.

Douglass was careful to pay for his own meal. As he departed, he asked Caleb to consider why anyone might have a beef with the Seattle Super-Sonics.

When Douglass got back to Quantico, he learned that the three people in Herkimer had been killed with the same DSMO poison as those in Trenton. The perpetrators had even used the same delivery system. So the baseball murderers were back. Where would they strike next?

Douglass surfed the Internet to learn about DSMO. He found that colorless DSMO is commonly used in veterinary medicine as a liniment to carry medicine into a horse's body. It can penetrate the skin rapidly, and it evaporates slowly. Maybe the individual was a veterinarian or a horse rancher, he thought. He found an article in *Muscle Mass Magazine* about DSMO use in sports and body building. Its one notable side effect is that it causes bad breath. So the bad guy could be a body builder. The bad news was that anyone could buy it cheaply: 99.9 percent pure at a low price of $12.32 a bottle.

Product

A *product* is anything that can be obtained through the process of exchange to satisfy a need or a want. A *product* can be a tangible (a good) or an intangible (a service). It can include ideas, information, places, events, organizations, or even real or financial property.

For marketers, it is valuable to separate products into *consumer* or *business* products because the two categories are bought differently and therefore need different marketing strategies. Consumers buy to satisfy a personal need, while business products are bought for non-personal business use.

Types of Consumer Products

Consumer products are categorized based on the degree of shopping effort a consumer is likely to exert to buy the product. This categorization, in turn, assists the marketer in developing a marketing plan to reach the target market.

1. *Convenience products* are products for which the consumer wants to spend as little effort as possible to purchase. Thus, they must have intensive distribution with many retail outlets that provide convenience of purchase. Accordingly, there is likely to be a longer channel of distribution, with a low purchase price and mass-media advertising. Examples include milk, chewing gum, and tobacco products.

2. *Shopping products* are products for which the consumer has incomplete knowledge and is willing to shop around and compare prices. If the customer is willing to shop and compare products, there is not the need for as many retail outlets as there are for convenience products. Accordingly, personal selling may be required to assist the consumer in learning more about the product. Prices are generally higher, and sellers may need to provide credit programs to encourage purchases. Examples include smart phones and flat-screen televisions.

3. *Specialty products* are products for which the buyer is willing make a special effort to buy. Generally speaking, the buyer has complete

knowledge about the product sought and will not accept substitutes. Thus, there will perhaps be only one or a limited number of outlets selling the product in each market. Examples could include yachts or very expensive automobiles.

4. *Unsought products* are products the buyer does not seek until the need arises. Personal selling may be necessary to seek out the buyer and make the sale. Examples include insurance policies and burial plots.

Four competing philosophies strongly influence an organization's marketing activities. These philosophies are commonly referred to as production, sales, marketing, and societal marketing orientations.

—C.W. LAMB, JR.
—JOSEPH F. HAIR, JR.
—CARL MCDANIEL

A tall, redheaded woman wearing glasses, a heavy, bulky brown coat and a Pistons hat ate at the McDonald's on Lapeer Road. It was cold outside, but there was no snow on the ground in Auburn Hills, Michigan. She noticed McDonald's most recent marketing campaign to give rewards to schoolchildren with good grades and perfect attendance. She liked a campaign based upon rewards for a job well done. When she finished her Big 'N Tasty hamburger combo, she left to go to the Palace of Auburn Hills. She wanted to be at the Hawks and Pistons game early.

The Palace has been home to the Detroit Pistons since 1988. The sporting and entertainment venue has also hosted the Detroit Shock of the WNBA since 1998. One of the oldest arenas in the NBA, the Palace, at 5 Championship Drive, has a capacity of 22,076, with 193 luxury suites. The "5" in the address refers to the Pistons' 3 NBA titles and the Detroit Shock's 2 titles. With the largest arena in the NBA, the Pistons had the highest NBA home attendance from 2002–06. The team is one of only five NBA teams not to sell its naming rights to a sponsor, and it has one of only eight basketball arenas owned by an NBA franchise. The Western Forum in Los Angeles started the trend of selling naming rights to a sponsor. Now sponsorship is an important revenue stream for many franchises.

Some people call the Pistons arena "the Malice at the Palace" after November 19, 2004, as a result of one of the worst fan-player brawls in the history of basketball, during an Indiana Pacers and Pistons game. With 49 seconds remaining in the game, Pacer Ron Artest fouled Piston Ben Wallace as Wallace drove to make a lay-up. Wallace shoved Artest, and several other players became involved. Ron Artest climbed on a scorer's table and pretended to be giving a radio interview. Ben Wallace threw an armband at Artest, and a spectator threw a beer cup at him. Artest charged the stands and confronted the wrong person. Stephen Jackson and Wallace went into the stands. During the brawl, several Pacers punched spectators. Around nine fans were injured, and two were taken to the hospital. Ron Artest was suspended for the remaining 86 games in the season, and 8 other players received suspensions.

Public relations and publicity, part of the promotional mix, is one of the promotion tools of marketing that helps companies communicate to customers, suppliers, stockholders, employees, government officials, and the community at large. Other promotion tools are personal selling, sales promotion, and advertising. But no advertising or other promotion is as beneficial as free, favorable publicity. Likewise, free unfavorable publicity is devastating. The Pacers-Pistons' fight became the NBA's PR nightmare.

The redhead, wearing heavy make-up and glasses, purchased a ticket with cash and did not go to one of the luxury suites. She headed to the upper level, behind the basket, in section 221. This purple section was clearly the nosebleed area. But for only $45, it would serve her purpose. After finding her seat, she walked to the opposite side of the arena and then down a level. When she bought her first hot dog she was extremely scared, especially when she placed several of the tampered packages of mustard, ketchup, and relish on the condiment table when no one was looking. She had to get her weaker poison into food. The HeadOn product did not cause her formula to be absorbed through the skin. She knew that now, and wondered if she could get her money back, as their commercials suggest. She could even repeat the commercial: "If you are not 100 percent satisfied, we will give you your money back. We will give you your money back."

Shirlee Ann personally liked the funny Allstate TV commercials. The latest one involved a small, wimpy student who is the field-goal kicker for a high-school football team. He is in chemistry class, and an attractive coed asks him if he is going to the game Saturday night. He says, "I'm on the team." She laughs and says, "That's a good one." During the game he is shown sitting all alone on the bench until 4 seconds are left with the score tied. When the coach tells him to go in to kick the field goal, the coach does not know his name. He kicks the field goal and becomes the star of the game. Dennis Haysbert, of Fox 24 fame, infers in his deep voice that you are in good hands with Allstate. Allstate is "there when you need us."

Allstate is, of course, fighting Geico's animated gecko ads, which suggest that Geico has lower insurance rates. Even though the gecko is a memorable icon that assists in promoting Geico, a good message that better addresses the customer's needs and is effectively presented will usually win out.

Shirlee Ann made her way to another concession stand and repeated the process. The third time she became more confident. She was careful to leave no fingerprints. She ate only the third hot dog.

Back at her seat she heard a person in front of her say that the Atlanta Hawks were the league's worst team in the 2004–05 season. They had the longest tenure for the most consecutive seasons without a playoff appearance at eight years. The Pistons' mascot, a horse named Hooper, symbolizes horsepower. Hooper came out on the court wearing a Pistons jersey.

A professional basketball court is 94 feet long and 50 feet wide. Five players on both teams run up and down the court trying to shoot the basketball through the opponent's hoop, which is mounted ten feet from the floor on a 6-by-4 foot fiberglass backboard. Tonight the foul lane, or paint, which is 19 feet by 16 feet in the pros, was painted dark blue.

There was a dark red circle around the foul line, which is 16 feet from the backboard. The basket hangs over the paint. There was a 23 feet, 9 inch semicircle drawn around the center of the basket. A player who gets a field goal by shooting a live ball from beyond this second circle gets 3 points rather than the normal 2 points for a field goal. Even if only a toe is on the 3-point line, the shot counts as 2 points. In the case of a successful penalty shot, called a foul shot or free throw, a player scores 1 point.

No offensive player can be in the lane or paint more than 3 seconds, even if only one foot is in the lane. Otherwise, the player will be whistled for a 3-second violation and the other team gets the ball. There is not a similar restriction on a defensive player. A player has 5 seconds to pass the ball in bounds to a teammate after taking possession. Only 5 seconds are allowed for inbounding the ball once it goes out of bounds or a basket is scored. The offensive team has 10 seconds to move the ball over the center line.

While dribbling, a player cannot touch the ball with two hands at once. A player may not dribble (bounce) the ball, clearly hold it, and then proceed to dribble again without first either attempting a field goal or passing off to a teammate. This violation is called a double dribble. Moving both feet without dribbling is called traveling. Also, while dribbling a player may not turn the ball over in his hand between dribbles. If this is done, it is called palming. If these events occur, the other side gets the ball, which is called a turnover. When guarded, a player should not dribble the ball above the knees and the ball should not bounce above the waist. On defense, players are trained to watch the opponent's waist and not the eyes in order to determine which way a player is going to cut or move. Eyes may be used to trick a defender.

A professional game is composed of four 12-minute periods, or quarters. A college game is made up of two 20-minute halves. If a game ends in a tie, there are as many 5-minute overtime periods as necessary to break the tie. Because of timeouts and penalty shots, games can last well beyond 80 minutes.

The Hawks came out on the floor wearing navy, red, and white uniforms. The Pistons were leading 24 to 19 at the end of the first quarter, but by halftime the Hawks were ahead 48 to 45. The redhead heard sirens during the half. She did not get up from her seat, even though she was nervous and felt she might pass out. During halftime Hooper, the Pistons' racehorse mascot, wearing double zero on his red jersey, and the Flight Crew put on a trampoline dunk show.

Atlanta led by 9 points entering the fourth quarter, but trailed by 7 with one minute to play. However, Atlanta's 6'7" guard Joe Johnson (who earned $16 million in 2011) shot two 3-pointers to pull the Hawks within 1 with 40 seconds to go. In the end, the red, white, and blue Pistons won the game 92 to 91 as a result of free throws by 6'3" point guard Chauncey Billups. The point guard or ball handler is generally shorter than the other guard, the shooting guard. The point guard brings the ball down the court and tries to create shooting opportunities for his teammates. The point guard is often evaluated by the number of assists per game. Nicknamed Mr. Big Shot, Billups had a 2011 salary of $13 million.

As the redhead made her way away from the Palace, she decided that a wig and make-up was not enough of a disguise. She had to consider prosthetic make-up or a male disguise for her next date with the New York Knicks. She hoped that the people only became sick. She laughed when she thought about Bill Douglass trying to figure out why there were no basketball cards. "Keep them guessing" was her motto. There were no fingerprints or DNA on the letter that she would mail to Douglass tomorrow.

She knew about ink tagging. Manufacturers of ink change their ink formula regularly, so a white-collar criminal should not backdate a 2001 document with a pen manufactured in 2007. Likewise, most laser printers now encode the serial number of each machine in tiny, invisible yellow dots in every printout, nestled within the printed words and margins. The number tracks back to the printer like a license plate.

The next day the *Detroit Free Press's* summary of the game was headlined "Billup's Free Throw in Final Seconds Lifts Pistons in Home Opener." However, the Pistons' third straight win was marred by a number of fans falling ill, apparently from food poisoning. One person died.

The moment that Douglass heard on Fox News about the sick fans in Detroit, he knew for sure that the baseball murderer was back. He called the owner of the Pistons, William Davidson, and set up an appointment to speak with him. Bill Davidson bought the team from the original owner, Fred Zollner, for $7 million in 1974. The franchise is now estimated to be worth $284 million. Davidson is chairman of Guardian Industries, a manufacturer of glass. He is estimated to be worth $3.5 billion.

At 4:45 p.m., Douglass was sitting in Davidson's office. He explained his suspicions to the owner: that the sickened fans were probably poisoned by the baseball murderer. Davidson told Douglass that under no circumstances should any money be paid to the sickos. "Not a dime from me for an extortionist," Davidson said. "You have to catch them fast. My organization will help you. Just tell me what we can do."

Douglass asked for a list of employees or former players that might have a grudge against the Pistons. Davidson mentioned the names of several Pistons players, but indicated that he would prepare such a list for the FBI.

Next, Douglass went to the hospital that had treated most of the sick fans. The autopsy results of the fan who died showed oleander, fingernail-polish remover, potassium dichromate, white bryony, and wax. The report indicated that the last three items may have come from a product called HeadOn.

Douglass talked to three of the fans who were still in the hospital and learned that each of them had eaten a hot dog or hamburger at the game. They had seen no basketball cards. After obtaining a list of sick fans, he faxed the list to the Detroit FBI office at 477 Michigan Avenue, asking them to contact all of the fans to determine what they ate and if they had seen a basketball card lying around.

On the flight back to Quantico, Douglass kept debating a number of questions:

1. Why was there a new type of poison?

2. Why were there no basketball cards?

3. Why was the poison weak?

4. Why did she pick the Pistons? Detroit?

5. Did she dislike the Pistons or the Hawks?

6. Was there more than one murderer?

7. Were they terrorists? If this was a case of terrorism, he needed to contact Homeland Security.

8. What was the pattern?

9. Was this a copycat attack?

As in addressing marketing issues, it is important first to identify the problem. If ticket sales are down, that is not the real problem. The problem to be addressed is, "What is causing ticket sales to go down?" If someone has a headache and treats the symptom, the pain may go away. However, the problem has not been addressed if the pain is caused by a brain tumor.

Douglass's right arm still hurt. It had started hurting about four days ago. His wife said that he had arthritis or a torn rotator cuff. His arm had pain from the top of the shoulder shooting down toward his elbow. "Both your older sister and mother have arthritis. They use ice each night," his wife said. "You need to ice your arm at night."

Douglass noticed an advertisement on television about Therma Wrap—both hot and cold wraps. So which should he use? Heat or cold? Miami Heat Shaquille O'Neal had been advertising the heat strip on the tube. Douglass's wife had given him a frozen Blue Ice Rubbermaid Lunchpack the evening before he flew to Detroit.

He rubber-banded the ice pack to his upper arm as he worked at his desk and then walked on his treadmill for 40 minutes. When he took off the new white shirt he had been wearing, the blue water had spotted his shirt. Would the blue stuff come out of the shirt? Had he really addressed his pain problem?

Oh well, what did he tell his kids when they complained? "The world is run by people with headaches. Suck it up, Douglass." But how could a macho FBI agent protect the U.S. from dangerous criminals when he was obsessing about his shoulder and arm pain? Maybe he should use heat.

Early the next morning, Douglass called Caleb Pehrson and gave him the details of the Detroit incident. He asked him to develop some theories as to why the criminal had decided to strike at Detroit. Caleb said he would.

Later that afternoon, the Detroit FBI office confirmed his fears. The sick fans had all eaten a hot dog or hamburger. They had used either mustard, ketchup, or relish from the small packages on the condiment tables.

Around 4:30, Caleb Pehrson called and gave Douglass his thoughts. "As far as history is concerned, the original Basketball Association of America was the forerunner of the NBA. Terry Pluto, in his 1992 book *Tall Tales*, says the NBA came into existence for three reasons:

1. Ned Irish in New York and Walter Brown in Boston were making money with pro hockey but needed to fill up the year with another sport.
2. College basketball was popular and drawing crowds.
3. World War II was over, and men were home with money in their pockets.

So eleven arena operators met on June 6, 1946, at the Hotel Commodore in New York City. These eleven teams were divided into two divisions, the East and the West. The teams then were:

EAST	WEST
Boston Celtics	Chicago Stags
New York Knickerbockers	Cleveland Rebels
Philadelphia Warriors	Detroit Falcons
Providence Steamrollers	Pittsburgh Ironmen
Toronto Huskies	St. Louis Bombers
Washington Capitols	

"I'm faxing you the list now," Caleb said, "because the Detroit Falcons are not the Pistons of today. Before the 1948 season, four of the best National Basketball League teams jumped to the BAA—the Fort Wayne Pistons, the Indianapolis Jets, the Minneapolis Lakers, and the Rochester Royals. The Fort Wayne Pistons are the forerunner of the Detroit Pistons.

"On August 3, 1949, the BAA merged with the National Basketball League, expanding the number of franchises to 17. The BAA had the biggest arenas in the larger cities, but the NBL in smaller Midwestern cities had the better players. I am faxing you the NBA family tree from the official *NBA Basketball Encyclopedia*. You should buy the book."

Caleb continued, "The NBA considers the game on November 1, 1946, between the New York Knicks and the Toronto Huskies to be the first game of the NBA. In Toronto the Knicks beat the Huskies before a crowd of 7,900 by a score of 68–66. The New York press gave the Knicks little coverage. Leo 'Ace' Gottlieb was New York's high scorer with 12 total points." Caleb stopped his discourse for a moment.

"So where was the second game played?" Douglass asked.

"Hold on, Bill. If you go to a Fort Wayne Pistons' Internet site, someone can find out that the Fort Wayne Pistons played their first game in November 1941. So the bad guys may have mistakenly felt that the first game was played in 1941. Understand? I looked at all of the original teams' websites, and the November 1941 date may be believable."

"Good work, Caleb. So you're saying the second game would have been between the Knicks and Huskies, and the third game would have been between . . ." Douglass asked.

"The Boston Celtics played the Chicago Stags on November 5, 1946. The game started one hour late because Boston's Chuck Connors splintered a wooden backboard with a practice dunk before the game," Caleb said.

"Chuck Connors, the star of the television series *The Rifleman*?" Douglass asked.

"You bet. The same guy. The first broken backboard in professional basketball history. The 4,329 fans at the game saw the Stags beat the Celtics 57 to 55. The Celtics had a 22–28 record at the end of the first season in a last-place tie with the Toronto Huskies."

"Anything else, Caleb?" Douglass asked.

"That's about it," Caleb said. "We have to catch these people. I have to go teach tonight. The real problem is that we play the Knicks on the 29th of this month. I'm really worried."

"Where do you play them?" Douglass asked.

"Here at home."

"I better be there with some agents, but we'll catch them before then."

"Thank you," Caleb said quickly, but with little confidence. "I'll have some extra security personnel, too."

"When is the Knicks' next home game?" Douglass asked.

"Just a moment." There was a short pause, and Douglass heard paper shuffling. "Friday night against the Orlando Magic," Caleb finally said.

"Could you go with me to the game?"

"Sure," Caleb said.

"Who can I contact with the Knicks? Someone with discretion," Douglass asked.

"I'll email you a contact later today," Caleb said.

* * * * *

Caleb Pehrson was a part-time adjunct professor in The Carroll School of Management at Boston College. The Carroll School of Management is organized around six departments: Accounting, Business Law, Finance, Marketing, Operation, Information and Strategic Management, and Organizational Studies. BC is one of the oldest Jesuit universities in the United States, with about 8,500 undergraduate and 4,000 graduate students. The St. Ignatius Gate welcomes visitors to the lower campus, and the O'Neill Library is named after former Speaker of the U.S. House of Representatives Thomas P. "Tip" O'Neill, Jr., Class of 1936.

Caleb was in front of his basic marketing class. He liked to add excitement and interest to the classroom. Tonight he was covering the concept of "exchange." His first PowerPoint slide showed a model of the sports-marketing exchange process developed by Professor Matthew Shank of the University of Dayton.

"In theory, a sporting event will pull in people like bees to honey. Sports have a tremendous ability to excite emotions. A profitable sports franchise is, however, dependent upon the successful operation of the event (owners), the participants, the sponsors, and the audience (fans), as is shown in this marketing diamond," Pehrson told his class.

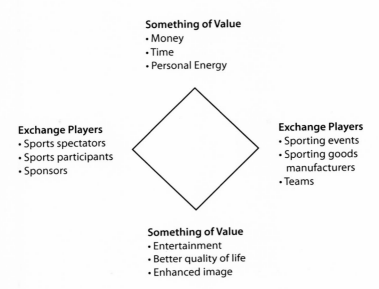

Something of Value
- Money
- Time
- Personal Energy

Exchange Players
- Sports spectators
- Sports participants
- Sponsors

Exchange Players
- Sporting events
- Sporting goods manufacturers
- Teams

Something of Value
- Entertainment
- Better quality of life
- Enhanced image

"In sports marketing, many exchanges may be occurring at the same time. Exchanges may occur with ticket purchases from the team ownership, caps or shirts purchases from licensed vendors, money to concessionaires, and money to media to broadcast the game.

"*Forbes* lists the world's most valuable sporting events brand each year. For 2010, the top ten sporting events in value were as follows." Caleb put up another slide.

RANK	EVENT BRAND	VALUATION (IN MILLIONS)
1	NFL Super Bowl	$379
2	Summer Olympic Games	$176
3	Soccer's World Cup	$103
4	NASCAR Daytona 500	$91
5	Rose Bowl	$88
6	NCAA Men's Final Four	$82
7	Winter Olympic Games	$82
8	Kentucky Derby	$69
9	MLB World Series	$56
10	NBA Finals	$47

"In terms of total revenue, the 2008 Beijing Olympics pulled in around $3 billion, with $1.7 billion from broadcasters," Caleb said. He put up another slide that listed *Forbes'* top ten most valuable sports-teams brands:

RANKS		VALUATION (IN MILLIONS)
1	Manchester United	$270
2	New York Yankees	$266
3	Real Madrid	$245
4	Dallas Cowboys	$208
5	Bayern Munich	$200
6	Arsenal	$195
7	Milan	$175
8	Barcelona	$170
9	New York Mets	$159
10	Boston Red Sox	$57

"As you can see, worldwide soccer is king," Caleb said. "They call it football. Soccer dominates because of their ability to obtain money from jersey sponsorship, stadium sponsorship, and merchandising.

"Due to the interdependency of the four variables in the concept of exchange, any one of the four can squander almost overnight any goodwill produced by a sporting event. George Shinn, owner of the former Charlotte Hornets basketball team, is an example of this negative goodwill. The rabid fans were willing to pay a fee for the right to buy tickets when the Hornets first came to town. Once they had procured the right, the tickets still had to be purchased. There were rumors that eight season tickets for Hornets games were auctioned for $160,000. A series of personal actions by Shinn caused the fans and local governmental officials to turn on him.

"Another example is the spygate affair involving the New England Patriots' videotaping of the New York Jets' sideline in 2006 in order to steal their hand signals. NFL commissioner Roger Goodell fined Patriots' coach Bill Belichick $500,000 and the Patriots $250,000. The team also had to forfeit their first-round draft pick in 2009. Their pattern of secretly videotaping the signals of opposing NFL coaches may have begun as early as Belichick's first pre-season in 2000—a total of seven years.

"Sports columnist George Solomon titled one of his stories about spygate as follows: 'If you are not spying, you're not trying.' Maryland basketball coach Gary Williams said, 'Coaches look to get any advantage they can.' In racing, Formula One Team McLaren was caught with technical information which belonged to its chief rival, Ferrari. They were fined $1 million.

"Almost two dozen Florida State University football players were suspended in 2007 before the Music City Bowl due to an academic cheating scandal involving a three-hour online music history class. A rogue tutor provided inappropriate help on the examination. FSU ended up losing to Kentucky in a close game, 35 to 28. The St. Petersburg Times editorialized that coach Bobby Bowden should retire. He is 'padding the career victory total at the expense of a remarkable legacy and a dignified exit. Dadgummit, Bobby, it's time.'

"Then there was Texas A&M football coach Dennis Franchione, who had to resign because of a scandal involving a newsletter he published that sold inside information to big-time supporters.

"There are a number of examples where players have shot themselves in the foot. Kobe Bryant of the Los Angeles Lakers was eventually able to overcome the unfavorable publicity from an alleged rape. Only time will tell if the most highly paid and electrifying NFL player, then Atlanta Falcons' quarterback Michael Vick, can recover after being sentenced to 23 months in federal prison and 3 years' probation. The disgraced NFL star was convicted of running a dogfighting operation. Many fans have been willing to forgive his past behavior, while others want to see him kicked out of the league altogether.

"An entire sport can be tarnished by a major labor dispute. The drug allegations against Barry Bonds and some other baseball players have tarnished the players and the sport of baseball."

Caleb put a third PowerPoint slide on the screen. "Marketing mix is used to strategically position a service or product in the marketplace. As the marketing mix diamond indicates, there are four P's: product (service), price, place or distribution channel, and promotion. This mix was developed by Neil Borden in 1964."

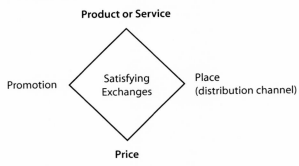

"Let me talk about the product of sporting events. The product in sports marketing can be the pure entertainment of the events, as well as the goods and services associated with the athletic event. Ticket sales, parking fees, broadcast rights, event entitlement, endorsement sales, and concession sales can result in revenues to owners of the event. Revenue from sponsorship rights is important for many event owners. For the sponsors, there is a means of getting their products and services in the minds of consumers.

"Many of the professional sports have franchise rights, such as basketball, baseball, football, and hockey. Franchising means that someone, such as a possible team owner, pays money to a league for the right to have a team in the league. In return the league grants the privilege, but the owners must abide by the clauses in the franchise agreement. Franchising puts some money into the owner's pockets, plus franchising allows the valuation of the team to increase over time. For example, even though the New York Knicks has had such a terrible win-loss record in recent years, the franchise is still worth approximately $592 million in 2007." Caleb repeated, "$592 million.

"NASCAR racing may be the number-one spectator sport in the U.S., with as many as 75 million fans. Sports racing has a free-market system rather than a franchise system. Richard and Lee Petty are pushing for a franchising system for NASCAR that would limit the number of teams competing in the Sprint Cup. A franchise system would guarantee starting berths and give owners equity in their team. For example, a new entity such as Honda would have to buy an existing franchise. Thus, a sports team over time hopefully will increase like an investment. Also, the racing teams could attract investors. NASCAR has resisted a franchise system so far because the privately held racing organization would have to give up some authority to the racing franchise owners.

"In the Sports Marketing Diamond, sponsorship is merely one of the elements of promotion in the Marketing Mix Diamond. Promotion includes such elements as advertising, public relations, sales promotion (e.g., two-for-one deals), direct marketing, and personal selling. A balance of the five tools is called the promotional mix. Some major forms of advertising include television, radio, newspapers and magazines, travel trade press, videos, posters, cinema, exhibitions and trade fairs, and the Internet." Caleb paused.

"Three researchers—J. Zarick, J. Grant, and K. Dobie—have argued that sponsors and organizers must agree on the identification of the sponsor's objectives, how they are to be measured, and the organizer's responsibilities regarding the attainment of sponsor objectives. Unless both parties have a clear understanding of the responsibilities of each, misunderstandings and unmet objectives will be commonplace. In their study, they found a statistically significant negative relationship between the dollar value of the sponsorship and the success of the sponsorship. Their research suggests that it is not the amount of dollar value, but rather other factors that determine the success of the sponsorship effort in achieving organizational objectives.

"Sponsorship alone is less effective than leveraging the sponsorship by spending additional resources on communication and promotional activities, such as advertising, sales promotion, on-pack signage, point-of-purchase, and production merchandise. Some researchers suggest leveraging up to three to five times the initial expenditure. Otherwise, a sponsorship may not be as effective as, say, advertising and sales promotion. Merely paying the sponsorship fee without advertising the sponsorship is like buying a page of advertising space in a magazine and leaving the page blank. The effect of the media coverage on consumers' attitudes or behaviors toward a particular brand is now weak.

"Leveraging a sponsorship is necessary in order to overcome ambush marketing, which reduces the benefits of a sponsorship of an event. Ambush marketing refers to the practice of associating a company with an event without paying the huge sponsorship fee. Viewers may identify a particular brand with a particular event even though the company is not in fact a sponsor.

"A great example of ambush marketing occurred during the winter Olympics in Japan several years ago. A Japanese film company bought the franchise rights to be the official filmmakers of the Olympics and to receive exclusive promotion rights in the film-product category. They spent millions of dollars in TV advertising, signage, and sponsorship events. However, a famous American film manufacturer bought TV air time for commercials immediately before and after the sponsored events appeared on TV. These commercials and other advertising for the events prior to the Olympics gave the false impression that the American company was the official sponsor of the Olympics. To combat this ambush marketing, a company may have to expend even more funds. For example, a company may have to buy all outdoor-advertising sites within a 3-mile radius of a stadium.

"In the April 2004 *Schmalenback Business Review,* Reinhard Grohs suggests these tips for sports marketers who want to maximize their sponsorship fees." Caleb put a slide upon the screen.

1. Try to ensure that exposure is high (e.g., by signing coverage contracts with television channels) and use this information when negotiating sponsorships.
2. Approach sponsors that have the closest fit with the event.
3. In the long run, try to promote sports with high fan involvement.

"Jeff Burton has driven a bright-orange No. 31 Chevrolet with the trademark jack of Cingular Wireless for a number of years. Cingular paid $150 million to showcase their brand before the NASCAR crowds. However, in 2006, AT&T merged with BellSouth and the Cingular brand was retired. When the Cingular jack was to be replaced with the AT&T trademark globe, NASCAR objected. The reason: in 2003, NASCAR signed a 10-year deal with AT&T competitor Sprint/Nextel for $700 million to rename the series of races formerly known as the Winston Cup.

"AT&T went to court and argued that if AT&T cannot replace the Cingular trademark with the AT&T globe, NASCAR has 'in effect, gotten us booted out of the sport.' The NASCAR lawyers argued that 'AT&T is using the merger to engage in ambush marketing that would erode NASCAR's semi-exclusive sponsorship agreement with Sprint/Nextel. AT&T attorneys cited marketing studies that show 72 percent of an estimated 75 million NASCAR fans consider racing sponsorships when making purchasing decisions.

"AT&T won at the lower-court level, but the Eleventh Circuit agreed with NASCAR that AT&T cannot put their brand on Jeff Burton's car." Caleb turned the page of his notes.

"In November 2006, Kia Motors unveiled a multitiered marketing program to sponsor nine NBA teams, including the Atlanta Hawks, the Boston Celtics, the Miami Heat, the New York Knicks, and the Seattle SuperSonics. In 2007, 7-Eleven signed 18 sports sponsorships, including four NBA teams: the Chicago Bulls, the Dallas Mavericks, the Los Angeles Lakers, and the Miami Heat.

"*Promo Magazine* gives an example of Wrigley, the gum company, pumping up their NBA sponsorship through sweepstakes on Wrigleyhoops.com. Their 'Do You Have the Real Stuff' instant-win promotion allowed fans to win prizes by entering a code from any Plenty Pak of Wrigley's assorted flavors of chewing gum. Around 80,000 instant prizes included $25 to $250 gift certificates for NBA merchandise and free Wrigley's chewing gum. At the end of the regular season, two registered participants won two tickets to the NBA finals in June. Wrigley also sponsored a mobile Jam Van tour across the U.S. after unveiling its multiyear NBA sponsorship. They have a weekly video-entries contest, and at the New Jersey Nets games they have installed branded courtside gum bins so players have easy access to something to chew on during the game." Caleb laughed and said, "I wonder who cleans up the chewing gum from the court.

"There is a difference between a sweepstakes and a contest. In a contest, the winner must exhibit some degree of skill. This skill may be as simple as guessing the number of beans in a jar. In a sweepstakes, each participant has an equal chance to win. In either of the two situations, the sponsor cannot require a person to purchase a product in order to participate.

"Companies give away free gifts, such as t-shirts, hats, calculators, and hundreds of other items. Drug companies give free drugs to doctors. Some psychologists argue that these small gifts that drug representatives give to doctors are very effective. When someone believes that a gift is not a bribe, but a token of friendship, the doctor or person feels the subconscious need to reciprocate."

Caleb paused and looked around the room. He wondered how many of the students were listening. Oh, well. "Let me summarize. There are several categories of sponsorship rights." Caleb moved to his next slide:

Title rights: placing the sponsor in the title of the sponsorship vehicle.

Presenting rights: acknowledges the sponsor alongside the title rather than incorporated into the title.

Naming rights: a long-term agreement associated with physical structures (e.g., arenas or stadiums).

Sector rights: exclusive representation from a sponsor's trading sector.

Supplier rights: products or brands are a function of the event.

"Possibly the first naming right was when Rick Corporation paid $1.5 million in 1973 for a 25-year relationship with Rick Stadium, the home of the NFL Buffalo Bills.

"Let me cover briefly sponsorship rights of superstars. In the past, many superstars have signed $50 or $60 million endorsement deals with Nike and other companies. Of course, some athletes choose not to do so because they are already wealthy. Japanese center-fielder Ichiro Suzuki, who has played for the Seattle Mariners for seven years, has taken a low profile in respect to endorsements. He has given up $50 million in deals in order to become one of the best baseball players. Many athletes choose not to pursue a second job while playing their sport.

"In the future, I believe superstars will ask for equity in deals. Rather than a short-term deal, they will demand a long-term piece of the action. Their playing time is a finite period of time, and they need to leverage their relationship into an equity deal rather than a short-term endorsement. They need to carry their worth beyond the playing field or arena. For example, former San Francisco 49ers All-Pro safety Ronnie Lott, offensive lineman Harris Barton, and quarterback Joe Montana founded a sizable hedge fund called HRJ Capital at the height of the tech bubble. They lost money initially, but they survived. HRJ is called a fund of funds because it invests in other venture funds.

"A sports star must plan ahead, much like Jennifer Azzi, who runs a fitness center in Salt Lake City called Azzi Training. She was the point guard for the Stanford University Cardinals when they beat Auburn University in 1990 for the NCAA Divisional I Basketball Championship. She was a member of the gold medal–winning U.S. women's basketball team in the 1994 Goodwill Games and the 1996 Summer Olympics in Atlanta. She played for the Detroit Shocks and the Utah Starzz. She planned for retirement long before she retired from the WNBA, and is now a motivational speaker."

Caleb stopped and asked if there were any questions. There were none, so he said, "Don't forget your homework for next time. Before you go, I'm handing out a document put out by the state of Virginia that talks about career opportunities in sports marketing."

Part of the handout is as follows:

It's the playoffs. L.A. versus Detroit. Whether you're watching the game on television or sitting directly courtside, there's probably one thing you can't help but notice—lots and lots of ads. "Gatorade" is scrawled across the court floor in gigantic letters.

Frequently, TV ads cannot be seen if you are at the event. An analogy is the yellow first-down line you see on TV in a broadcast football game. The TV broadcaster has the ability to show a logo on a basketball court or behind home plate as if it were actually there. And they can change the image as often as they wish, or at least as often as the number of times they sell the advertisement "space." This phenomenon has become known as "virtual advertising."

Advertising is prevalent at the actual sport event. Often, big Budweiser and Coke signs festoon the arena walls. Prominent players wear uniforms with equally prominent corporate logos, like those of Nike or Adidas. And it doesn't stop between quarters. You see dozens of TV commercials featuring star basketball players pushing everything from cars to shoes to life insurance to breakfast cereal. The sports arena itself is named after a bank, a group of stores, or some other corporation that agreed to sponsor the care and upkeep of the facility.

Welcome to the world of sports marketing.

Although we may think of sports as fun and pure pleasure, sports is nothing if not a big business. Each year, sports organizations pull in billions of dollars from fans and corporate sponsorships, enough to reward their players with handsome multimillion-dollar contracts. Every year, corporations plan advertising and promotional campaigns built on the endorsements of sports celebrities, from Dorothy Hamill to Michael Jordan to Tiger Woods. Sports organizations offer hospitality events and fantasy camps for fans and corporate sponsors. Players nurture their careers to eke out the maximum amount of profit from endorsements, motivational speaking tours, and personal appearances. Businesses hope to win over potential investors by hosting sports events.

* * *

In short, there are a lot more players in sports than just those on the playing field.

For the near future at least, the ball is squarely in the court of sports marketers.

Specific duties in this field include:

- Negotiating and preparing contracts for athletes
- Strategizing about how best to leverage sponsorship
- Planning and coordinating sports events
- Conducting market research and analysis
- Producing promotional material, including mailings and webpages
- Talking with athletes and sports organizations about their needs
- Monitoring sports activities and new trends
- Overseeing the development of new merchandise and products associated with a team, player, or a particular sport
- Overseeing the upkeep and maintenance of a sports facility
- Overseeing ticket sales

While education in this area depends on the exact job, people in this field usually need a master's degree in business administration with an emphasis in sports marketing or sports management. Certainly, the most prestigious jobs with well-known organizations, teams, and companies go to people with MBAs. However, smaller teams, organizations, and agencies often accept students with only a bachelor's degree in sports management or business.

The University of North Carolina at Charlotte recently implemented an MBA program with a concentration in sports marketing. This program drew students from across the country and even from some foreign countries. MBA students attended full-time, and during the course of their time at UNCC they spend at least one semester in an internship at a professional sports team or organization.

New York University also offers a Master of Science in Sports Business, reflecting the fact that it is a $200 billion industry. They also offer a Graduate Certificate in Sports Business.

The Exchange Process

Exchange occurs in the marketing process when the buyer gives something of value to the seller in return for a product (a good or service). For exchange to occur, there are at least five conditions that must exist:

1. There must be at least two parties involved.
2. Each party must have something of value to offer the other.
3. The two parties must be able to communicate with each other.
4. Each party must be free to accept or reject the offer.
5. Each party must believe it is desirable to transact with the other.

The increase in the number of television and radio networks available created added clutter in the marketplace and the competition between advertisers to attract consumers' attention was fierce. For many, sponsorship became an effective and less costly alternative to break through the clutter in order to reach specific targets.

—BENOIT SEGUIN

—NORM O'REILLY

he letter got to Douglass's desk on the morning of the Knicks-Magic game. The outside of the envelope was addressed with block letters. Inside was one page with the following message in words cut from newspapers and magazines:

Like   Freddy   Krueger   I   am   back   Douglass

Sandy   Kojak

His name was spelled right, and the letters had apparently been cut from an old newspaper article published during the baseball murders. Douglass called Pam Olson at the Department of Homeland Security and explained the situation. She agreed to send two female DHS agents with knowledge of exotic poisons to the Knicks-Magic game that night.

Madison Square Garden, or simply the Garden, opened February 14, 1968, on 7th Avenue between 31st and 33rd Streets in New York City. The Garden hosts at least 320 annual events, including the Knicks and N.Y. Rangers of the National Hockey League. It can hold 19,763 basketball fans. Seating is arranged in five ascending levels, with the lowest level called courtside for basketball games. Being a monolithic grandstand, distance from the ends of the arena to the playing floor is significant, especially when sitting behind tall spectators.

Basketball arenas are often shared with ice-hockey teams. Basketball teams need a wooden floor, and hockey teams need an ice rink. Since it is time-consuming and costly to melt and refreeze ice, many basketball games are played over ice. The rink stays frozen, and for a basketball game a layer of insulation is created between the ice and the wood. The wooden floor is made in sections that are stored in the arena, so the Madison Square Garden workers must turn the ice rink into a basketball court by fitting the wooden panels and insulation together like a jigsaw puzzle.

The Knicks Legend Section includes 30 prime tickets approximately 20 rows from the court. Fans can start their evening off by entertaining clients with a pre-game meal in the Club Bar & Grill restaurant. They can enjoy in-arena food and drink service during the game and possibly collect an autograph from a former Knicks star. The cost for 30 guests is a mere $22,500. The smaller groups charge $750 per seat. Douglass did not get to sit in this section, which is located at Gate 63, Lodge level.

The term Knickerbockers comes from the Dutch settlers who came to America and settled in New York in the 1600s. These settlers wore pants that were rolled up just below the knees. A character called "Father Knickerbocker," wearing a cotton wig, three-cornered hat, buckled shoes, and knickered pants, became synonymous with New Yorkers. The Knickerbocker name was first attached to Alexander Cartwright's Manhattan baseball team in 1845. When the Basketball Association of America granted a franchise to Ned Irish in 1946, a group put possible names into a hat, and most of them said "Knickerbockers." The team's colors, except for two seasons, have been orange, blue, and white.

The New York Knicks is one of only two charter members of the NBA still in their original cities, the other being the Boston Celtics. On December 16, 2006, the Knicks had the most penalized on-court brawl since the infamous Pacers-Pistons altercation. Knicks coach Isiah Thomas became mad at the Denver Nuggets coach running up the score after the Nuggets were comfortably ahead. Knicks player Mardy Collins reached around the Nuggets' J. R. Smith neck and threw him down as he went for a lay-up. A number of fights broke out on court, and even after the brawl appeared to be over Carmelo Anthony punched Mardy Collins in the face. The officials ejected all 10 players who had been on the court at the time.

On December 18, 2006, NBA commissioner David Stern issued these fines and suspensions:

- The Knicks and Nuggets organizations were fined $500,000 each as a result of the altercation.
- Nuggets forward Carmello Anthony was suspended for 15 games.
- Nuggets guard J. R. Smith was suspended for 10 games.
- Knicks guard Nate Robinson was suspended for 10 games.
- Knicks guard Mardy Collins was suspended for 6 games.
- Knicks forward Jared Jeffries was suspended for 4 games.
- Knicks center Jerome James was suspended for 1 game for leaving the bench during the on-court altercation.
- Nuggets forward Nene was suspended 1 game for leaving the bench during the on-court altercation.

Neither coach was fined or suspended. On the front page of the *New York Daily News* blared the huge headline "His Fault," with the statement, "Mike Lupica says finger of blame points at Isiah Thomas for causing Garden brawl." Lupica wrote a column called "The Garden of Evil," accusing Thomas of creating an uncontrollable atmosphere. The *Wall Street Journal* said Thomas was attempting to resurrect the rough, physical "Bad Boys" tactics of the late 1980s Pistons, of whom Thomas was a member.

Isiah Thomas was coaching today for the Knicks as Shirlee Ann made her way to Section 227 in the "Garden of Evil." She had eaten at the Knickerbocker Pizza in order to test her disguise. She was carrying a card that explained she could not talk. She then wrote her request on a pad of paper. She had paid $100 for a ticket from someone outside the arena, which was a difficult task without speaking. Her hair was cut short under her Knicks baseball hat. She was wearing the bulky brown coat, but she was dressed like a man, wearing glasses. She found her seat early and sat down to observe the Garden of Evil.

Isiah Thomas is a retired professional basketball point guard with nicknames like the Baby-Faced Assassin, the Smiling Assassin, and others. He is a partner in the New York–based gourmet-popcorn chain Dale and Thomas Popcorn, and he appeared in the basketball documentary *Hoop Dreams*. Shirlee Ann had read reports of Anucha Browne Sanders's sexual harassment lawsuit against Thomas and the Madison Square Garden.

Sanders's lawsuit said that Thomas had refused to stop making unwanted sexual advances toward her, had used offensive language, and had turned others in the organization against her.

Sanders had been Senior Vice-President of Marketing and Business Operations and the second highest-ranking executive in the Knicks' organization. After she filed the charges, she was fired. She maintained that Thomas engaged in "demeaning and repulsive behavior." A court awarded her $11.6 million, one of the largest sexual harassment judgments in history (later reduced to $11.5 million).

* * * * *

Douglass met with Caleb Pehrson, five FBI agents, Pam Olson, and two DHS agents in the office of the Knicks' Executive Vice-President of Facilities. Douglass gave them some simple instructions, which the VP then related to his security personnel. They were to pay special attention to the women's bathrooms. They were given latex gloves and warned not to pick up any basketball cards.

On the side, the VP asked Douglass if any of this might have to do with the Thomas lawsuit or the Knicks and Nuggets incident. Douglass told him he did not think so, but that anything was possible.

During the game, Douglass, Caleb, and the assembled security group were constantly going from bathroom to bathroom and concession stand to concession stand.

* * * * *

Shirlee Ann was watching the Orlando Magic mascot, Stuff the Magic Dragon. Stuff is a green dragon with red wings with a white bib on its stomach. The white bib has "Stuff" written on it.

Tonight Billy Donovan, who had agreed to a 5-year, $27.5 million contract earlier in the year, was not the head coach of the Orlando Magic. Donovan was the University of Florida's men's basketball coach who led his team to back-to-back NCAA championships. Two days after agreeing to the Magic contract, Donovan decided to go back to the University of Florida. Eventually the Magic agreed to allow Donovan to back out of the deal in return for a 5-year noncompete clause, which said that Donovan would not coach for another professional basketball team. Some experts argue that since Donovan exchanged something of value—the release for the noncompete clause—he had approximately $2 million in taxable income.

Similarly, the flagship university in one of the poorest states in the union pays its football coach, Les Miles at Louisiana State University, at least $4.3 million. More than the governor of Louisiana or the president of the United States. Go figure.

Whatever the case, the Orlando Magic hired Stan Van Gundy, a former Miami Heat coach. Van Gundy was the coach for the Knicks in 2001 when San Antonio Spurs player Marcus Camby threw a punch at Danny Ferry, missing Ferry but hitting Van Gundy. Van Gundy needed 15 stitches to close the cut over his left eye.

During the first quarter, Shirlee Ann was able to watch the 17 Knicks City Dancers do their thing. They were dressed in blue with an orange vertical stripe down both sides, a wide white belt, and white boots. She enjoyed their dance routine.

At the end of the first quarter with the score tied 28–28, Shirlee Ann went to a snack bar and bought a hot dog and a coke. She was so nervous she could not eat the hot dog. However, she noticed some well-dressed men walking around with earphones. The FBI, maybe? She checked out the bathrooms, and most of them seemed to be under surveillance.

She decided to go into one of the men's bathrooms that were not being watched. In two of the stalls she was able to carefully put a basketball card on the toilet-paper holder. With a little more confidence, she went down a level and placed two more cards in stalls. She left a written message in two of the stalls. She then went back to her seat.

At the end of the second quarter the Knicks were ahead by 1 point, 49 to 48. But the two big men for the Knicks, center Eddy Curry and power forward Zach Randolph, were in foul trouble, and they sat out the last 4:18 before the half. Curry, a 6'11" center, had a 2009 salary of $10.5 million, and Randolph, a 6'9" power forward, had a $17 million salary in 2010. Near the end of the third quarter, both of the Knicks big men received their fourth foul. During a time-out in the third quarter, former NBA center Patrick Ewing, the Knicks scoring leader, was given a loud ovation. He is now one of four assistants with the Magic team.

During the third quarter Shirlee Ann heard sirens, so she left the Garden. She was not there to see the Magic outscore the Knicks in both the third and fourth quarters. The Magic won, 112–102. This was the Magic's fourth road game, and they had won them all.

Douglass found the SuperSonics basketball cards and messages, but it was too late to save the afflicted fans. The cards were in men's restrooms, and he had felt that any cards would be left in the women's restrooms. A fatal mistake.

The message read as follows:

> Retribution for the cruel U.S. occupations in Iraq and Afghanistan. Long live Osama Bin Laden. There will be more to come!

The initials "SK" were printed on the notes and basketball cards.

Douglass and Pam Olson called their respective directors and suggested they inform the U.S. President that the so-called baseball murderers were back attacking professional basketball teams. The President told the director of the FBI, "You better find these crazies fast. Your job is on the line."

A partial write-up in the *Daily News* the following day went as follows:

REVENGE AGAINST THE GARDEN OF EVIL
Claude Berger

Not only did the Orlando Magic and coach Stan Van Gundy hand the Knicks a 112 to 102 loss, but two fans died from apparent food poisoning at the Garden of Evil. There is some indication that the two fans were killed by poison. Two others are in serious condition. There is speculation that either the Knicks/Nuggets altercation or the awful handling of the sexual harassment lawsuit by Anucha Browne Sanders may have caused someone essentially to attack the Garden.

There are unconfirmed reports that both the FBI and Homeland Security agents were at the game. Two of the deaths occurred in men's bathrooms, and two other fans were found unconscious outside a bathroom. There may be some parallel to the many so-called baseball murders two years ago. During the game, Coach Van Gundy was not attacked by any players.

When Douglass reviewed videotapes of the men entering the two bathrooms, nothing of importance could be gleaned. Dead end.

There simply were not enough FBI agents or DHS agents to go to all of the professional basketball games. Douglass told his director that the President must decide if the general public should be told about the threat. If the public was told, there would be panic, and the NBA revenue stream would be significantly affected.

The President decided not to go public until more information was obtained.

The medical reports and autopsy results showed that the poison on the basketball cards was a mixture of sarin, nicotine, and dimethyl sulfoxide. The same as the Trenton and Herkimer murders.

Nothing happened for several days, but around 11:00 one morning Douglass answered the phone and a woman spoke.

"Hello, Douglass, did you find my messages and basketball cards? I really do hate involving other people, but you killed my friend, and we never received our payment."

"But . . ." Douglass tried to speak.

"We will call you shortly and ask for $3 million in diamonds. Just like last time. Stay tuned."

She hung up.

Douglass traced the call to a pay phone in Charlotte, N.C., on the campus of the University of North Carolina–Charlotte. The phone had been wiped clean. Not many pay phones were left, with so many cell phones in use today.

Douglass looked in *The Official NBA Basketball Encyclopedia* and found that the Charlotte Bobcats played in Charlotte.

Douglass called Caleb Pehrson and asked him to work on any leads in respect to the Supersonics cards. "Be sure to look at any events that could have angered anyone. I'm talking about teams that the SuperSonics may have played during the 1977–78 season."

"Will do," Caleb promised. "Don't forget that we play the Knicks at the end of this month. It's a home game."

"I know," Douglass said. He told Caleb about the call from Charlotte. Caleb indicated that the Hornets team had played in Charlotte for about four years before the owner, George Shinn, moved them to New Orleans. "I'll check on the Hornets and Bobcats," Caleb promised.

"Two other items of interest," Caleb added. "Starting on January 1, 2007, Commissioner Stern announced that the league would return to the traditional leather basketball. There had been a number of players' complaints about hand injuries caused by the new Spalding microfiber ball. The players even filed a lawsuit against the NBA about the ball. They said that the microfiber ball was too sticky when dry and too slippery when wet. This episode shows poor public relations on the part of Stern, but he knew how to get out of it."

Douglass joked, "Did they argue that the new ball caused global warming?"

"Well, Shaquille O'Neal said that the new ball felt like one of those cheap balls that you buy at the toy store," Caleb said.

"I don't want to argue with Shaq. Is he shooting free throws any better?" Douglass laughed.

"Second," Caleb continued, "as of 2006, official NBA jerseys are now manufactured by a German company, Adidas, and not the previous supplier, Reebok. Maybe some ill-feeling there. Adidas's 11-year licensing agreement is worth about $400 million. Reebok had a 10-year licensing agreement that was signed in 2001 for about $200 million. Reebok will still furnish NBA-branded footwear. Reebok has a roster of basketball endorsements, such as Yao Ming and Allen Iverson."

"Thanks, Caleb," Douglass said. "Millionaires complaining about the basketball. Go figure. A lawsuit to get a leather basketball."

"We can probably eliminate the National Basketball Retired Player Association as the bad guys. They recently signed a 5-year licensing agreement with the NBA that is worth about $5 million to the association. This deal doubles the previous agreement, which allows the NBA to use the likenesses of retired players such as Elgin Baylor and Moses Malone."

"So that would include Elvin Hayes?" Douglass asked.

"Yes. The players whose likenesses are chosen to create promotional items such as retro jerseys, bobblehead dolls, video games, posters, and t-shirts will receive 4 percent of the revenues that the league earns on those items."

"So the NBA gets a lot of revenue from licensing agreements?" Douglass asked.

"You bet. In the middle of 2007, the NBA signed a $7.4 billion deal with ESPN, ABC Sports, and Turner Network Television covering the seasons 2008–09 through 2015–16. Streaming live games are part of the eight-year deal. ESPN will be able to televise up to 75 regular season games and 29 playoff games."

Under a franchise, a franchisee, such as ESPN, is granted the right to engage in the business of offering, selling, or distributing goods or services (e.g., showing a basketball game). The franchisee is associated with a franchiser's trademark, trade name, advertising, or some other commercial symbol. In return, the franchisee must pay directly or indirectly a franchisee fee to the franchiser. Under a licensing agreement, a company's logo or a university logo can be placed on collectibles, apparels, furniture, and many other novelties.

Channels of Distribution

Products are transferred from seller to customer through channels of distribution. A *channel of distribution* begins with the seller and includes *intermediaries* who resell to others or facilitate the sale within the channel until the final exchange takes place with the final customer. Consumer-product channel intermediaries include wholesalers, retailers, agents, and brokers. Their functions are to facilitate the flow of goods and ownership between the producer and the buyer. These functions include:

A. Transactional functions:
  1. Contacting and promoting
  2. Negotiating
  3. Risk-taking

B. Logistical functions:
  1. Physically distributing (transporting)
  2. Storing
  3. Sorting (overcoming discrepancies of quantity)

C. Facilitating functions:
  1. Researching (gathering information about customers and other channel intermediaries)
  2. Financing (extending credit to facilitate the efficient flow of products through the channel to the ultimate customer).

When the great teams of any professional sports league are discussed, none can
approach the Celtics' dominance. Not the New York Yankees. Not the Montreal
Canadiens. Not the Green Bay Packers.

—DALE RATERMANN

ouglass called the NBA commissioner David Stern and asked for a
meeting with the basketball owners as soon as possible. The NBA is
located at 645 Fifth Avenue, N.Y., in the Olympic Tower. The league
has 30 teams, 29 in the U.S. and one in Canada. Training season
begins in October. The teams play some pre-season games as they
try to get to a 12-man roster, with a 3-man inactive list. The regular season
begins November 1, and each team plays a brutal 82 games, divided equally
between home and away games. During the season a team will play every
other team. In February there is the NBA All-Star Game, and the regular
season ends near the end of April, with the start of the NBA playoffs.

David Stern began his tenure as the fourth NBA commissioner in February 1984, taking over from Larry O'Brien. The NBA was struggling at
that time, with 17 of its 23 teams losing money. The league's reputation
was so bad that in 1980, CBS showed the final game between the 76ers and
the Lakers on tape-delay at 11:30 p.m. With little basketball background
other than playing hoops on local basketball courts, Stern became a savior
to the NBA. He is credited with being the creator of the roadmap for the
commercial maximization of major-league sports in the U.S. He studied
political science and history at Rutgers and received a law degree from
Columbia Law School while working behind a counter in his family's New
York delicatessen.

This shoot-from-the-hip guy has been called both a savior and dictator
on AskMen.com. His success has made him feel immune to criticism, and

he dictatorially controls the players, the owners, and the NBA entry lottery draft. His success, however, has increased the NBA's revenue by 500 percent since 1984. He also has added franchises, introduced collective bargaining (which led to revenue sharing), opened international offices, created the Women's National Basketball Association, introduced the salary cap, and negotiated a 24 percent increase in North American TV contracts. Market values of franchises had increased as much as 500 percent by 2007.

Before the 2005–06 season, Stern announced a new NBA dress code. The new code bans players from wearing headphones, chains, shorts, sleeveless shirts, indoor sunglasses, t-shirts, jerseys, and headgear such as baseball hats during public appearances.

In 2007, Stern was facing something of a crisis with eight of the small-market franchises. He had received a letter from eight of the owners stating that "the current economic system whereby local television revenue and gate receipts are not shared among the 30 franchises works only for the large-market teams and a few teams that have extraordinary success on the basketball court." Owners in Charlotte, Memphis, Milwaukee, Indianapolis, Orlando, and New Orleans had signed the letter.

One of the best-run small-market franchises had not signed the letter. Although the San Antonio Spurs is in the third-smallest market in the NBA, this franchise is worth approximately $390 million. In the past season they had an operating profit of $11.7 million, versus the NBA average of $6.9 million.

Apparently, what the eight owners were complaining about involved the revenue-sharing formula. Whereas baseball gives $20 million checks to their smaller-market franchises, Stern and the NBA allow a consulting firm, McKinsey & Co., to develop a sharing plan based upon how well the franchise is run. According to Stern, run your team well, and you are eligible for a handout. Run your team poorly, you get nothing. The bottom five teams in term of valuation in 2010 were:

TEAM	VALUE (IN MILLIONS)
Charlotte Bobcats	$281
New Orleans Hornets	$280
Indiana Pacers	$269
Minnesota Timberwolves	$264
Milwaukee Bucks	$258

Shirlee Ann did not feel sorry for the owner of the New Orleans Hornets. Since she grew up in Concord, N.C., she knew that the Hornets' owner, George Shinn, had only paid about $33 million for the franchise in Charlotte.

The top five teams in terms of valuation in 2010 were:

RANK	TEAM	VALUE (IN MILLIONS)
1	N.Y. Knicks	$665
2	L.A. Lakers	$643
3	Chicago Bulls	$511
4	Boston Celtics	$452
5	Houston Rockets	$443

Stern's latest scheme is the NBA's subsidiary in China, which is one of the few notable U.S. imports into that country. Chinese stars such as Yao Ming have legions of fans in their homeland. NBA China has the right to create teams in China and will own all broadcasting rights and merchandising. It is valued at about $2.3 billion. Walt Disney Company will own 5 percent of the subsidiary, and four other Chinese investors will own together 6 percent.

* * * * *

On the day before the meeting with the basketball group, Caleb Pehrson called Douglass.

"Bill, we may be wrong about the history that our character is following. She may not be using the timeline in the NBA family tree. I called a friend with the Atlanta Hawks, and he said that at a pre-season game between them and the Philadelphia 76ers, there were basketball cards found in a number of locations. Get this, Seattle SuperSonics cards. You'll need to check out the Los Angeles Lakers pre-season game with the Sacramento Kings."

"Can you explain why?" Douglass asked.

"Sure. It is confusing. There were five teams that were in existence when the original Basketball Association of America was formed in 1946 that did not join at that time. Three of these teams joined the BAA in 1948, and two of them became members in 1949."

"Who were these teams?" Douglass almost shouted.

"I faxed you a list with their history."

"Let me go get the fax, and I'll call you back on my dime," Douglass said.

Douglass found the fax and read it. "Wow! Wow! And double wow!" he said aloud.

- Syracuse Nationals (1939) became Philadelphia 76ers, joined Basketball Association of America in 1949 season.
- Fort Wayne Pistons (1941) became Detroit Pistons, joined BAA in 1948 season.
- Rochester Royals (1945) became Sacramento Kings, joined BAA in 1948.
- Detroit Gems (1946) became L.A. Lakers, joined BAA in 1948.
- Tri-Cities Blackhawks (1946) became Atlanta Hawks, joined BAA in 1949.

Douglass called Caleb back. "OK, I'm looking at the fax. You said that basketball cards were found at the 76ers' and Hawks' pre-season game. They hit the Pistons' game, so that leaves the L.A. Lakers and Sacramento teams, right? So they'll hit there next?" Douglass asked.

"Not necessarily. There was a pre-season Lakers and Kings game after the 76ers/Hawks game. I don't know if anyone got sick there, or if there were any basketball cards," Caleb said.

"But they wouldn't be going in the proper order," Douglass suggested.

"True, but we do not know where the bad guys are located. Where do they start? Where is their base? Besides, why have a pattern that we can anticipate? If I were the bad guys, I would hit in random areas," Caleb said.

"Correct. So they start out in Atlanta. Go to the West Coast and swing back to Detroit," Douglass said. "They may be located in the South."

"Also, keep in mind that the bad guys are probably getting much of their information about the teams from the Internet, and probably from Wikipedia, the free encyclopedia. That's how I did it. They can make mistakes, maybe on purpose."

Douglass paused for a moment. "I'll check out the Lakers and Kings pre-season game and also try to get more information about the Hawks and 76ers game. Please be prepared tomorrow at the owner's meeting in New York to outline this pattern that may be emerging," he said.

"I will," Caleb answered firmly.

"Wait a minute. Where was the Lakers-Kings game played?" Douglass asked.

"At Sacramento," Caleb answered.

Douglass was thinking as he hung up the phone. The people were killed by a batch of deadly poison at the first two sites. At the Pistons site a new mild poison was put into the food. There were basketball cards at the Hawks-76ers game, and maybe at the Lakers-Kings game. Suppose she ran out of the old poison and had to make a batch of new poison from oleander bushes. The HeadOn product did not work at the two pre-season games, so she had to add it to the food. What was his motto? Look below the tip of the iceberg. Look below the waterline, where two-thirds of the iceberg rests. Think outside the box.

* * * * *

Commissioner Stern called the meeting of the owners to order the next morning with Douglass and Pehrson present. An exceptional dresser, Stern was wearing an expensive blue suit and red tie. Of course, with $7 million in income and a personal tailor, what could one expect? Stern turned the meeting over to Douglass.

Douglass calmly told the assembled basketball elite about the $3 million extortion call and the similarities between the baseball murders two years ago and the current threat. He did not explain to them that the caller knew about the initials "SK" printed on the baseball cards, but he did say that some of the poisons were similar. He emphasized the killings at Trenton and Herkimer. Douglass then asked Caleb to explain about the possible pattern with respect to the dates.

Caleb showed the group an outline of the beginning dates of the franchises:

1. Syracuse National (1939) became the Philadelphia 79ers.

2. Fort Wayne Pistons (1941) became the Detroit Pistons.

3. Rochester Royals (1945) became the Sacramento Kings.

4. Detroit Gems (1946) became the L.A. Lakers.

5. Tri-Cities Blackhawks (1946) became the Atlanta Hawks.

Douglass pointed out that although there had been no deaths, basketball cards were found at both the Atlanta and Sacramento games. He explained how the murderer or murderers might be experimenting with the various poisons.

Next Caleb gave a theory as to the order of the next possible teams that the extortionist might strike.

1. N.Y. Knicks (1946), already hit.
2. Boston Celtics (1946).
3. Golden Gate Warriors (1946).
4. Washington Wizards (1961).
5. Chicago Bulls (1966).
6. Houston Rockets (1967).
7. Seattle SuperSonics (1967).
8. Phoenix Suns (1968).
9. Portland Trailblazers (1970).
10. L.A. Clippers (1970).
11. New Orleans Jazz (1974).
12. Denver Nuggets (1976).
13. San Antonio Spurs (1976).
14. Indiana Pacers (1976).

He emphasized that there was no assurance that the killers would follow this pattern.

After Caleb sat down, Douglass opened up the meeting for questions and suggestions. He indicated that baseball did not pay the extortion demands two years ago.

Michael Jordan, part-owner of the Charlotte Bobcats, asked about the mechanics of any payoff.

Douglass said, "I do not know. The caller has not given me any instructions."

Ted Stepien, owner of the Cleveland Cavaliers, asked, "Why are they calling you? Are you involved with them? I thought you FBI guys caught them two years ago."

Douglass explained that he was the high-profile fellow during the last baseball disaster, and said, "No, I am not part of the group, Mr. Stepien."

Christopher J. Cohan, owner of the Golden State Warriors, whose team was next on the list after the Celtics, stood up and said, "Look, we have to do something about the problem immediately. Can we not get the President to activate the National Guard?"

"Calm down, Chris, my team is high on the list, too," Susan O'Malley of the Washington Wizards said. "We certainly must keep our mouths shut about this situation when we leave this room. Look what happened to baseball's revenue two years ago."

Several people in the room agreed.

The outspoken owner of the Dallas Mavericks, Mark Cuban, stood up and said, "I make a motion that we do not pay any extortion money, otherwise we'll have every nut in the country trying to shake us down."

A representative from the Detroit Pistons seconded the motion, and in a voice vote the proposition passed. But a number of people kept quiet.

A folded note was passed to Caleb near the end of the meeting. The note said that $200,000 cash would be delivered to Douglass tomorrow to pay off the killers. "Please stop this," it concluded.

Douglass asked each of the teams to send him a list of employees, players, or others who might have a grudge against their team or the NBA in general.

Someone whispered "Major League Baseball."

* * * * *

The next day the proverbial crap hit the fan. The *New York Times* ran a front page story about the meeting.

BASEBALL MASS MURDERERS BACK?
Samuel Essec

The basketball elite met yesterday at the Olympic Tower in New York to learn from the FBI that the so-called baseball mass murderers have returned.

Anonymous sources indicate that these diabolical terrorists have struck at least three times. First, they struck in Trenton, then in Herkimer, N.Y., and three nights ago at the Knicks-Magic game in the Garden. Apparently, one or more individuals are poisoning fans at basketball-related functions.

The moment Douglass entered his office that morning, the director of the FBI called and said that the President of the United States had told him to remind Douglass that the President could lose his re-election bid if these psychos were not caught soon.

Then he had a call from the Vice-President, "encouraging" him to find the killers.

His administrative assistant did not put through any of the phone calls he received from numerous reporters.

Later in the morning Douglass received a call from the "SK" woman. When he picked up his phone, she said, "Hello, Douglass, I wanted to get our transaction done before all of the headlines. But I guess it's too late."

She continued, "Tomorrow evening I want you to spend the night at the Fairfield Inn by Marriott, 3033 Cloverleaf Parkway, Concord, North Carolina. It's near Interstate 85. Rent a solid blue Chevrolet or Ford. Do not use a government car. Register under your own name. Stay at least three nights.

"I hope you are recording my message. Like last time, put the $3 million in diamonds inside a briefcase, which should be placed inside a silver metal suitcase. You should have two suitcases left from our baseball conflict.

"The diamonds should be one to two carats, at least eye clean—e.y.e.— and I color. No junk. Do not lock the outside suitcase or the briefcase, but label the suitcase with the following warning: 'Caution: Radioactive Material Inside.' Remember, Fairfield Inn in Concord, North Carolina. Be there by 4:30 p.m."

"Wait, how do I know who you are?" Douglass asked. The caller was trying to disguise her voice.

"You do. SK. Sandy Kojak. Seattle SuperSonics. 1977–78. By the way, Douglass, do not try to cheat me like last time. Remember what happened in the Tokyo subway system on March 20, 1995. Do not put a tracking device in the package." The phone went dead.

After hanging up his phone, he said, "Bingo. She's in the South." But he knew what had happened in the Tokyo subway system. Sarin was released.

The phone call was traced to another pay phone on the University of North Carolina–Charlotte campus. The phone had been wiped clean.

Douglass obtained a briefcase, filled it with Herkimer diamonds, and placed it inside a silver suitcase. He added a handful of cubic zirconias for good measure. Known as CZs, they are the most inexpensive and widespread diamond simulant on the market. Although discovered in 1937 by two German scientists, they only made their way into the jewelry market in the 1970s. Grown under tremendous heat around 5,000 °F, they are mass-produced at a fraction of the cost of diamonds. CZs have a higher dispersion than diamonds, which gives them a greater brilliance. CZs can fool the unaided and untrained eye. Douglass hoped the double-terminated quartz crystals and CZs would give the FBI some more time.

At the last moment, he added a handful of synthetic moissanite. Sources told him that moissanite reads as "diamond" by most standard diamond-tester devices. One needs a specific moissanite detector to tell it from a real diamond.

The entire mixture looked beautiful to Douglass. "Buyer beware" was one of the oldest marketing principles. Before closing the briefcase, he put in the $200,000.

He took an FBI jet to Charlotte, rented a blue Ford at the airport, and drove down Billy Graham Parkway to Interstate 85. He anticipated a two- or three-day stay. At least he would be away from the reporters.

Along I-85 he noticed a billboard with the advertisement, "Two Bobcats Season Tickets with the Purchase of a New Home." Another billboard said, "Hey, Dude, You Have Just Missed Hundreds of Customers." He passed the Poplar Tent Road exit and eventually took the number 58 exit to the Fairfield Inn in Concord. He noticed that North Carolina license plates proclaimed "First in Flight," advertising the fact that the Wright brothers flew the first plane at Kitty Hawk, N.C.

He caught himself drumming on the steering wheel to the beat of the "Music Box Dancer." He really liked that song. He had not changed channels on the radio when he got into the car. The next song was "I Can't Stop Loving You" by Ray Charles. "What a great station," Douglass thought. The next song was the sad but great song "El Paso," sung by Marty Robbins.

Paul Harvey with the news came on next, with his page 1 advertisement, followed by his patented page 2, page 3 style. Then Douglass noticed a bumper sticker on the back of a truck: "Work is for people who do not fish." Douglass always liked Paul Harvey's "The Rest of the Story" radio stories.

* * * * *

Caleb's phone rang. When he answered, the caller on the line identified himself as Jacob Johnson, legal counsel for Upper Deck.

"Mr. Pehrson, I hate to bother you, but we need to talk. I know how concerned you must be for the Celtics and the NBA with this mass murderer on the loose. However, my client has a particular concern about protecting the brand equity of Upper Deck. We are afraid the public is going to shy away from the purchase and collection of our sports cards due to the unfavorable publicity generated by people dying from poison on basketball cards at NBA games."

"I can certainly appreciate your concern. What can I do for you?"

"I was wondering if the NBA would consider a press release or press conference to allay the fears of our customers. Anything you can report from the ongoing investigation that will assure the safety of our customers would certainly be appreciated."

"Mr. Johnson, rest assured I am just as concerned about public safety as you are," Caleb said. "We are doing what we can from a PR standpoint without interfering with the ongoing criminal investigation. However, I believe it would be in the best interest of your client if they were proactive themselves and addressed this issue directly.

"Do you remember the Tylenol scare a few decades ago? Some crackpot placed cyanide in three bottles of Tylenol in a Midwestern city store. One person died. Johnson and Johnson, the parent company of the Tylenol brand, was extremely proactive. They immediately announced a recall of all Tylenol products from retail shelves worldwide. Of course, this recall cost the company millions of dollars. They subsequently changed their product from capsule to solid spansule–product format and introduced the tamper-proof bottle for their product. While the changes cost them millions of dollars in the short run, their action won them acclaim from the public for the way they handled the situation.

"In contrast, a few years ago the news media made much ado about Ford Explorer SUVs rolling over as a result of tire blowouts. Ford sat on this information for a long time before addressing the issue, and when they finally did, they blamed Firestone for faulty tires as the cause of the accidents. Firestone and Ford kept blaming each other and people continued to die.

"I recommend you act more like Johnson & Johnson and take the initiative to address the problem yourselves. We will certainly do what we can to calm the public."

Integrated Marketing Communication

The term "marketing promotion" has been replaced with the concept of *integrated marketing communication (IMC)*—the coordination of all marketing promotional activities such as media advertising, personal selling, public relations, publicity, sales promotion, website design, point-of-purchase displays, and other tools designed to produce a unified customer-oriented message. IMC informs, persuades, or reminds potential buyers of a product with the intent of influencing an opinion or eliciting a response. In short, IMC is used to reach the target market and meet the organization's marketing communication/promotional goals. All of these promotion elements are assembled around a central coordinating theme. The key elements are as follows:

Advertising: Impersonal, one-way mass-media communication from the seller to the potential buyer. The sponsor of the message is readily identified and the medium is paid for the space or time utilized.

Personal Selling: Direct communication between two people in which one attempts to influence the other in a sales situation.

Sales Promotion: An effort to produce a direct response to a promotion. Includes such elements as coupons, product samples, contests and sweepstakes, premiums, loyalty programs, and rebates.

Public Relations: Efforts to strategically convey messages to stakeholders such as investors, consumers, media, government, employees, and the general public. Tools include news releases, feature articles, press conferences, event sponsorships, and product placement.

The mission of a sports team is not just to play games, but to serve the interest of its fans.

—CORBIS/BETTMANN

hirlee Ann was born and grew up in Concord, N.C., the county seat of Cabarrus County. With a population of around 55,000, it is the home of Lowe's Motor Speedway, which is in the heart of NASCAR country. In 2000, a pedestrian bridge across Highway 29 to the racetrack collapsed, injuring more than 100 fans.

Shirlee Ann played on the Concord High School basketball team. Concord athletic teams are called the Spiders. For two years she dated a boy from nearby Kannapolis who was a student at A. L. Brown High School. Its students were called the Wonders. Each year the Spiders and the Wonders would play the Battle of the Bell. The winner of the football game would receive the railroad bell, which they would then paint their school colors.

She still remembered the stories about the Kannapolis Christmas parade —oops, the "holiday parade" for the politically correct. The children always knew when the Santa Claus float was near because of the barking coon dogs. There was always a 'possum float that had a tree with 'possums hanging from branches. There would be hunters on the float with their coon dogs on leashes barking at the 'possums. When the dogs stopped barking, the hunters only had to shake the tree to start them barking again. PETA probably stopped the second-favorite float in the Christmas parade in Kannapolis. Shirlee Ann's boyfriend worked briefly in Cannon Mills, and he would laugh about the refreshment cart that came around the mill during his shift. Most mills operated twenty-four hours a day, in three eight-hour shifts. The refreshment truck was called the dope cart, and the dope man would come around three times during a shift. How times have changed.

Until recently, Kannapolis, with a population of 37,000, was a textile mill town. James William Cannon, the founder of Kannapolis, built Cannon Mills Company in 1888. Many poor employees worked their entire lives as "lint heads." William Cannon, however, lived in Concord with other wealthy people. As cheap foreign textile goods flooded into the U.S., eventually Cannon Mills and other textile mills across the U.S. closed their doors.

David H. Murdock purchased Cannon Mills and stripped the cash from the pension-plan trust. Keeping the real estate around town, he sold the mill to Fieldcrest. Fieldcrest later sold the mill to Pillowtex. Eventually Murdock repurchased the mill buildings, tearing down more than 1.2 million square feet. Today he is building a huge North Carolina Research Campus on the site. Most remnants of William Cannon's company have been eliminated, including the famous Cannon Mills smokestacks.

In spite of Kannapolis's long history as a low-wage mill town, it gave birth to a number of Horatio Alger success stories. George Shinn, owner of the NBA Hornets; Robert Tucker, founder and owner of the large Shoe Show retail chain; internationally famous composer Jackson Hill; and the most famous of them all, Dale Earnhardt, launched their careers from there.

Earnhardt became known as "The Intimidator" for his aggressive style of driving in NASCAR races. Typical of most drivers, he raced under contract for a team owner, who in Earnhardt's case was Richard Childress. The contracts for drivers specify how compensation is to be determined. A driver may get a salary and any combination of team earnings, including bonuses for wins or where they place in a race. The owners generally receive millions of dollars from corporate sponsors. In return, the major sponsor has its name on the hood, trunk lid, side panels, or other exterior parts of the car. There are also minor sponsors, who, for less money, have their logos printed on the car's quarter panels or fenders. Sponsors especially like NASCAR sponsorships because the fans are extremely loyal and support the sponsor by buying their products.

To make the big bucks, drivers usually form their own marketing company and generate revenue from licensing arrangements with businesses. Dale Earnhardt, Sr., who became affectionately known as "Big E" when his son Dale, Jr., began racing, made millions of dollars each year from the sale of licensed merchandise from t-shirts to anything else on which the signature "Dale Earnhardt," his visual likeness or the stylized number "3" could be placed. The number 3 was the number owned by the race team, which was painted on the roof and sides of Earnhardt's Chevy Monte Carlo race car. The number 3 has not been used on a NASCAR car since Earnhardt's tragic death in the infamous race at Daytona.

Many old timers resent the fact that the only statue in Kannapolis is one of Dale Earnhardt, Sr. Exit 60 off of Interstate 85 is now named Dale Earnhardt Boulevard. In 2004, the movie *3: The Dale Earnhardt Story* was released by ESPN. His son, Dale Earnhardt, Jr., is carrying on his father's racing tradition.

Dale, Jr., seemed to inherit the hearts of his father's fans and quickly became the most popular driver on the NASCAR circuit, driving car number 8. He drove for a DEI team owned by his father and stepmother, but due to a disagreement with his stepmother he left DEI and joined Hendrick Motorsports, owned by Rick Hendrick. Of further interest was the fact he could not take the number 8 with him since it was owned by DEI.

Dale, Jr.'s, sponsor at DEI had been Budweiser, even though the company sponsored the team and not the driver. Although Budweiser had invested millions of dollars in the team and had capitalized on Dale, Jr.'s, popularity among NASCAR fans, the company lost that investment when he left to drive for Hendrick Motorsports. One indication of his worth to Budweiser was reflected in the point of sale. Point-of-purchase (sale) displays with Dale, Jr.'s, likeness proved this point. Beer distributors had to buy their POP displays from the parent company, Anshauser Busch. Obviously, they would not buy the displays to be placed in retail locations unless they work. And work they did. Budweiser sales increased, and Budweiser distributors all over the country began buying these POP displays. These sales proved the popularity of NASCAR racing, but more importantly they pointed to the association of the Budweiser brand with Dale Earnhardt, Jr. and the value of sports sponsorships. But as things go, when Dale, Jr., left DEI, the sponsorship stayed behind. His current sponsor is the National Guard.

* * * * *

Douglass brought his computer along with briefing papers about professional basketball with him to Concord. Since the town is only about 20 miles from Charlotte, he hoped to determine if the Charlotte Bobcats or the Charlotte Hornets had anything to do with the extortion plot.

He learned that the Bobcats were a new franchise established in 2004 as an expansion team. Black Entertainment Television's Robert T. Johnson, one of the first African-American owners in professional sports, was awarded the Bobcats franchise. In 2006, NBA legend Michael Jordan became the second-largest shareholder in the Bobcats. The Hornets had left for New Orleans when the city refused to build a new arena downtown.

Since the Bobcats seemed to be fairly noncontroversial, Douglass focused on the Hornets. Could someone be mad because the Hornets had left town? Certainly the controversial owner of the Hornets, George Shinn, has led a confrontational, roller-coaster life in his rags-to-riches career. Could he be the target or reason for this attack on basketball?

Shinn was born 25 miles from Charlotte in Kannapolis. His father died when George was eight, and Shinn graduated last from A. L. Brown High School in a class of 232 students. He worked in a textile mill for three years before working part-time as a janitor to help pay his tuition at Evans Business College.

His big break occurred when he was doing his cleaning duties. Two young girls showed up at the door and asked for information about the business college. He gave them a tour. The next day four girls arrived who were interested in enrolling in the school, but would only talk to him. The director then hired George to recruit students, and his selling skills were so good that he was given part-ownership of the college. After graduation, he purchased the school.

After doing so, he built more than 30 schools, known collectively as the Rutledge Education System. He sold the empire in the early 1980s for $30 million. He invested in real-estate development, an auto dealership, publishing, and a traffic reporting company. In 1975, at age 35, Shinn was one of the youngest people to win the Horatio Alger Award.

Only eight basketball arenas are owned by an NBA franchise, and most are public facilities. Obviously, public funding reduces the costs to a team, especially for smaller franchises. The Minneapolis Timberwolves built their facility in 1990 for $104 million, but the debt was so burdensome that the city had to take it over. The Target Corporation is its corporate sponsor.

Shinn was able to convince NBA executives to grant Charlotte a franchise, and on August 12, 1985, work began on a state-of-the-art arena six miles outside of Charlotte. Although the building was financed by voter-approved bonds, Shinn was able to rent this new coliseum for five years for a fee of one dollar per game.

Fan support was phenomenal, and Shinn organized a name-the-team contest to replace the original name, "Spirit." The team was named the Hornets because during the Revolutionary War, the North Carolina militiamen were compared to hornets by British General Cornwallis, who said, "It's a veritable nest of hornets down here." The Hornets' first game was on November 4, 1988, and they led the NBA in attendance for eight consecutive years (1988–96).

Trouble began almost immediately, however. Shinn had elicited three partners to help pay for the franchise—Rick Hendrick, Felix Sabates, and Cy Bahakel. In 1989, Shinn decided to enforce a buyout clause. Although Hendrick and Sabates agreed to sell their shares back to him, Bahakel took the dispute to the courtroom. Even though Shinn eventually won, the newspaper headlines eroded his popularity.

Douglass read an article in the *Charlotte Observer* entitled "The Rise and Fall of George Shinn and the Hornets," dated February 7, 2002. "From hero to hated, George Shinn has fallen hard—and he has taken his beloved Charlotte Hornets with him. Today, this man is despised, viewed as a traitor and hypocrite who should be run out of town, or run up a rope." Lynn Wheeler, a city council member was quoted in the article as saying, "The dislike, the hatefulness, for George in this town right now is incredible."

What caused George Shinn to become a pariah in Charlotte? He seemed to have a dual persona. On one side was his Horatio Alger rise to fortune, his family values, and his religious personality. He had a prayer read over the arena's public-address system before each game. Around Christmas time he would invite senior citizens from all the area churches to come to the arena for finger food and ice cream. People could listen to Christian singing, and Shinn would walk around talking to people. Sometimes the coliseum was full. He also would give new shoes to homeless people in shelters. His speeches and writings were laced with Christian statements.

But a media circus began when his wife divorced him following rumors that he was having an affair with one of the Hornets' cheerleaders, called the Honey Bees. Then Leslie Price accused the 58-year-old Shinn of luring her to his house on September 5, 1997, and sexually assaulting her, knowing that she was vulnerable while being treated for addiction to prescription painkillers. Price said that Shinn forced her to have sex with him. No criminal charges were filed, so Price sought damages in a civil lawsuit. After an 11-day civil trial, on December 17, 1999, a South Carolina jury rejected Price's claim, agreeing with Shinn that the sex was consensual. But the marketing damage had been done.

George Shinn became dissatisfied with his current coliseum because of the limited number of luxury boxes. In 1987, Joe Robbie Stadium (now the Miami Dolphins stadium) started the era of luxury suites and club seats. The importance of luxury boxes can be found in the testimony of former San Francisco 49ers coach and general manager Bill Walsh. He testified for the Oakland Raiders, who were suing the Oakland-Alameda County Coliseum for more than $1 billion in a fraud suit over a 16-year lease agreement. According to Walsh, luxury suites allow an organization to spend money on players that a competitor might not have. With large salaries and a restrictive salary cap, luxury suites allow a team to get extra funds to use as signing bonuses that do not count against the cap.

The Hornets were now near the bottom of NBA attendance. Miami center Alonzo Mourning said that the Hornets simply lost their charisma. Shinn issued an ultimatum demanding that Charlotte build a new arena at no cost to the team, or he would move the team. A referendum to build a new arena was defeated, but the city said that they would build a new coliseum if Shinn would sell the team.

Most leagues frown upon movement of teams from one city to another because it denotes instability. However, owners won the right to move in 1982 in the court decision *Raiders v. NFL*. Thus, Shinn moved the Hornets to New Orleans for the 2002–03 season.

Three years after moving the Hornets to New Orleans, the New Orleans Arena still had not been able to find a sponsor in order to fulfill the right to collect from naming rights. In December 2004, the Hornets hired the Bonham Group to find a sponsor. As of January 2008, no sponsor had been found. Thus, the state of Louisiana must pony up as much as $2.5 million annually to give to the Hornets. The amount is based upon a sliding scale determined by attendance. If the Hornets sell the naming rights in excess of $1.5 million but less than $2.5 million, the state has to pay the Hornets the difference until it reaches the total of $2.5 million. If the naming rights are more than $2.5 million, Louisiana is in the clear and the Hornets keep the difference.

Several other named arenas are:

Atlanta Hawks—Philip Arena
Chicago Bulls—United Center
Cleveland Cavaliers—Quicken Loans Arena
Miami Heat—American Airlines Arena
Orlando Magic—T. D. Waterhouse Centre
Denver Nuggets—Pepsi Center
Utah Jazz—Delta Center

So there were people who did not like George Shinn, but they would have to go to New Orleans to act on their grievances, Douglass concluded.

When the Carolina Panthers moved to Charlotte, they created a personal seat license (PSL), which is the same to an individual as a luxury box is to a business organization. A person must make an advance payment to purchase the right to a particular seat for a certain period of time. Some universities even have personal seat licenses.

After making this one-time payment, the person still must pay for the tickets each year. The Dallas Cowboys are asking their fans to pay as much as $150,000 for the 30-year right to buy season tickets for their new stadium. They will get cushioned seats on the 50-yard line, food and drinks on game days, and access to premium parking. The Cowboys' cheapest license is $16,000. The average PSL for the NBA is $1,000 to $5,000, and Major League Baseball's average PSL is $3,600 to $15,000.

* * * * *

Shirlee Ann had selected two alternative drop sites for the diamonds. The first one was near the North Carolina dam across the Catawba River, which created Mountain Island Lake. This lake has more than 60 miles of shoreline and a surface area of more than 3,235 acres, providing millions of gallons of water for the City of Charlotte. Shirlee Ann's thought was to have the FBI agent toss the suitcase off the bridge across the Catawba

River on Brookshire Drive or Highway 16. Taking the opposite direction on Brookshire Drive from I-85 took one directly to the Bobcats arena.

Once she retrieved the loot from the suitcase at the bottom of the bridge, she could scuba toward the Mountain Island Lake dam and come into the boat docks on Mt. Isle Harbor Drive. There were private boat docks up and down the river where she could hide if necessary. Also, near the dam is a small wooded island, which is actually the top of the mountain that was almost completely covered by water when the dam was built by Duke Power in 1923. This area was below the flight pattern for the many planes landing at the Charlotte-Douglass International Airport, which might restrict the FBI helicopters looking for her.

Shirlee Ann had read about Mountain Island in a story in the *American Philatelist*. She had been a stamp collector for a number of years before high school, but her stamps had disappeared when she went off to the University of Georgia. According to the author of an article entitled "Rediscovering the Confederate Treasury: Mountain Island, North Carolina History," the island still may contain hidden Confederate gold. Near the end of the Civil War, Confederate president Jefferson Davis and his cabinet had made their headquarters at a Bank of North Carolina branch, located on the west side of Tryon Street, midway between Trade and Fourth Streets. Along about April 20, 1865, some 3,000 pounds of gold bullion and money belonging to the branch bank were removed and buried about 18 miles from the bank.

Uncle Jim, an African-American slave, told this story to children about the buried gold:

> I remember the day as if it was yesterday. My poppa and I spotted a troop of Confederate soldiers coming from the direction of Charlotte. They were escorting a horse-drawn wagon down Rozzelles Ferry Road. There were about a dozen soldiers on horseback riding on each side of the wagon. They were in a hurry to get where they were going. The wagon the horses were pulling was so heavy that I could see where its wheels cut deep ruts in the dirt road.
>
> I saw them turn off the road toward where the steam plant sits today. They were gone a pretty long time.

Then he would half-whisper, "long enough to bury something."

Then, an hour or so later, they came flying back down the road. They were riding like the Devil himself was chasing them, and they didn't slow down when they got to the big road where they turned towards Lincolnton. The wagon was empty this time, and it was flying all about behind them like a June bug on a string.

He would lean close to the kids and say, "Some say they buried gold that day, and some say the gold is still buried deep in the ground. It could be buried beneath your feet where you are standing right now."

Is the gold still hidden on the underwater mountain covered by millions of gallons of water that now form the reservoir for the city of Charlotte? While she was exploring the area before the drop, Shirlee Ann would scuba around the island looking for possible caves that might hold the hidden gold. She did not find the gold.

Shirlee Ann paid cash for two cell phones of the buy-use-and-toss variety containing prepaid SIM cards worth $40 each.

* * * * *

Douglass did not receive a phone call from the bad guys during his first evening in the Fairfield Inn. He spent some time reading the *Charlotte Observer* and the *Independent Tribune*. In the *Tribune* there was a story about Barry Bonds arguing to keep his all-star legal team intact. Bonds was shown leaving the Philip Burton Federal Building in San Francisco where had had been fighting the perjury and obstruction of justice charges for allegedly lying to a federal grand jury about his steroid use.

A story in the *Tribune* entitled "Expert Worries About Safety at College Stadiums" was about Jim McGee, a professor at the University of Southern Mississippi. As part of the university's Spectator Sports Security Management, his job is to teach others about the dangers facing event managers. He believes that it is only a matter of time before another domestic or international terrorist targets a sport event.

Douglass mused, "If they only knew what I know already."

Another story was about L.A. Lakers Kobe Bryant, who had complained about the lack of talent on the Lakers the past spring. He had asked to be traded. The Lakers had just beaten the Phoenix Suns, 122 to 115, their ninth win in eleven games. "Who sang the country-western song 'Thank God for Unanswered Prayers'?"

Another story, entitled "Boy Scout Holds Title as Popcorn Salesman," was about 14-year-old Anthony Aldrich, a freshman at Myers Park High School. He claimed the title of Popcorn Salesman King in the Boy Scouts last year, and was trying to win for a second year in a row "That's a tough goal, but I'm very competitive," Anthony said. "When I heard no Scout had been top seller two years in a row, I knew I had to achieve that. I love a challenge."

He pitched microwave popcorn to tailgaters at the Carolina Panthers' football game against the Dallas Cowboys in full Scout uniform. "My secret is keeping eye contact," he said. "I don't just read from a sheet. I talk to them about what the popcorn is good for. If they're on a diet, I talk about low-calorie popcorn. If they don't like popcorn, I talk about making a donation. I always try to have an answer." He sold $19,458 worth of gourmet popcorn last year.

But around 5:00 Wednesday evening the phone rang, and the same female voice asked, "What kind of car did you rent?"

"A blue Ford," Douglass answered.

"OK, here is your agenda. Go to your blue Ford and carry the suitcase with the diamonds. Put the suitcase in the trunk. I worry about robbers. There should not be a tracer in the suitcase or briefcase. Take them out now. The cases should not be locked. Go north on Interstate 85. Take exit 63 to Kannapolis. You will go left on Lane Street until you come to the first traffic light. Cut left again onto Wright Avenue in Kannapolis. Almost immediately you will see a church on the left. Franklin Heights Baptist Church. I repeat. Lane Street. Wright Street. Park on the right side of the church.

"There will be a church service going on when you arrive. On the right side of the church is a ten-foot-deep concrete trench surrounded by a metal guard rail. Near the front of this trench is a tiny wire attached to the guard rail. By pulling up the wire you will find a package. Only you should get the package. No one else. We are watching. Follow the instructions in the package. Franklin Heights Baptist Church. Enjoy the service, Douglass.

"Surely hope you have my diamonds. Did you see the movie *No Country for Old Men* with the psychopath Anton Chigurh? He says, 'I know where your wife, Jenny, lives.'" The connection broke. Douglass's wife was named Jenny.

After about a 16-minute drive, Douglass reached the church and parked on the right side. There were cars in the paved parking lot, and the church was lit up. He noticed a sign that said, "No loitering and skateboarding." He heard singing as he walked to the concrete trench which allowed sunlight to get to the basement windows. There were six beautiful stained-glass windows along the upper side of the church.

With his Maglite he searched for the wire attached to the pipe fence, found it, and pulled up a brown, padded envelope. He took the wire and package back to his blue Ford. Douglass opened the brown mailing envelope and found a cheap throw-away phone and a hands-free device that slips over one's ear. One sheet of paper had this message.

> Go to the front of the church, read the sign, and remember the name of the minister. Wait 5 minutes and go down Clay Street toward Kannapolis. Almost immediately on the left is the name of a hotel. Remember its name. Further down Clay at the corner of Clay and Evelyn on the left you will see a house surrounded by a unique fence made of covered wagon wheels. Count carefully the number of wagon wheels in the fence. Next go right over to Lane Street, turn right on Lane Street, and then drive back down Lane Street towards I-85. Keep the phone on. Before the lake on the right is Lane Street Baptist Church. Pull into its parking lot. Wait 10 minutes *or* until someone who speaks your name comes to your car. There is someone with a rifle watching you. If nothing happens within 10 minutes, get out of your car and walk to the back of the portable carport. There is a note taped to the back, right side. Be careful. Do not get a speeding ticket.

After getting the name of the minister, Douglass waited 5 minutes, put his gun down within reach on his seat, and drove down Clay Street. He saw a sign over a driveway saying "Hotel California." At the corner of Evelyn he counted 78 wagon wheels. "This is crazy," he thought. "Was she a tour director?" He then drove down Lane Street and parked in the Lane Street Baptist Church's parking lot. He tried to slump down in his car seat and moved his head from side to side to make it more difficult for a sniper. He kept his hand on his gun.

The phone rang, and he jumped. "Hello, Mr. Douglass. Glad you could make it," the familiar female voice spoke to him. "What is the minister's name?"

"Jim Grigg," Douglass answered.

"What was the name of the hotel?"

"Not a hotel. Just a large, weird sign over a driveway that says 'Hotel California.'"

"Right. How many wagon wheels?"

"Seventy-eight," he said.

"Horse feathers, Mr. Douglass. You missed five. You should be more careful."

"What is your cell phone number?" she asked.

He told her.

"Please get out now and go behind the portable carport in the parking lot. Keep the phone on so I can hear you. Start counting from one to 100."

Douglass started counting.

"I want you to pull off the white envelope taped to the back of the carport. Do not open the envelope. Remember my shooter."

Douglass did as he was told. He retrieved the envelope and returned to the car. Before he entered his car, she said, "Please get the silver suitcase from your trunk, and put it in your front seat. Then put the envelope into the briefcase. Is the suitcase locked? Is the briefcase locked?"

"No and no." Douglass did not put the envelope in the briefcase.

"Now I want you to start your car, go back out to Lane Street, turn right, and head toward Interstate 85. Keep the phone on, but start counting softly from one again. When you turn onto Lane Street, do not speed. They give traffic tickets along here. Oh, I forgot. You are the FBI."

As he turned right onto Lane Street, Douglass started counting from one again. When Douglass saw the bridge ahead he anticipated her next instructions.

"Douglass," she said, "in the middle of the bridge ahead, stop on it. Take the suitcase and the phone and throw them in the water on the right side of the bridge. Do not bring your gun with you. Leave immediately. One of my shooters has you in range," she warned.

Douglass did as instructed, tossing the suitcase into the water. He heard it hit the water. Douglass got into his car, punched a number on his cell phone and said, "The Eagle has landed." He turned on the GPS tracking system, which was working. Both tracers were going slowly down the lake.

He gunned the gasoline pedal, but after about 1,000 feet he stopped his car and got out. He could hear the helicopters in the distance, but for some reason he was not optimistic because of the darkness.

Douglass's pessimism was well-founded. They did not find the female extortionist, only the silver suitcase and briefcase, which were empty. She had allowed both to float down the lake with the tracking devices. So the FBI began reverse 911 calls to the houses around Lake Fisher to see if anyone had seen anything suspicious. There were no leads. Douglass had not thrown the cell phone into the water, and the cell phone had been activated with the name Elvin Hayes. He decided to get a list of everyone in the past 5 years that had gotten motor vehicle tickets along that stretch of Lane Street.

K-9 units from both Kannapolis and Concord were used to search the shores around Lake Fisher. The Belgian Malinois and Dutch Shepards found the buried scooter. Canines can track lost persons, detect illegal drugs, search buildings, find people under debris, and apprehend suspects in crimes.

Douglass began second-guessing the wisdom of putting fake diamonds into the suitcase. At least she was $200,000 richer. But would she stop? Douglass thought not.

* * * * *

Shirlee Ann was grateful that she had spent time on the back porch and in the backyard kissing her Kannapolis boyfriend a number of years ago. They would sneak down to Lake Fisher some nights and take a swim in the moonlight. Illegal, of course.

Once she retrieved the silver suitcase from under the bridge, Shirlee Ann took out the briefcase and opened it. She took out the diamonds and put them in a large pouch, making sure there were no tracers. She dipped the diamonds in the water because she knew the water would short out any GPS tracker. She kept the package of $100 bills after checking for a tracker. She then put several strands of hair in the briefcase. She tied the briefcase to her waist with a rope.

She had two choices. To the north was Moose Road. If the Kannapolis Intimidators, a Class A–affiliate of the Chicago White Sox, had been playing tonight in the Fieldcrest Cannon Stadium, she might have gone north about a mile. Instead, she headed south along Lake Fisher Reservoir, which was 3 miles in length and about 534 acres in area. Water pumped from the lake goes to a filter plant to be used by the citizens in and around Concord.

The underwater scooter carried her down the reservoir at about 3 miles per hour. After a short distance, she let the briefcase float up and away. The darkness hid her few bubbles as she went under the Brantley Road bridge. Her lighted underwater compass allowed her to get to the end of the reservoir near Lake Fisher Road. She again checked the diamonds and money to make sure there was no tracker. Finding none, she placed the scooter inside a large plastic bag and buried the scooter in a hole that she had previously dug. She hoped to come back and get the scooter after several days. Shirlee Ann put her diving gear in the two saddle bags and drove the motorcycle down Lake Fisher Road, turned right onto Centergrove Road, and immediately crossed over the unlucky Lake Concord bridge.

The bridge has been the site of two bizarre events. About 26 years ago, a father left his house early one foggy morning to go to work and never returned home. He disappeared and was presumed to have left his family. About 14 years later, the lake level receded because of a drought. Someone noticed a car antenna sticking out of the lake. When the car was pulled from the lake, his body was found. He had driven off the bridge in the fog, and no one had noticed his car submerged in the water.

Several years later, a woman went to have her hair done at a beauty shop after work. That morning, she had told the person working beside her at Terry Products that she did not know why she had worn her old shoes. Later that afternoon, she drove her car down Centergrove Road and parked it near the bridge. Someone saw her jump from the bridge and commit suicide.

After crossing the unlucky bridge, Shirlee Ann headed toward Interstate 85, then went north to Salisbury where her RV was parked. She saw several helicopters searching the banks and lake with searchlights.

* * * * *

Once Douglass learned that Elvin Hayes was a former professional basketball player, he called Caleb Pehrson and asked him to research any possible connections between Hayes and the extortion plot.

Caleb received another phone call that day. It was a second call from Jacob Johnson, the lawyer for Upper Deck collector cards.

"Hello, Mr. Pehrson. This is Jacob Johnson again. I have recommended to my client that we be prepared to file suit against the perpetrators of the murders pending their arrest. I need some help from a forensic-marketing consultant and thought you might be able to recommend someone to me. I need someone not only with expertise, but also experience in assisting attorneys in the preparation of cases in which there have been substantial financial losses from the intentional actions of either competitors or other third parties."

Caleb responded, "Well, you may be jumping the gun. But I need to make sure what you mean by someone experienced in forensic marketing. There are a number of definitions in the marketing literature, and I need to make sure we are talking about the same thing. If you are looking for someone to gather data and provide analysis that is one thing, but if you are looking for someone to provide testimony as an expert witness you may be looking for someone with a more sophisticated background and certainly a wealth of experience on the stand in the courtroom.

"I believe I can provide you with some names of excellent people, but I would like a little time to think about it. Are we on the same wavelength? I'll write you a summary statement for you to review and respond to, if that is okay with you. Give me a week and I will be in back in touch. I still have your phone number."

Caleb was rather excited at the prospect of perhaps being involved in the case himself, since he had the credentials he felt Johnson needed for the dispute. He first had to decide if he had the time to adequately devote to the research and preparation that would be required. Furthermore, the dispute itself might take months and even years if it went into appeals. He really wanted to get involved, but he was concerned about the amount of time it might take him away from the college marketing course he was teaching. First, he would have to familiarize himself with the collector-card industry and its market. He made a list of what he thought the effort would entail:

1. The history of the industry, including sales trends.

2. Size of the market.

3. Number, size, and market share of the competitors.

4. Any possible sales projections that the industry may have made.

5. Sales figures for the industry as a whole, and Upper Deck in particular, leading up to and during the span of the recent murders.

6. A review of the literature and perhaps any precedent setting court cases in remotely similar situations.

He was also concerned about any uncontrollable variables that may have had an impact on the sales of the cards. Was there a decline of fan interest in NBA basketball in general that would perhaps lead to a decline in the purchase of player collector cards? What other factors could have influenced fluctuations in the sale of the cards? It was certainly going to take time gathering and analyzing any secondary data he might need. He thought, "Wouldn't this be a great time to have a graduate student to assist me with all of the grunt work?" Of course, that would be unethical.

Caleb knew that the conflict would be a civil suit, not a criminal action. In a civil dispute, the plaintiff only has to provide about 51 percent of evidence to win. Thus, the plaintiff must move the football from the zero-yard line across the center of the field onto the 49-yard line. In a criminal case, the evidence needs to be at about 95 percent in order to convict a person.

For example, O. J. Simpson was acquitted in his criminal trial, but he lost in the civil dispute against him. The Ron Goldman family won at least $33.5 million in the civil suit, but O. J. has not paid this amount. Robert Blake lost $35 million to the family of his murdered wife, but he declared bankruptcy.

Caleb liked the grueling task of preparing beforehand and participating in a courtroom battle over marketing principles. It was a challenge to react and respond to the many innuendoes and leading questions asked by the opposing attorney during deposition and trial. The stress probably was not worth the daily fees he received, but he enjoyed it. He sometimes imagined the opposing attorney to be a black-clad medieval knight racing toward him on horseback with a long, sharp lance. He always toppled the vicious knight in his daydreams, though not always in court.

His motto was former Louisiana Governor Huey Long's old campaign slogan, "Nail them to the wall. Give me the hammer, and I'll nail them to the wall." Hard to be impartial, however. He started humming, "I don't care what they say, but forensic marketing is here to stay." An expert witness job paid well, but it took a pretty thick skin. The job certainly was not a sideline for the faint-hearted.

Pricing

There are two perspectives to pricing of products: the seller's and the buyer's. From the seller's perspective, pricing is a major determinant of revenue. In setting price, the four issues of *cost, demand, competitor prices,* and customer *value* must be considered.

A firm that does not cover both direct and indirect costs in its pricing structure is doomed to lose money on each sale. How much product can be sold at different price levels is also important. Just because a firm sets a price that covers its costs does not mean the customer will buy the product at that price. If a firm does not consider the prices of competitor's products, it may find itself operating at a competitive disadvantage if the competitor's price for a similar product is noticeably lower.

Price also influences how the potential buyer perceives value. Perceived value is the total customer benefits received from the product divided by the total customer costs, of which price is an important element.

$$\text{Perceived Value} = \frac{\text{Customer Benefits}}{\text{Customer Costs}}$$

A key consideration for the seller is the relationship between price and revenue. This relationship is known as "price elasticity." It refers to the customer's sensitivity and responsiveness to changes in price. It is the relative impact of price on volume purchased.

The formula for measuring price elasticity of demand is:

$$\text{Elasticity} = \frac{\text{Percentage Change in Quantity Demanded}}{\text{Percentage Change in Price}}$$

If the above formula produces a result less than 1, the product has *inelastic demand.*
If the formula produces a result of 1, the product has *unitary demand.*
If the result is greater than 1, the product has *elastic demand.*

The Celtics left the Boston Garden after 1995. In 2000, fans could buy pieces of the past basketball palace. Sold through the team, a 4-inch square of the famed parquet floor cost $99. Prices for two actual seats from the Garden, mounted on a 14 by 36 inch piece of parquet, ran from $2,500 to $3,000.

—THOMAS OWENS

T he director of the FBI, along with Douglass, spoke to the President the next day. They asked the President if he wanted the FBI to go public with the extortion plot. The President said no.

The director told Douglass that this problem was beginning to look like the CIA's waterboarding disaster. "The President will jerk the rug out from under us if we do not catch the extortionist soon," he said.

Douglass agreed. "Hindsight is always 20/20."

Waterboarding became a huge issue during 2007 for the CIA. Although members of Congress, including House Speaker Nancy Pelosi, were given demonstrations of waterboarding as early as 2002, objections to it were not raised at the time, and at least two lawmakers asked if the methods were tough enough. Politicians having oversight during this period were Democrats Nancy Pelosi, Jane Harman, Senator Bob Graham, and Senator John D. Rockefeller. Over time, other members of Congress were briefed on this interrogation technique.

Although waterboarding was used on only three people, including Abu Zubaida in 2007, a number of Democrats began to condemn this technique as torture and illegal. Much to-do was made of the destruction of two videotapes of an interrogation of one of the waterboarded detainees. Congressional leaders used waterboarding as a symbol of the excesses of the George W. Bush Administration's counterterrorism efforts. Politics as usual.

That afternoon Caleb Pehrson called Douglass about Elvin Hayes, the name registered to the cell phone left by the bad guys.

"There may be a connection between the SuperSonics cards that are being thrown down at the basketball events," Caleb said. "As the NBA history states, the Washington Bullets and Seattle SuperSonics will forever be linked in opposition until the two franchises win another title with someone else as the opponent.

"I am sending you a write-up of Hayes, but let me give you some highlights. You need to obtain a copy of his 1978 book entitled *They Call Me the Big E*. You can get it on Amazon."

Caleb paused. "Anyway, Elvin Hayes was inducted into the Basketball Hall of Fame in Springfield, Mass., in 1990. He played for 16 seasons, scoring 27,313 points and 16,279 rebounds in 1,303 games. He was born in Rayville, in the northeast corner of Louisiana.

"He tells a story in his book about going to a girls' basketball game in the seventh grade when the Rayville girls were playing the Tallulah girls. He made the mistake of picking up a rolling ball before it went out of bounds. He threw it back to the referee, who asked him where he lived. When he said Rayville, the referee called a technical foul on Rayville. Rayville lost by one point, the free throw from the technical foul. After that event, Hayes said everyone in Rayville seemed to be out to get him.

"I'll skip his high school and the University of Houston career, but you can read it in my faxed copy to you. In the pros he played three years with the San Diego Rockets, four years with the Houston Rockets, and the remainder of his playing time with the Washington Bullets.

"So here is the SuperSonics connection. During the all-important seventh game in the 1978 NBA playoffs against the SuperSonics, he fouled out with only 12 points. He apparently was upset about two 'cheap' fouls called against him by a referee."

Douglass said, "So I better put a tail on Hayes and that referee. I can do that. He could be throwing down those SuperSonics cards, right?"

"There's more. Center and Bullet captain Wes Unseld was named the playoffs' MVP by *Sport Magazine*, which gave him a new car. Unseld sank a free throw with 9 seconds left to give the Bullets a 3-point lead. He had missed 3 consecutive foul shots in the final minute of the game. The final score was 105–99. Wes Unseld had 15 points, 9 rebounds, and 6 assists in this seventh and final game. A *New York Times* write-up of the game went as follows:

> For Hayes, as often criticized as admired despite his performance in nine NBA seasons, it was sort of vindication, even though he was on the bench at the end.

"During the regular season, Elvin Hayes scored 19.7 points per game for a total of 1,598. Unseld only scored 7.6 points per game for a total of 607 points."

"I can see why he might be mad," Douglass said. "Who were the referees?"

"A Jack Madden and Earl Strom. Consider this," Caleb said. "Hayes received his nickname 'The Big E' after the U.S.S. *Enterprise* carrier. He had been hounded over a number of seasons about his poor performance in the playoffs. A reporter wrote after this game that 'the difference between Hayes in the playoffs and the regular season is like the difference between 'E' and 'e.'"

"Ouch," Douglass said. "I better put a tail on that reporter too," he joked. "Fax me the material so I can read it."

"By the way," Caleb said, "Hayes became a reserve detective for the Liberty County Sheriff's Department in November 2007."

"So he knows about DNA, fingerprints, guns, and maybe poisons," Douglass said. "What did he do after he retired in—?"

"He retired from basketball in 1984. He has been an automobile dealership owner," Caleb answered.

After the telephone conversation, Douglass read the write-up from Caleb.

> Elvin Hayes began playing basketball in the eighth grade when another teacher saw Hayes in the principal's office. Reverend Calvin put him on the school basketball team, but Hayes was awkward and clumsy. As a ninth grader at 6'5" he was a benchwarmer, but he practiced and developed his trademark turnaround jumper. (Joe Fulks of the Philadelphia Stars started the jump shot in the late '40s and early '50s.) In his senior year Hayes led the Rayville team to the championship, averaging 35 points during the

regular season. He scored 45 points and obtained 20 rebounds during the championship game.

His basketball talents got him a free ride out of the segregated southern town and onto the University of Houston campus. Houston coach Guy Lewis mentored one of the school's first African-American athletes. (Chuck Cooper was the first black player drafted in 1950 by Boston in the second round.)

Hayes rose to national attention with the January 20, 1968, game against the No. 1 UCLA basketball team. Some call it the greatest college basketball game ever because the Bruins had a 47-game winning streak behind Lew Alcindor (Kareem Abdul-Jabbar), and Houston seemingly did not have a chance. With 52,693 fans in the Astrodome and the score tied 69–69, Hayes sunk two free throws to make the score 71–69 with 28 seconds left. His free-throw average was around 60 percent. The statistics for the two players were as follows:

	Points	Rebounds
Elvin Hayes	39	15
Kareem Abdul-Jabbar	15	12

Hayes was named the College Player of the Year by *Sporting News*.

He was the first pick in the 1968 NBA draft, and he became a premier power forward. One of the larger players on a team, the power forward is supposed to aggressively pursue rebounds and score most of his points within six feet of the basket. On offense they play with their back to the basket, which made Hayes's unstoppable turnaround jump shot, both from the baseline and outside the paint, important to his career. At 6'9", Hayes is on the NBA's 50 Greatest Players list. Peter C. Bjarkman says Hayes was one of the finest shooting big men in all basketball history. He is eighth in all-time points (27,313) and sixth in all-time rebounds (16,279).

There are reports that he did have difficulties with some coaches, such as Alex Hannum and Tex Winters. Some quotes from NBA history:

Critics felt he had an attitude problem that sometimes short-circuited the teams he played for and gave him a Jekyll-and-Hyde personality.

John Lally, a trainer with the Washington Bullets, said, "For some players and coaches, being around Elvin every day is like a Chinese water torture.

It's just a drop at a time, nothing big, but in the end, he's driven you crazy."

Hayes himself said, "There is one reason I get into trouble. I speak what I feel. Other people are more diplomatic, but I don't feel, by doing that, that I'm a man."

Hayes said that racial prejudice in Rayville when he grew up was "thick as cotton in a field."

Caleb Pehrson had included some quotes about Hayes's 9-month, 809-hour course at the LCSO's police academy from two recent articles in the *Cleveland Advocate* and the *Beaumont Enterprise*.

When Hayes left Rayville, crossing the bridge out of town, he said, "I didn't try to tear down the bridge and never go back. Instead I have continued to build bridges."

When asked if there are parallels between all three of his careers, Hayes thought for a moment and then said, "Basketball laid a foundation that I was able to build upon. I think the hard work, dedication, and sacrifice made it possible for me to achieve and accomplish things in the car business, and it has enabled my life so that I will be ready to take this next step [as a reserve detective]."

Hayes will be speaking to high school students. He said, "I want to show them there are two roads they can take. I can either go down the road that will help them dedicate themselves to working hard and achieving success, or they can go down this other road, where I will be waiting to enforce the laws. I would much rather help the kids choose the right road."

He had this to say about setting an example for youths. "When people only see the rappers talking about shooting and killing and they glamorize all that, I think there has to be a counteraction to all that. Everybody's not gonna be a professional athlete, a professional rapper, [an] actor, but here's something you can do. You can give back to your community, to the kids out there as they grow up."

An article from the *New York Times* dated February 1, 2004, said that he wanted to play baseball and not basketball as a child. But he could not play baseball because his family could not afford shoes. He said that he "didn't own shoes from first grade to ninth grade. I went barefoot in the winter and summer. When I first started playing basketball, I wore two left-footed tennis shoes I pulled out of the trash and taped to my feet."

Basketball is not part of his life now. His life is in the business world. When not working, he mainly does three things: he jogs six miles at 4 a.m., takes cruises as often as possible, and follows his athletic passion, baseball. He goes to some Houston Astros games.

When Douglass put down the faxed pages from Caleb, he said to himself, "Hayes is not involved. But why are they setting him up for the fall? Once I know Mr. E is not involved, how can I use him to help catch her?"

But just to be careful, Douglass arranged for an agent to stake out the former basketball player.

* * * * *

Nothing. Nothing happened for five days. Even the media firestorm subsided. Douglass had no call from the mystery woman. But to his regret, November 29 soon arrived—the dreaded match-up between the Boston Celtics and the New York Knicks at TD Banknorth Garden.

Before the game, Douglass met with Caleb Pehrson, ten FBI agents, Pam Olson, and four DHS agents in the office of the Celtics' Executive Vice-President of Facilities. Douglass gave them detailed instructions, which the VP then relayed to his beefed-up security personnel. They were to pay attention to all bathrooms and concession stands. They were given latex gloves and warned not to pick up any basketball cards.

* * * * *

Shirlee Ann had tried to improve her disguise by going to the Internet site called "The Make-Up Gallery." She used the character Shannen Doherty had played in "She's a Man, Baby, a Man" as a model. Using some of Sandy's props, she added a small mustache and a small beard around her chin. She still used the glasses and a Celtics baseball hat. Using a card saying, "I have laryngitis," she was able to purchase a ticket below TD Banknorth Garden for $130.

Formally known as the Fleet Center, the arena was built on top of Boston's North Station, a major transportation hub. It took over 29 months to complete at a cost of $160 million. Of course, the commuter rail area becomes crowded during Celtics and Bruins games. The Boston Bruins are a National Hockey League team.

Inside the arena at 100 Legends Way, Shirlee Ann saw the parquet floor, originally built after World War II because of the cost and scarcity of lumber. Target Center in Minneapolis and the Amway Arena in Orlando also have parquet floors. The arena has a basketball capacity of 18,624, and it has had 32 different names. Some sportswriters still call it "The Vault," because of its tall, square shape. While Shirlee Ann was walking in the concession area, she passed William Douglass talking to a Celtics executive.

Back at her seat, she looked at the new HD entertainment board, with complete 360-degree LED technology. Shirlee Ann had read that the Celtics had won only 24 games during the past season, and that the New York Knicks had an eight-game losing streak before their current two-game winning streak. The talk was that Knicks' coach Isiah Thomas would soon be fired. The Knicks, with the second-highest payroll of $81 million in the 2006–07 season, had won only 33 games.

Tonight's game would not help Isiah Thomas. At the end of the first quarter the Celtics were up 27–16. Early in the second quarter the 6'8" Celtics forward James Posey took out the team's radio announcers when he went over the scorer's table for a loose ball. There are five position players. Position 1 is the point guard. Position 2 is the shooting guard. Position 3 is the smaller forward. Position 4 is the power forward. The center is Position 5. A forward or small forward is shorter, quicker, and leaner than power forward. Often small forwards are prolific scorers and excellent defensive players. By taking the ball to the basket, small forwards score many points from foul shots. So small forwards must be accurate foul shooters.

By halftime the score was Boston, 54, and Knicks, 31. When Boston was ahead 69–34 in the middle of the third quarter, Celtics power forward Kevin Garnett left the game, playing only 22 minutes. Garnett was drafted directly out of high school and had a 2008 salary of $22 million.

Although the Celtics did not try to run up the score, Boston beat the Knicks, 104 to 59. Celtics guard Rajon Rondo dribbled out 24 of the last 26 seconds and turned the ball over on purpose rather than go for a 50-point win. As it was, this game was the Knicks' third-worst loss and their second-worst scoring performance of the shot-clock era. The shot clock was introduced into the NBA in 1954 to speed up the game and add more excitement. In the NBA, the offensive team has 24 seconds to shoot a ball which touches the rim. Otherwise, there is a shot-clock violation, and the other team gets the ball. Danny Biasone invented the shot clock, but he never played the game.

Knicks guard Nate Robinson, at 5'9" with an $8.9 million salary, made a 37-foot 3-pointer at the final buzzer to save the Knicks from scoring the fewest points in their franchise history. Was it because of the murders in their arena against the Orlando Magic? Were they worried about their own safety?

Listed at 5'9" but probably only 5'7", Nate Robinson is the shortest player in the NBA today. There is height discrimination in the NBA, because even most point guards are generally 6 feet to 6'4". But there have been some vertically challenged players in the NBA. Muggsy Bogues, at 5'3" and 136 pounds, played for five teams over 14 years, and Spud Webb was about 5'7"and still won the NBA Slam Dunk Contest in 1986. Earl Boykins, at 5'5", has played for at least seven professional teams.

The Knicks' Nate Robinson won the NBA Slam Dunk Contest in 2006 with help from Spud Webb, becoming only the second player under six feet to win the contest. In the contest, Webb tossed the basketball to Robinson, and Robinson then jumped over Webb to stuff the ball.

* * * * *

Shirlee Ann left the game at the start of the fourth quarter. At the end of the fourth quarter, both Douglass and Caleb were smiling like alligators lying around all day on the shore of a bayou. Nothing had happened in the arena during the game. Caleb was especially happy about the final score.

Their happiness did not last long, however, because soon there were a number of sirens. People were dying and becoming sick below the arena in Boston's North Station. The North Station has a food court and waiting area, MBTA commuter rail for northern routes, a local bus station, and the Orange and Green lines of the Boston subway at its eastern entrance.

Someone had placed deadly SuperSonics basketball cards in the men's restrooms and in the subway area, along with poisonous peanuts, mustard, and ketchup in the fast-food area. A total of seven people died, and five more were hospitalized but recovered.

No one was a happy camper, except maybe the perp.

Marketing Research Process

Stage One:

1. Develop questionnaire
2. Test questionnaire
3. Print questionnaire
4. Write cover letter
5. Print cover letters
6. Print return envelopes
7. Print return postcard
8. Purchase postage for envelope, return envelope, and postcard
9. Apply postage to each
10. Fold and insert letter, questionnaire, and postcard
11. Hand-address envelopes
12. Seal envelopes

Stage Two:

1. Set up software program for tabulation
2. Scan and conduct cross-tabulations
3. Perform analysis
4. Write report
5. Present oral report

11

Corporate sports sponsorship seems like a win-win proposition. But as several companies have discovered recently, there's also a big element of risk. Consider the BMW and Oracle team sailboat, eliminated in May from the America's Cup qualifying competition in Valencia, Spain, before the main event even started. German press reports put the cost of the failed Cup bid at nearly $200 million.

—JACK EWING

By 10:34 a.m., both Fox News and CNN began running security camera shots of a "person of interest" with respect to the basketball murders at the Garden the previous night. There were several photos of a tall, thin male wearing a Celtics baseball cap and glasses. The images from the security cameras showed the individual wearing gloves, with a small mustache and small beard around his chin. The FBI had not released any photos that showed the individual putting down any basketball cards or food.

Soon the FBI had the image of the "person of interest" flashing in twenty major cities on their eye-catching, roadside digital billboards. Wanted posters have been used to catch criminals since paper sketches were tacked onto trees during the Wild West. Within 15 minutes of getting a suspect's photograph, these digital billboards can display the sketch to thousands of viewers. So, along with ads for auto insurance, fast foods, hotels, banks, and car dealers, the digital photo of Shirlee Ann dressed as a man was shown on the FBI's 150 digital wanted posters. "Our partnership with the FBI to use our digital networks to assist in the apprehension of fugitives and provide other critical security messages is a logical extension of this invaluable community service," said Paul Meyer, president and chief operating officer at Clear Channel Outdoors.

Caleb had told Douglass that effective crisis management involved a rapid response to the crisis. Luckily for Douglass and the FBI, the news cycle helped them the next day. The 409-page report by former Senator George Mitchell was released at 2:00 p.m., which linked 85 baseball players to the illegal use of steroids and other performance-enhancing drugs. This list included seven MVPs, two Cy Young Award winners, and 31 All-Stars. Yankees Roger Clemens, Andy Pettitte, and Kevin Brown were on the list. How would baseball respond to this unfavorable publicity?

President George W. Bush, a former managing partner of the Texas Rangers, had this to say about the steroids mess, which was being compared to the infamous Black Sox scandal: "I understand the impact that professional athletes can have on our nation's youth. I just urge those in the public spotlight, particularly athletes, to understand that when they violate their bodies, they're sending a terrible signal to America's youth."

Commissioner of baseball Bud Selig said, "If there are problems, I want them revealed. His report is a call to action, and I will act."

The players' union was uncooperative with Mitchell. Union head Donald Fehr said, "Many players are named. Their reputations have been adversely affected, probably forever."

Former Toronto Blue Jays and New York Yankees strength coach Brian McNamee fingered Roger Clemens, and Clemens sued McNamee for defamation. The seven-time Cy Young Award winner denied using any performance-enhancing drugs. His lawyer said that Clemens "is outraged his name is included in the report based on the uncorroborated allegations of a troubled man threatened with federal criminal prosecution." Curt Schilling suggested, however, that if the allegations were true, "Clemens should return his Cy Young Awards."

Pete Rose, who has been suspended from baseball for 18 years for betting on his Cincinnati Reds team to win, said that he "never thought anybody could make me look like an altar boy. If the allegations are true, they are making a mockery of the game."

An article by Tom Sorensen titled "Charlotte, Pro Sports A Lousy Mix" said that the biggest loser, next to the commissioner and the head of the baseball union, was Roger Clemens. "When Clemens reached his mid-30s, he looked thick and pitched as if he was used up. And then he was great again. His fans attributed his late-life turnaround to his warrior workouts."

Headlines across the nation were as follows:

New York Daily News: Cheaters.

Washington Post: Baseball is Called Out.

Seattle Times: Knockdown Pitch.

L.A. Times: Two-Strike Count.

Houston Chronicle: Dark Day for Baseball.

Kansas City Star: Out of the Shadows.

Rocky Mountain News: On Needles, Pin.

Philadelphia Inquirer: Scarred Stars.

Boston Globe: Tainted Gloves.

Sacramento Bee: Steroids Era Hits Home.

Milwaukee Journal Sentinel: Gagne Faces Accusation.

Orlando Sentinel: Bottled Rocket.

* * * * *

Douglass called a brainstorming session with several profilers at Quantico. Caleb Pehrson in Boston, Mel Wales in Trenton, and Sarah Stamp in Herkimer all joined in the session via conference call. The out-of-town participants could observe the relevant charts and materials through the Internet.

Douglass first asked the participants to compare the similarities and differences between serial killers, mass murderers, and spree killers. This chart shows up on several Internet sites:

Comparison Chart

ATTRIBUTES	SERIAL KILLERS	MASS KILLERS	SPREE KILLERS
Victim Count	5+	3+	4–5+
Victim Rate	Months/Years	Hours/Day	Days/Weeks/Months
Kills at Victim Rate	1–2 At One Time	Many At One Time	1–2 At A Time
Common Killer	White/Male/20–30	White/Male/25–40	White/Male/20–30
Common Kill	Stabbing/ Strangulation	Shooting	Stabbing/Shooting
Common Weapon	Knife/Binding	Gun	Knife/Gun
Common Victim	Females (Trait)	Females (Mostly) & Males	Females & Males
Organization Type	Disorganized/ Organized (3/4)	Disorganized	Disorganized
Motive	Sex/Rejection	Rejection/Revenge/ Deranged	Rejection/Revenge/ Deranged
Rape/Sadism	Yes (Org.)/Yes (Disorg.)	Rare/No	Maybe/No
Killing Attitude	To Go Uncaptured	Uncaring/Suicidal	To Go Uncaptured

"Let me summarize. A serial killer murders five or more people over a period of time, often for sexual reasons. The killings take place one after another, like the old-fashioned newspaper serial. That's how the term came about. Generally, there is a cooling-off period between the kills, becoming shorter and shorter.

"The serial killer's motive tends to be sexual, control, domination, power, and manipulation. Some experts do not classify criminals who commit multiple murders for material gain (e.g., hit men) as serial killers. I disagree, however.

"A mass murder or massacre occurs when someone murders a large number of people over a short period of time or at the same time. Genocide would not be included in this category. Examples in this category would be the Columbine High School massacre and the Omaha, Nebraska, mall massacre in 2007. Charles Joseph Whitman, a University of Texas student, launched America's modern age of mass murders when he killed 14 and wounded 31 from the observation deck of the University's Main Building. He killed his mother and his wife the night before.

"Seung-Hui Cho killed two people before embarking on the slaughter of 32 people with two pistols on the Virginia Tech campus in 2007.

"I do not believe we are looking here at mass murder by terrorists even though we had a note to that effect. At least two-thirds of terrorist murders are religious.

"A spree killer kills a number of people over a relatively short period of time at different locations. This person is like a serial killer at warp speed without a sexual motive or a mass murderer at a snail's pace.

"The Beltway sniper is an example of a spree killer. Ten people were killed and three others were critically wounded around Washington, D.C., by Lee Boyd Malvo and John Allen Muhammad. Earlier deaths in Louisiana, Alabama, Georgia, California, Arizona, and Texas ran their spree death total to 16.

"As grotesque as it may sound, there is a market for serial killers' memorabilia, such as clown paintings of John Wayne Gacy and poetry of Jack Unterweger. There are even trading cards and action figures of the predators.

"I've talked too much," Douglass said. "Let me hear from you. We need to profile this basketball murderer. Anyone?" He looked around the room.

Harold Jacob, a profiler said, "We need to consider that we are also dealing with an extortionist. There is a profit motive. What we have is a horrible extension of the email extortion that says pay the sender or risk the alternative of some unfavorable event to your business. Often attached to the attack is something like this:

> I have followed you closely for one week and three days now. . . . Do not contact the police or FBI or try to send a copy of this to them, because if you do I will know, and might be pushed to do what I have being [*sic*] paid to do.

"So you do not believe that I have to worry about the threat to my wife?" Douglass asked.

"Now, I didn't say that," Jacob said. "I would get her and your kids out of Dodge until we catch them."

Janice Reese spoke up. "This person, who I believe is a woman, may have gotten the idea from a 1995 film called *The Basketball Diaries*. The protagonist, a high-school basketball player, is played by Leonardo DiCaprio. He has a dream sequence where he is wearing a black trench coat, and he shoots six classmates with a shotgun in the school hallway while his friends cheer him on."

"Janice, why do you think she's a woman?" Douglass asked.

"The way she walks. The motions she makes when she bends down. I bet you she was an athlete at one time. She looks to be about six feet tall. Maybe a volleyball or basketball player in high school or college."

"We have not released this information yet, but we did find a buried underwater scooter on the shore of Lake Fisher. We found some hairs in the suitcase, at least two from a black man. So once we catch them, we do have evidence. No fingerprints, however," Douglass said. "Give me more."

Another profiler spoke. "I believe we are dealing with a spree killer. As the chart shows, they plan to go uncaptured, and they kill males and females—even kids. Of course, he or she is killing many victims at a time, and is not using a knife or a gun. By using poison, I believe we are dealing with a woman. But clearly, he or she is not disorganized. By using poison, the perpetrator can rationalize that the victims are collateral damage—like the mass murders by terrorists."

The profiler paused and continued, "The killer or killers are organized, with at least one person with an IQ in the 120 plus range. They are planning their crimes methodically. The escape in Lake Fisher and discarding the tracers prove that. They must be scuba divers, since the scooter was buried more than two miles from where you threw the suitcase. To throw down the poison below the Boston arena shows intelligence. Did you get any glimpse of the individual when you threw over the suitcase?" The profiler looked at Douglass.

"No, it was dark. I only heard the suitcase hit the water. I immediately got back into the car and left. The instructions said that a sniper was watching me." Douglass explained. "We don't know if there is more than one. Any thoughts on that?"

"Before we get to that," Sarah Stamp said over the conference phone, "let's talk about the monetary gain. How common is it for spree killers or mass murders to have a profit motive?"

"Sam, you prepared some material on that." Douglass gestured to Sam Torne.

"Let me first cover how the FBI classifies homicides." Torne put up a chart.

FBI Crime Classification Manual
1. Personal Cause Homicide
2. Sexual Homicide
3. Group Cause Homicide
4. Criminal Enterprise Homicide
   • Contract killing
   • Gang-motivated
   • Criminal competition
   • Kidnap murder
   • Product tampering
   • Drug murder
   • Insurance/inheritance
   • Felony murder
   • Commercial profit

"Our killer falls into the commercial profit category, Torne said.

"Surprisingly there have been quite a few mass murders or spree killings for a monetary gain, such as money, property, insurance, or inheritance. The obvious examples are the hit men for the Mafia and the killers for hire. I would not include mass murders as a result of a robbery going wrong. But there was an interesting case involving a bank robbery in Japan. Sadamichi Hirasawa poisoned 12 bank workers with cyanide during a bank robbery in January 1948.

"Hirasawa, posing as a government health worker, told the 16 employees in a Teikoku Bank branch in a suburb of Tokyo that the post–World War II occupation forces had ordered them to drink medicine because of an outbreak of dysentery. The employees lined up and drank the medicine with cyanide. As they died, he stole between $600 and $720.

"He was convicted and sentenced to death. But because of doubt surrounding the evidence or the law at that time, none of the Japanese Justice Ministers would approve the execution. After being on death row for 30 years, he was given amnesty at age 88. He died at age 95 from pneumonia in May 1987."

Sam continued. "There is, in fact, criminology slang for multiple murders for monetary gain or a profit. "Black widow" is associated with women who kill for money, often with arsenic in food. Females use poison about 80 percent of the time, and money is the motive 74 percent of the time, followed by control at 13 percent. Wikipedia lists 14 women who have murdered their husbands out of a total of 62 female serial killers, or about 20 percent. American female serial killers make up about 75 percent of all female serial killers.

"The Kellehers, in their 1998 book *Murder Most Rare: The Female Serial Killers,* say that females are more successful, careful, precise, quiet, and methodical. They are twice as likely to kill a husband, boyfriend, or child, and it takes twice as long to catch them.

"Anna Marie Hahn was America's first female serial killer to die in the electric chair, in December 1938. She poisoned and robbed elderly men and women in Cincinnati's German community. Arsenic was her weapon.

"One of the recent infamous black widows was North Carolina's Velma Bullard, who murdered five people—husband, boyfriend, mother, and others—with arsenic-based rat poison. She was executed in 1984.

"Another North Carolina female serial killer was Blanche Taylor Moore, who used arsenic hidden in food as her modus operandi, resulting in four deaths—including her father and first husband. Although sentenced to death, she is still alive in prison. A television movie made from the book *Preacher's Girl* starred Elizabeth Montgomery in *The Black Widow Murders: The Blanche Taylor Moore Story.*

"Insurance was the apparent motive for Jamie Lou Gibbs to kill her three sons, a grandson, and her husband by poisoning them with arsenic between 1966 and 1967. The 35-year-old grandmother, who ran a day-care center, admitted to killing her family. She was released from a life prison sentence in 1999 with Parkinson's disease.

"A bizarre one was Dana Sue Gray who murdered three elderly women by strangulation, bludgeoning, and stabbing in 1994. Her motive was to fund her shopping sprees.

"An argument can be made that Florida's Aileen Wuorno's seven killings were driven by money. This prostitute preyed on truck drivers. After her business was transacted, she would kill and rob them. She was executed in October 2002. Two documentaries and the movie *Monster* were made about her life.

"So let me point out two flaws in most charts and profiles about serial killers. Women have been murdering serially maybe as long as men. Likewise, there have been and will be black serial killers. An Earl P. Holt III has a list on his Internet site of at least 43 African-American serial killers. That's more than 10 percent.

"Now let me switch gears," Sam Torne said. "The name given to males who serially kill for profit is "bluebeards," derived from the fifteenth-century, powerful French nobleman Gilles De Rais. This predator confessed to killing 80 to 200 children, mostly blond-haired, blue-eyed boys, over a 10-year period. He had blue-black facial hair, and he fought alongside Joan of Arc.

"An example of a bluebeard early in the twentieth century is Helmuth Schmidt. He ran personal ads in newspapers to find lonely women. Most of the women were immigrants seeking sponsorship. He is suspected of killing 31 women he found through his personal ads. He committed suicide in prison.

"The profit motive was certainly relevant for another French serial killer, Henri Desire Landru. A secondhand furniture dealer in Paris, Landru would place personal ads in the local newspapers: 'Widower with Two Children.' After getting the lady's assets, he would kill her by strangulation, dismember her, and burn the body parts in his stove. He was guillotined in February 1922 for the murder of 10 women.

"Police found in his villa the personal effects of many unknown women.

Letters from around 283 women were sorted into seven group headings: 'No reply'; 'Without money'; 'Without furniture'; 'To be answered poste restante'; 'To be answered in initials poste restante'; 'Possible fortune'; and 'In reserve for future investigation.'

"One more. South Texan Joe Ball ran a saloon called the Sociable Inn in Elmendorf, Texas. He had a pond behind the saloon with five alligators. Called the Alligator Man, he possibly killed 20 women." Torne sat down.

Douglass said, "Thank you, Sam. Now back to the question. Is there one or more person involved in this? What do you think, Mel? I haven't heard from you."

"I also think we are dealing with a woman because she first hit women's bathrooms. As she got more publicity, she had to use disguises. With the photos of him/her running on all the news channels, I predict she'll go back to a female disguise, maybe an older woman.

"It is possible she is working alone. Really too soon to know," Mel said over the conference phone. "She appears to plan ahead."

"Anyone else?" Douglass looked around the room. "OK. I am also wondering if the perp may have had a conflict with a sports team. For example, could the individual be an earlier baseball or basketball player who was not paid much, or perhaps his pension payout is low? Could compensation be a motive? Could it be a mad fan? I asked Caleb Pehrson, vice-president for sales for the Boston Celtics who has been acting as an unpaid consultant, to prepare some information about payrolls in the NBA. Hopefully, this data will jog someone's memory. Go ahead, Caleb."

"Thank you, Douglass. As I tell my sports-marketing students, when one or several employees have huge salaries compared to the other employees, the business may not succeed in achieving its mission. Matt Bloom, a management professor at the University of Notre Dame, says that the bigger the pay difference between a major league baseball team's stars and scrubs, the worse its record. According to Bloom, more parity in payment for performance will result in a better baseball or basketball team. Big pay differentials sow the seeds of discord rather than promoting team unity.

"Big pay differentials also may sow the seeds of discord rather than promoting a team's success in other sports, as well as business. Once again, in 2007 high salaries did not guarantee success in professional basketball.

"Please look at the chart that I have prepared."

2006–2007 Season

RANK	TEAM (PAYROLL RANK)	PAYROLL*	GAMES WON**	COST PER WIN
1	Toronto Raptors (29)	$42,223,168	47	$898,365
2	Dallas Mavericks (8)	$64,821,094	67	$967,479
3	Chicago Bulls (22)	$54,699,276	49	$1,116,312
4	San Antonio Spurs (6)	$65,645,095	58	$1,131,812
5	Utah Jazz (19)	$60,325,348	51	$1,182,848
6	Houston Rockets (12)	$62,627,349	52	$1,204,372
7	Cleveland Cavaliers (11)	$62,992,678	50	$1,259,854
8	Philadelphia 76ers (28)	$44,407,250	35	$1,268,779
9	Charlotte Bobcats (3)	$41,961,743	33	$1,271,568
10	Phoenix Suns (1)	$82,440,784	61	$1,351,488
11	New Orleans Hornets (25)	$53,171,676	39	$1,363,376
12	Detroit Pistons (4)	$75,517,622	53	$1,424,861
13	Denver Nuggets (7)	$65,000,230	45	$1,444,450
14	Los Angeles Clippers (20)	$58,202,032	40	$1,455,051
15	Golden State Warriors (14)	$62,120,690	42	$1,479,064
16	Los Angeles Lakers (13)	$62,251,869	42	$1,482,187
17	Orlando Magic (18)	$60,527,557	40	$1,513,189
18	New Jersey Nets (10)	$63,772,329	41	$1,555,423
19	Washington Wizards (15)	$61,853,822	41	$1,581,801
20	Atlanta Hawks (26)	$47,812,036	30	$1,593,735
21	Indiana Pacers (16)	$61,526,247	35	$1,757,893
22	Miami Heat (3)	$78,203,790	44	$1,777,359
23	Seattle SuperSonics (21)	$56,647,817	31	$1,827,349
24	Sacramento Kings (17)	$61,065,219	32	$1,908,288
25	Milwaukee Bucks (23)	$54,633,510	28	$1,951,197
26	Portland Trail Blazers (9)	$64,751,726	32	$2,023,491
27	Minnesota Timberwolves (5)	$66,734,452	32	$2,085,452
28	Memphis Grizzlies (27)	$47,055,458	22	$2,138,885
29	Boston Celtics (24)	$53,620,490	24	$2,234,187
30	New York Knicks (2)	$81,672,615	33	$2,474,928

*taken from USAToday.com
**taken from NBA.com

Note: The Suns, Heat, Pistons, Spurs, Nuggets, Mavericks, Nets, Cavaliers, Rockets, Lakers, Warriors, Wizards, Magic, Jazz, Bulls and Raptors made the Playoffs

Note: The Spurs won the Playoffs.

"Although the Phoenix Suns, who had the highest NBA payroll of $82 million, did make the NBA playoffs, the N.Y. Knicks, with the second-highest payroll of $81.5 million, did not make the playoffs. The Knicks were at the bottom with respect to efficiency (highest cost per regular season win). The Minnesota Timberwolves, with the fifth-highest payroll and the 27th least efficient record, did not make the playoffs. The San Antonio Spurs won it all and were the fourth most efficient team, but they were the sixth highest payroll team. The Cleveland Cavaliers, who were eleventh in terms of total payroll and seventh in terms of efficiency, lost to the Spurs in the playoffs.

"In most major league sports, even the lowliest teams, such as the Memphis Grizzlies or baseball's Tampa Bay Devil Rays, can dream of a championship. Equalization formulas, such as salary caps and higher draft picks for losing teams, can overcome economic factors. However, the NHL salary cap after the 2004–05 lockout did not change hockey's competitive balance. The salary cap was supposed to keep big-market teams from buying their way to success. In 2003–04, the Detroit Red Wings had the best regular-season record and also the highest payroll (around $80 million). The lowest payroll club had a total of only $26 million. By the All-Star Game in 2008, the Red Wings were still the number-one team with a total payroll of only $46.1 million, ranked 18th out of 30 NHL teams.

"NHL deputy commissioner Bill Daly says, 'Detroit's success is an example of what good, committed ownership and astute management can accomplish. The team's success is especially impressive given the nature of our new system, where teams are competing on a much more level playing surface than ever before.'

"Peter C. Bjarkman, in his *Encyclopedia of Pro Basketball,* had this to say about the San Antonio Spurs in the mid-nineties: 'The eighteen seasons that have marked the history of the San Antonio Spurs in the NBA began on a mountain top, eventually slipped into a deep, dark valley, and have finally scaled partway back up the steep sides of the rugged peak. But the early and late phases of the team history have been sufficient to leave the Spurs unchallenged as still the very best among ABA refugee teams [Pacers, Nuggets, Nets, and Spurs] attempting to play competitively in the NBA.' The Spurs, of course, made it to the top of the mountain in 2007."

Douglass concluded the brainstorming session with the request that everyone send him any and all suggestions about the killer or killers. "How do you think he or she is traveling? Were diamonds somehow related to the perp? Are there any former players in the diamond or jewelry business? Where are they getting the poison? Were they an old-time sports player? Was a fan the perp? Anything that will help will be appreciated," Douglass pleaded.

Marketing Plan Structure

1. Executive Summary
   A. Synopsis
   B. Major aspects of the marketing plan

2. Mission/Value/Vision Statement

3. Situation Analysis
   A. Analysis of the internal environment
   B. Analysis of the customer environment
   C. Analysis of the external environment

4. Swot Analysis
   A. Strengths
   B. Weaknesses
   C. Opportunities
   D. Threats
   E. Analysis of A.–D.
   F. Establishing a strategic focus

5. Marketing Goals and Objectives
   A. Marketing Goals
   B. Marketing Objectives

6. Marketing Strategies
   A. Primary target market and marketing mix
   B. Secondary target market and marketing mix

7. Marketing Implementation
   A. Structural issues
   B. Tactical marketing activities

8. Evaluation and Control
   A. Formal marketing control
   B. Informal marketing control
   C. Financial assessments

For every seller, there's a buyer.

For every buyer, there's a seller.

—ROBERT CRAIS

he word came back to Douglass from Texas that Elvin Hayes had not left his area during the Boston Celtics game. Douglass suggested they continue to follow Hayes in case he was working with someone. Should he attempt to get DNA from Hayes to see if the hairs in the suitcase matched? How long could he wait? Would a judge allow him to put a tap on Hayes's phone? He doubted it, but he would try. He would have a better chance if he could surround the request with possible terrorist implications.

The FBI and even Douglass became the butt of jokes on the late-night talk shows. Even Fox's *Best Damn Sports Show Period* and ESPN's *Sports-Center* made fun of Douglass. *The Best Damn Sports Show Period* airs around 11 p.m., Monday through Friday. The show's NBA expert host and four-time NBA champion John Salley was extremely critical of the FBI. He said that Tom Arnold, the comedian, could do a better job of finding the killer than Douglass. Tom Arnold was a previous host on the show. The show normally features fun interviews with top athletes, coaches, celebrities, and entertainers. *SportsCenter* has been shown more than any other show on U.S. television—more than 30,000 times as of February 11, 2007. The show is aired up to twelve times a day. The anchors began predicting a sharp drop in attendance at professional basketball games.

Chris Myers, a prior sports anchor, was noted for saying that "they scored (a number of points) off the bench. Had the player been on the bench, he'd been out of bounds." Another anchor, Craig Kilborn's favorite roundball sayings were:

- The lost art, the bounce pass.
- Take care of the onion, or it will make you cry.
- Messed around and got a triple double. [A triple double occurs when a player accumulates double digit totals (e.g., 10 or more) in any of three categories: points, rebounds, assists, steals, or blocked shots.]

* * * * *

When Sandy had worked as a maintenance person at the college in Denver, he collected and labeled hair from the professors' offices, which Shirlee Ann now had. Sandy had told Shirlee Ann that he had gone into several SuperCuts, told them that he worked for a movie company, and asked for hair. They would gladly give him a bag of hair. Beauty salons like Super-Cuts had certainly depleted the supply of barbers.

She had learned that until recently when hair roots were not available, scientists thought analyzing the hair shaft was of relatively little use, as it contained so little DNA. However, she read a story by Anna Salleh from the Australian Broadcasting Corporation, entitled "Ancient Hair Gives Up Its DNA Secrets," which said that a new method allowed DNA extraction and sequencing from hair shafts. This new method was helpful when dealing with ancient hair. Apparently, DNA from hair was protected from water by the hair's hydrophobic keratin, especially from human sweat. How could she get some of Elvin Hayes's hair?

Shirlee Ann did not believe that the diamonds Douglass left at the drop were real, so she drove south and spent the night in Greenville, S.C. The next morning she visited several jewelry stores and carried in three of the stones that looked different. She told the jewelers that her husband had bought the stones at a flea market, and she wanted to know if the stones were diamonds. Three of the jewelers spotted the CZ and the Herkimer crystal. One of the jewelers thought that the moissanite was a real diamond, so she sold the stone to the jeweler at a deep discount. Two other jewelers had already told her that the stone was moissanite. They had a moissanite tester. One told her that moissanite costs approximately 10 percent of real diamonds. They are hard, durable, beautiful, and last a lifetime. Although the natural source of moissanite is from meteorites, the stone is now created in laboratories. The crystals, of course, were really cheap.

She decided that it was too risky to attempt to get the buried scooter. As she drove from Greenville toward Florida, she saw occasional Ron Paul and Mitt Romney signs along I-85 through South Carolina. She heard on the news that Fred Thompson had said that we had dangerous years ahead. "Terrorists will not rest until a mushroom cloud hung over a U.S. city." How could she get the terrorist threat back into her message?

On the radio she heard a lawyer advertising this message: "Success in business is what other people think of you." Even though it was misty and rainy, North Carolina, South Carolina, and Georgia were in a severe drought. Near Atlanta she saw a billboard that said, "Save water, shower in a different city. AirTran." She was shocked, however, when she drove past a digital wanted photo of her walking below the Celtics arena dressed like a man. "Oh well, I need another disguise," she said.

In the middle of Atlanta, after seeing her wanted poster, she decided to head for Houston. South of Atlanta she continued on I-85 towards Montgomery, Alabama. Montgomery is the capital of Alabama and was once the capital of the Confederacy. She had broken some of the $100 bills in North Carolina, so with the $200,000 she did not have to work. She still had more than $100,000 from Sandy's drop. When she was breaking one of the $100 bills, she passed a tractor supply store. Near the store the person running a fireworks stand was shooting rockets up into the air to get people's attention. Effective promotion.

Shirlee Ann had not expected to get the diamonds on the first drop, but it was nice of Douglass to try to trick her with the fake diamonds. She liked Douglass. He even threw in some Herkimer diamonds. "What a joker!" she said out loud. "Maybe I can unload the moissanite on some unsuspected jewelers or at a flea market. Caveat emptor." She smiled slyly.

Near the Shorter exit in Alabama, she saw a bumper sticker on a Honda that said, "Keep honking, I'm reloading." She turned left off of I-85 at Montgomery and headed toward Mobile on I-65. She chuckled when she saw the exit to Pine Apple. In Mobile she took I-10 toward Mississippi and Louisiana.

She crossed Mississippi. As a child she remembered M, eye, crooked letter, crooked letter, eye, crooked letter, crooked letter, eye, humpback, humpback, eye. Later that evening she stopped at the Frog City RV Park at Exit 92 in Louisiana. The next morning she was up early, crossing Louisiana, passing Crowley, the rice capital of the world, over the Sabine River into Texas. Close to the Texas border was the town of Orange, which advertised, "On the Right Side of Texas."

She almost ran into the back of a moving truck as she was observing the painting on its back. The back door looked as if you were looking into the inside of the truck, with furniture, blankets, and two children sitting down. The family-owned moving company, Atmosphere Movers, is headquartered in Covington, Louisiana.

Outside of Beaumont in the suburb of Vidor she saw a billboard. There was a picture of Steve Page with a long arrow pointing towards him. Along the top was "In '91, Here in VIDOR—He got by with MURDER."

- Found responsible for wife's death in Civil Court.
- Appeals Court Upheld Conviction.
- Pleaded Guilty of Desecrating Her Grave.
  CRIMINAL CASE: NO ARRESTS!
  Did the Police Take a Bribe???

Another billboard, about a dress shop, had a picture of a young woman with a large scarf of an animal or jungle print. The name of the dress shop was A Little Bit Gaudy. Something for Every Woman. "Why would a woman go there," Shirlee Ann thought. "Is this a good name for a dress shop?" Finally she thought, "It got my attention, and I'll probably remember it."

As she approached Beaumont, she picked up FM 97.1 on the radio, Country Legends. She was listening to "You don't have to call me darling, Darling; You never even call me by my name" as she passed several motorcyclists. She wondered why so many motorcyclists wore beards. Did she need a beard in Houston?

In Beaumont, the home of Lamar University, she left I-10 and took Route 90 toward Liberty, Texas. On the Internet she had read that the small town of slightly more than 8,000 people had an exact replica of the Liberty Bell, which was in Philadelphia, Pennsylvania.

Rebel David Allan Coe was singing, "I was drunk the day my mom got out of prison" as she passed the billboard "Skydive in Nome." The road was straight and flat as she drove through China, population 1,112. Near Nome, population 515, she noticed a new oil well being drilled. She passed the Brother & Sister Family Market, Saddle, Ropes & More, and the White Heron Motel before she reached Liberty. As she rolled into town, the group Alabama was playing on the radio, singing "If you're gonna to play in Texas, you gotta have a fiddle in the band." The Chamber of Commerce sign said, "Welcome to Liberty, Est. 1831." Driving through Liberty, she noticed Sassy's Detailing, AM Doughnuts, and West Palm Beach Tanning. Her food choices were Whataburger, Popeyes, and McDonalds. She chose Popeyes and the spicy chicken.

After eating, she drove over to Dayton, hearing on the radio John Conlie's "Friday Night Blues" and Linda Ronstadt's "When Will I Be Loved." The songs depressed her, so as she passed the Cowboy Palace and noticed its sign, "We Put the Cow in the Cowboy," she laughed and decided to return later that night for some entertainment.

A commercial on the radio by LifeLock impressed her. CEO Todd Davis gave out his social security number to demonstrate the value of their identity theft company. They promised to stop the thieves cold. "But you cannot stop me," she said out loud.

She turned around and headed back to Liberty. She parked her RV and rode her motorcycle to the Liberty Dayton GM AutoWorld, at 1100 North Main Street. The dealership sells Pontiacs, Chevrolets, GMCs, Cadillacs, and Buicks. She tried to see Elvin Hayes. No luck. They did not know when he would be back. "He is now a Liberty County reserve deputy," an employee told her. She knew that.

On the second day in Liberty, Shirlee Ann bought three magazines in Lewie's Grocery & Sporting Goods store: *Field and Stream, People,* and *Time.* She wanted *Sport Diver,* but the store did not have it. She picked up a free *Liberty County Outlook.* In *People* she saw a Welch's Peel 'n Taste strip. There was no way she would peel and taste the grape juice. She wondered how this new advertising technique would survive.

The Welch's peel 'n taste strip by First Flavor includes a thin, tamper-evident pouch with a Welch's 100 percent grape juice–flavored dissolving taste strip. Readers are encouraged to place the edible strip on their tongue to taste the bold, sweet taste of Welch's 100 percent grape juice. The instructions said to "Peel open from curved end. Place flavor strip on tongue. Enjoy!" Initially, Shirlee Ann had difficulty opening the strip, but she eventually placed the purple strip in her mouth. It did taste like grape juice.

Underneath the strip was the following advertisement: "Welch's grape juice has twice the antioxidant power of orange juice. It helps protect your immune system."

These taste strips are similar to the scent strips that are found in magazines for various perfumes, such as Calvin Klein's Obsession. A scent ad is coated with millions of tiny drops of fragrant oils, sealed inside specially designed capsules. The reader peels off the strip and smells the advertisement. Unilever used scent strips for its Snuggle fabric softener to fight Downy—the battle of the noses. Showtime pay-cable network promoted its drama *Weeds* about a drug-dealing mother by adding the scent of marijuana to strips in magazine ads. Scent ads tend to cost four to eight times more than a plain advertisement.

Madky EZ Scent Strips are advertised to help hunters bag a deer. "Just open the Madky EZ Scent Strip and place it on your portable blind, tree, bush, or tree stand. The right amount of premium scent will last a day."

By the third day, the Cowboy Palace, the magazines, and the sudoku puzzles in the local paper had not helped, and Shirlee Ann was antsy. But then she got lucky. Elvin Hayes came to the car dealership early, but he left and went to get a haircut. She followed him into the hair salon. After he received his haircut, Shirlee Ann was able to get some of his hair from the floor, picking it up and putting it in the novel she was reading, *Murder of a Botoxed Blonde,* by Denise Swanson. She was unbelievably lucky, and she was able to get her own hair colored black at the same time.

* * * * *

On Tuesday evening, Caleb Pehrson was in front of his sports-marketing class discussing the contingency framework for strategic sports marketing and how sports-marketing managers must understand how to face an ever-changing environment. He focused on understanding the importance of marketing segmentation and target marketing.

Marketing segmentation refers to an identification of the parts of the market that are different from one another. Segmentation allows a business to better satisfy the needs of potential customers. Rather than treating the market as a homogenous group and selling to the mass market, target marketing recognizes the diversity of customers and does not try to please all of them. Markets can be segmented by demographics, geographics, behavioralistics, and psychographics.

He asked his class, "What company has the slogan 'Just Do It?'" Almost every hand in the room went up, except for the students who were daydreaming.

"O.K., Janice. Who is the company?"

"Nike," she smiled.

"Right you are. These three words convey a powerful message for Nike." Caleb flashed up his next PowerPoint slide. "The top brand name in 2007 was Coke, according to *Business Week*."

Top Global Brand Names in 2007, from *Business Week*:

1. Coca-Cola
2. Microsoft
3. IBM
4. GE
5. Nokia
6. Toyota
7. Intel
8. McDonalds
9. Disney
10. Mercedes

"The top U.S. sports brand is probably the N.Y. Yankees, who are worth about $1.2 billion," Caleb continued. They have their own TV network and have a $95 million partnership with the German apparel maker Adidas. Peter J. Schwartz estimates the Yankees brand to be worth about $217 million.

"Branding includes image and prestige. Sports Business Associates says that global sponsorship of professional sports teams in 2006 was around $33.6 billion.

"As an example of branding, the accounting firm Grant Thornton recently unveiled a new global brand identity, logo, and Internet site. Their chief marketing officer said that the new brand will help differentiate them from both their largest and smaller competitors.

"Their new logo consists of three elements: the symbol, the color, and the Grant Thornton wordmark. The inspiration for the symbol was the Mobius strip, which was discovered by mathematicians in the nineteenth century. The symbol shows the qualities of a continuous band that looks three dimensional and is permanent, yet constantly flexible."

Grant Thornton

A wordmark, or brandmark, is a standardized graphic representation of a name of a business entity or its product. For example, FedEx is the registered name of Federal Express. When a brandname or brandmark is registered with the U.S. Patent office, it becomes a trade name or a trademark. A *brandname* is the part that can be vocalized. A brandmark is a distinctive design, symbol, or color that cannot be vocalized. Think "Nike" and "swoosh."

Caleb talked about market mix decisions (e.g., the 4 Ps). He emphasized the external and internal contingencies that affect the strategic sports-marketing process. He examined the following factors: compensation, technology, social and cultural trends, physical environment, legal and political conditions, demographics, and the economy.

At the end of his lecture, he gave his class a homework assignment called "Playing Marbles in Kannapolis." He told his class that his grandfather wrote the essay for a publishing company that publishes books about various counties in North Carolina. One of the books is entitled *Ain't No Bears Out Tonight and Other Cabarrus County Tales,* by Bob Lasley and Sallie Holt. "You are to read this interesting piece and answer the questions at the end of the essay," Caleb instructed his marketing class.

* * * * *

PLAYING MARBLES IN KANNAPOLIS
Samuel Pehrson

I was born January 16, 1941, to Carl Donald and Velvia Kelly Pehrson in the Cabarrus County Hospital. Dr. Wicker's delivery bill was $30. We lived on Patterson Street, initially on the right side of the road at 515. My parents rented the small frame house with four rooms, of course without a bath. My parents paid $11.00 per month to Mr. Clay Wright. We had running water only to the back porch, but it was free. We had an outhouse until we moved to Wright Avenue during my high-school years.

Since I was a traveler and wanderer by age 2, my mother said she tied me with a rope to the back porch to keep me in our yard. I could still ride my tricycle. She says that one time they could not find me, and they were worried that I had fallen into the outhouse. I had not. During the winter, as was the custom, we had a slop jar to use during the nights, which could be carried to the outside toilet the next morning. During the early years on Patterson Street we had an icebox. Each morning the iceman in his ice truck from the ice house in North Kannapolis would bring into the kitchen a block of ice. A hole was bored through the floor to allow the melting ice to run under the house. The milkman would deliver milk to the house, and we never locked either house on Patterson Street. We began locking our house when I was in high school in the late fifties, while living on Wright Avenue.

We would take a bath in a No. 2 tub once a week, generally on Saturday. Water would be heated on the stove and placed in the tub.

We had a reasonably sized back yard, which was used for a large garden —corn, tomatoes, green beans, carrots, cucumbers, squash, okra, onions, lettuce, and lima beans. Other staples were Spam, oyster soup, chicken, salmon patties, meatloaf, cod fish, hamburgers, hot dogs with cheese inside, fruit cake, and rocky-road cake. When there was no garden, the kids in the neighborhood would play football in the yard. One time when we were playing, my mother called me into the house to carry the garbage out. As I was carrying out the garbage, someone threw the football toward me. I threw a tin can at the ball, and being quite accurate, the football hit the tin can. The tin can came back, hit me in my mouth, and chipped a front tooth. I had the chipped tooth for many years.

My brother, Tony, was about eight years younger than I. When he was one and a half (1949), we had a wringer washing machine on our back porch. Somehow he was able to climb up on the washing machine and turn it on. His arm went through the wringer up to his armpit. He did not lose his arm.

I recall playing Monopoly, checkers, Chinese checkers, and dominoes with my younger sister by four years, Yvonne. We would play a Monopoly game over two or three days. We put together a number of puzzles. We played Red Rover, Simon says, hide and seek, hopscotch, jump rope, dodge ball, and kick the bucket with other kids in the neighborhood. We would catch lightning bugs and put them in jars or make rings out of them. We would catch June bugs, attach sewing thread to a leg, and watch them fly around. My sister, Yvonne, maintains that we would play Cowboys and

Indians by tying up Tony when our mother would go to work at Terry Products making baby clothes. Tony would want to play, and we would want to read. I do not recall such treatment, however.

We would make wooden stilts and walk on them. We would take two large juice cans, tie strings to each, and walk on them like stilts. Our Dick Tracy phones were merely two empty cans with a waxed string between them. We made our own kites from newspaper, branches, and water and flour (for the glue). We tied rags together to make the tail. We made slingshots from rubber tire tubes and played Cowboys and Indians with rubber guns. A piece of wood was cut in the shape of a gun, and then large rubber bands cut from tire tubes were stretched on the gun and shot. Where did all the tire tubes go? Patterson Avenue was on a slight hill and then made a sharp left turn at the bottom of the hill. We would get inside tires, and someone would roll us down the hill into a field at the end of the road. Great fun. In those days parents did not believe it was their responsibility to provide constant entertainment for their kids.

For Christmas we received clothes, a yo-yo, a book, a Slinky, Silly Putty, or a gun and holster set. My first bike was used, which we got from my older uncle who lived outside Ellerbe. We would put baseball cards in the spokes to make noise. My Mickey Mantle, Duke Snider, and other valuable cards disappeared when I went off to Pfeiffer College.

I still recall visiting my grandparents in Rockingham and Ellerbe. My mother and I were in Rockingham when the Pee Dee River Dam burst. She and I were on a hill watching the dam break and flood the Pee Dee Mill. My grandfather lived on six acres in a large house. My dad helped him tear down an elementary school and build the house. They dug a well, and you had to use a pump to get water. I remember my grandfather, Joseph Pehrson, had a large radio and a corn cob that he had shaped into a hand with five fingers. We would sometimes play with sand beside his house and make sand blocks with his cement block machine.

My other grandfather, Samuel Kelly, was a sharecropper, raising cotton and tobacco. When we visited there in the winter, it was cold. The only stove was in the kitchen, and you went to bed with many quilts. The floors had fairly large cracks in them, so when you woke up in the morning you could see and hear chickens underneath the house. The Kellys had a two-seater outhouse, with Sears & Roebuck catalogues and advertisements to use for toilet paper. To get to the outhouse, you had to go past the pig pen.

They would slaughter the pigs and eat the chickens that we saw under the house. They would wring the necks of the chickens and hang them by their feet on the clothesline.

I recall sitting on their front porch during a deadly storm watching the lightning hit the fields in front of me. They kept the grass away from the house by sweeping the yard with brooms made of sticks to keep the house from catching on fire. You had to pump water, and we would drink from the same dipper. I travelled throughout Russia during the mid-1980s, and the Russians still had huge water and juice containers in the streets, and the people would use the same cup. This adventure gives one a picture of how far behind the United States the Communists were, all because we had competition in the U.S.

I also remember sitting on my Grandfather Kelly's lap, and he would tell me riddles. What is hard water? Ice. What is colored water? Ink. What is black and white and red all over? Newspaper. He had a peg leg like a pirate, because he lost his leg from a shotgun accident as a teenager. His leg was simply a small tree attached to his body, with a round piece of tire attached to the bottom of the peg leg. He could still drive a car. He wore out two artificial legs.

I went to Jackson Park Elementary school and had Miss Massey as my first-grade teacher. We walked 1.2 miles to school, and when I got to school I had to run. We would take off our shoes as soon as we left home. There was a "dungeon" in the back of the school—concrete steps going down 10 to 12 feet with concrete sides. I do not know how one got chosen to be chased, but I suppose the bigger students would chase the smaller ones. If you were caught, you were thrown into the dungeon until the school bell rang or you escaped. I learned how to run fast.

I remember writing a term paper at Jackson Park on the country of Chile. I was only able to visit Chile when I was 65. The students who lived the farthest from Jackson Park were bused to Woodrow Wilson for seventh grade. If you missed the bus, you had to walk 2.4 miles. I did miss the bus occasionally, and I remember walking down the railroad tracks in front of Woodrow Wilson.

At both Jackson Park and Woodrow Wilson we shot marbles, because school yards did not have grass. You would draw a circle, and several kids would put an equal number of marbles in the middle of the circle. Each person would take turns trying to knock out one or more marbles. If you knocked one out, you kept it and got to shoot again. I do not remember how we selected who shot first. The best shooting device was a shiny ball bearing called a steelie. I won a lot of marbles (possibly 1,000), but when I went off to college my father used them to mix in cement to hold the posts for a clothesline. Oh, well. I was the first Pehrson to graduate from college and to get an MBA degree.

Aside from marbles, another form of gambling occurred in elementary and high school called pitching pennies. A straight line would be drawn in the dirt, and three or four participants would move five to seven feet from the line and toss pennies. The person's penny that came closest to the line got all of the pennies. Nickels or dimes could be used, but I could only afford pennies.

The Cannon Memorial YMCA was important to my development and learning. I learned to swim at the YMCA, and I also played basketball, volleyball, and bowled. Girls and boys swam at different times. The boys swam without bathing suits, but the girls wore bathing suits and bathing hats. Think about that.

Bowling was downstairs, and I sometimes set pins. Bowling pins had to be manually set up by someone after each bowler, and sometimes the bowler rolled the ball before the pin setter moved from the pit.

The YMCA had an excellent library, and during the summer there would be reading contests. During the summers I would often read as many as 125 books. I have had college juniors and seniors in my classrooms state in writing that they have read only one novel in their life: the one I required them to read.

Other things I remember about growing up in Kannapolis include the following:

- Picking blackberries and selling them for $1 a gallon. I had to wash with Clorox and alcohol to kill the red bugs and avoid getting poison oak.
- Playing football in the back of Zackie Moore's back yard. Most of the year we would play football or baseball from sun up to sundown in the large field next to Franklin Heights Baptist Church.
- Riding back and forth on the Old Concord Highway to get the necessary miles for the Boy Scouts biking merit badge. We had to go through the belt line at Scouts on occasion, but the troop disbanded before I could

get the swimming merit badge and advance to Eagle Scout. I had 40-some merit badges.

- Selling *Grit* papers, seeds, and shoes at Belk Bargain store, and cemetery lots, and working until 4:30 Saturday morning taking boxes off of the Winn-Dixie trucks and restocking the shelves. We would sometimes send a new employee to get a shelf stretcher. I would come back to work at noon on Saturday. I was both a bag boy and cashier.

- Hand-cranking the ice-cream freezer on a weekend to make peach ice cream. Mom made snow cream when it snowed.

- Trying to find the doodle bugs in their cone-shaped holes under the house.

- Seeing a television for the first time at Robert Compton's house the night that Eisenhower beat Stevenson. I recall being a Democrat then, but when I registered to vote as a Republican, I was only one of fourteen Republicans in my district, as opposed to 400-plus Democrats. It was a sin to be a Republican when I grew up. They had a saying about "Yellow Dog" Democrats. If they ran a yellow dog on the Democratic ticket, the yellow dog would beat the Republican candidate.

- My parents' first car was a '51 Chevrolet. Before that, walking and taxis were our modes of transportation.

- An occasional vacation was to Myrtle Beach, S.C., or the mountains. I have a black-and-white photo of Brenda and Gail Compton, Yvonne, and myself at the construction site of the Lake Fisher Dam in the late forties.

- After moving across the street to 522 Patterson, for which Dad paid $2,400, we would play ball in the dirt street. There was grass in the ditch in front of Glenn Scarborough's house, and I almost cut off one of my toes on a broken bottle in the grass. When I went to Dr. Guy Wicker, he asked me if I went barefooted. I said yes. He said that I should pee on the toe, which would help heal the cut.

- Yvonne and I would sometimes go to the movies at the Dixie Theatre (now Table Supply Store in Midway), Swanee Theatre (now Cannon Mills Visitors Center), and the Gem Theatre. When I was 15 and Yvonne was 11, she was taller than I. She would get mad because I would get in for under 12, and they wanted her to pay for 12 and over. There was always news and a cartoon before a movie.

- I remember dressing up on May 1 and participating in the May Day Dance at Jackson Park. I also remember wearing knickers and having flat-top haircuts.

In conclusion, we were poor but did not know it. There was no television, and everyone in Kannapolis was poor. We were happy, however. My life argues against the current welfare-oriented and socialist direction of the U.S. today. As Dolly Parton's song "Coats of Many Colors" says, "One is only poor if they choose to be. Now I know we had no money, but I was as rich as I could be."

1. Develop some marketing principles from this essay.

2. How would you market some of these products?

3. Why do some products disappear? What are the four stages of a product's life cycle?

4. Pick two products mentioned in the essay and suggest how they were marketed.

5. Could any products or services that have disappeared come back today? What are they?

* * * * *

After class Caleb began working on his next examination, but he kept thinking about where the madman or woman would strike next. The exam question before him was:

3. What is probably the second most important revenue stream for the New York Yankees sport franchise?
   a. Ticket sales
   b. Luxury suites revenue
   c. Television revenues
   d. Naming rights
   e. None of the above

Of course, the correct answer is C, television revenues.

Should he put a question on his examination about forensic marketing, a term being used in some literature? He picked up a copy of the Uciko

Group's website, labeled, "Forensic marketing supports the due diligence process for clients and considers acquisition, merger, or major investment. We have, to date, been at the forefront of rendering this complex service and have assisted many of our clients throughout times of merger and acquisition activity and at times IPO activity—known to excite shareholders and bring undue pressure on company executives. This service provides objective and realistic valuations in terms of market capitalization."

Their forensic marketing analysis typically includes:

- Marketing and sales capabilities—present and future
- Marketing strategy
- Channel strategy
- Promotional strategy
- Marketing resource cost and allocation
- Products and technologies
- Product strategy and pipeline
- Competitive products and technologies
- Forecasting

He was eating a Fig Newton by Nabisco, "2 Fruit Chewy Cookies." He noticed the wrapper on his desk where he had thrown it. On the side of the wrapper was printed, "Made with 100% More Real Fruit." He thought, "100% more of what?" He picked up the wrapper and in smaller letters he saw "than a Nutri-Grain Bar." There was an asterisk sign (*) that said in smaller print: "*Twice the level of fruit per bar vs. Nutri-Grain strawberry Cereal Bar, based on independent analysis. Nutri-Grain is a registered trademark of Kellogg North America Company."

"So," Caleb said out loud, "if Nutri-Grain has 1 percent fruit, a Fig Newton would have 2 percent. Was this misleading advertising? They were truthful, but possibly misleading. What if the Nutri-Grain had zero fruit? Zero times 100 percent equals zero." Had he just engaged in forensic marketing? Could he use the example on his exam?

* * * * *

Professor Cuneo had given much thought to Jacob Johnson's request for forensic-marketing assistance in his attempt to recover damages for Upper Deck. Cuneo had been informed that Upper Deck had engaged several expert witnesses, since Johnson's client was apparently convinced that the apparent recent decline in collector cards sales could be attributed to the scare from the poisoned cards. He picked up the phone and called Johnson.

"Mr. Johnson, this is Professor Murphy Cuneo at Herkimer Community College. I may not be the person you want for assistance in your suit for damages against the mass murderer when he or she is apprehended. You may want instead to talk with Professor Steve Thomason at the University of North Carolina at Charlotte, who is very experienced in this area. However, please allow me a couple suggestions and comments.

"First, let me say I don't mean to insult your intelligence, but please keep in mind the difference between 'correlation' and 'cause and effect.' Correlation only means that two factors appear to be related because a change in one is accompanied by a corresponding change in the other. There is an old story told in marketing classes about the fact that in college towns where there are a large number of professors there is a correspondingly high consumption rate of alcoholic beverages. This situation is correlation. You cannot conclude on this information alone, however, that the professors are drinking most of the alcohol and causing sales to be high. If that were true, then there would be a cause and effect. As a professor I hope you also would consider that perhaps fraternity parties, alumni at ball games, and other such factors could instead be influencing the consumption rate.

"I mention this example to caution you that just because collector card sales are down does not necessarily mean it is because of the scare from the deaths associated with the poisoned cards. I suggest that you get several years' sales records by month and compare the sales for each month. Perhaps there is a normal decline of sales in the months of the year where you are now experiencing decline. If there is a similar pattern of sales decline, you probably are going to have difficulty proving the 'cause and effect' of the current decline. If there is not a similar pattern, you have a better chance in court.

"Also, keep in mind there may be other factors causing the decline. I caution my students that they must first accurately define the problem. Too often, companies identify a decline in sales as the problem when it is only a symptom of an underlying problem. Perhaps the problem is an increase in a competitor's marketing activities, or perhaps too many of the company's sales personnel have been on vacation at the same time. In building your case, I would suggest you have the officials at Upper Deck look into other factors that may have influenced the decline in sales. Additionally, you may want to consider interviews with collector trade-show exhibitors to see if they have experienced a corresponding decline in demand.

"Also, have you spoken with the management at Topp's? Have they experienced a similar decline in sales? If so, perhaps you can get them to join into the suit with Upper Deck. Think 'lower legal fees'!!"

"Do you have any questions about what I have been saying?"

Professor Cuneo answered a few questions and then hung up. He had been told that Upper Deck had engaged several expert witnesses.

In exchange for higher prices than general admission seating, club seats offer
patrons various amenities such as wider seats, expanded menus with personal
delivery, preferred parking, and private restrooms. Since luxury suites are
considered to be the primary money maker among these nonshared revenue
sources, several scholars have considered it as the second most important revenue stream for sport franchises behind television revenues.

—DARYL WIRAKARTAKUSUMAH
—SOONHWAN LEE

Shirlee Ann arrived early at the elegant steel-and-glass Toyota Center
at 1510 Polk Street in downtown Houston in order to check out
the new arena. The Toyota Center replaced the Compaq Center in
October 2003. Costing $202 million to build, the center can hold
18,300 basketball fans. It is the home of the Houston Rockets, the
Houston Comets (WNBA), and the Houston Aeros (AHL). The arena has
2,900 club seats and 103 luxury seats.

The Silestone Rocket Club seats are located along the sidelines of the
lower bowl. Benefits include:

- First right of refusal to purchase tickets for concerts, family shows, and
  other exciting events that come to Toyota Center
- Extra-wide seats complete with cup holder and ample legroom
- A parking pass in the Toyota Tundra Garage, located next door to the
  arena, for every pair of club seats purchased
- Easy access to Toyota Center from the garage through the private sky-
  bridge entrance
- Concierge service

- Membership to Toyota Center's Rockets Club West and Rockets Club East loungers

The Rockets' advertising says the club seats are a great way to impress clients.

A review of Toyota Center by Karen Sommer asserted that the architects sank the lower bowl (60 percent of the seating) 32 feet below ground level, which puts fans closer to the action. She said the seats are two inches wider than most, and the scoreboard has the highest digital resolution of any built before the venue opened. The sound system is state-of-the-art. Whether a $10 or $500 stub, spectators have access to the Red & White Wine Bistro with their ticket.

Shirlee Ann did not buy wine after she purchased a single ticket outside and went inside. She was dressed as a woman tonight, but she had made herself heavy, with short, black hair. She wore glasses and a Rockets baseball hat.

Tonight the Houston Rockets were playing the Los Angeles Lakers. The franchise player for the Rockets is No. 11, Yao Ming. Center Ming, at 7'6" and 310 pounds, was born in Shanghai, China, playing five years for the Shanghai Sharks. In his fifth season in the NBA, he is the tallest player in the league. Born to a father, 6'11", and mother, 6'2", he lost his hearing in his left ear at age 7, and had his first dunk at age 15. He married his wife, Ye Li, who is 6'3", in 2007.

In order to be drafted by the NBA, he had to obtain nine signatures, including his own. His 2010 annual salary is $17.7 million, under a five-year, $75 million contract. In addition, Yao has sponsorships with the 2008 Beijing Olympics, McDonald's, Pepsi, Visa, Apple, Reebok, BMW, and Garmin. When he signed his initial contract, the Chinese government said that they would take 50 percent. The standard NBA agent contract allows a maximum of 4 percent, but few agents get that much.

In 2003, Yao was only the fourteenth rookie elected to start in the All-Star Game. Likewise, in 2005, Yao was named a "model worker" in his native China. His nomination as a "model and advanced worker" was approved by China's cabinet. In China, the annual disposable income of an urban resident is $1,025, and a rural citizen's annual per-capita income is $316. Yao's agent quoted Yao as follows: "I used to think that a model worker was a title for these ordinary laborers working hard, but now, apart from them, special migrant workers like me also can be awarded."

Although some teams do not have mascots courtside (e.g., the Lakers, Celtics, Knicks, Yankees, and Dodgers), the Rockets' mascot is a bear named Clutch. Clutch was named the most recognized mascot in sports by *USA Today* in 2005. Shirlee Ann saw Clutch on the court before the game.

At the end of the first quarter, the Lakers were ahead by 25 to 22, and Yao missed a free throw with 5:56 left in the half, snapping a streak of 35 consecutive makes. The second quarter was much worst for the Rockets. Tracy McGrady, seven-time All-Star and Houston's shooting guard, strained his right elbow near the end of the period, reaching in on Luke Walton. At the half the Rockets were down 61 to 49.

Although Yao Ming had 26 total points , he was harassed all night by Lamar Odom and Kwame Brown. Yao shot only 6 of 18 and was only 14 for 20 at the free-throw line. He normally shoots more than 90 percent at the free-throw line. Houston made a third-quarter run of 22 to 14, but at the end of the game Houston lost, 93–90. Lakers Kobe Bryant had 30 points.

Since Shaquille O'Neal left the Lakers, No. 24 Kobe Bryant, a shooting guard at 6'6", has been the Lakers' franchise player. With a 2010 salary of $24.8 million, Kobe started out with the Charlotte Hornets. With Shaq and Kobe, the Lakers won three consecutive NBA championships in 2000, 2001, and 2002.

Kobe is the son of a former player and coach, Joe "Jellybean" Bryant. His parents named him after the famous beef of Kobe, Japan, which they saw on a restaurant menu. Nicknamed the Black Mamba, he was drafted directly out of high school. He was the NBA leading scorer in the 2005–06 and 2006–07 seasons. He was the youngest player to reach 20,000 points.

Kobe is the only player in the NBA with a complete no-trade clause, which means that he can veto any trade deal. In the 2006–07 season he was demanding to be traded. In December 2007, Ken Berger said that "after an off season of 20,000 trade demands and just as many doses of animosity, the Lakers' superstar finally has settled down. But it seems only temporary."

Part of Kobe's trade-me tantrums involve the slow development of Lakers' center, Andrew Bynum. In this game Bynum played 17 minutes versus Kobe's 38 minutes. Bynum had 9 rebounds, 1 blocked shot, and scored only 6 points.

Tracy McGrady was on the way to the hospital by the time the third quarter started. The team doctor said McGrady, known as T-Mac, stretched a ligament and nerve in his arm.

Before the buzzer at the end of this game, five females died from poison on basketball cards in the women's restrooms.

Shirlee Ann had decided to go random.

Ironically, two days before her attack in the Toyota Center, the FBI released a press release encouraging the public to help them find another famous extortionist, D. B. Cooper. On November 24, 1971, a man calling himself Dan Cooper purchased a one-way ticket on Northwest Orient Airline, flight No. 305, from Portland to Seattle. The mystery passenger was about 5'10" to 6', 170 to 180 pounds, in his mid-forties, with brown eyes. In Seattle he hijacked the plane, maintaining he had dynamite, and demanded a ransom of $200,000. The airline gave him $200,000 in marked bills, along with four parachutes.

Cooper then told the flight crew to "fly to Mexico." Somewhere between Washington State and north of Portland, Oregon, the man parachuted out of the tail of the plane in a cold, driving rain with two parachutes and the money. One of the parachutes was a reserve chute to be used only for training and had been sewn shut. The hijacker could not see the ground due to cloud cover at 5,000 feet. The FBI release said that "no experienced parachutist would have jumped in the pitch-black night, in the rain, with a 200-mile-an hour wind in his face, wearing loafers and a trench coat. It was simply too risky."

During the hijacking, Cooper was wearing a black J. C. Penney tie, which he removed before he jumped. The tie provided the FBI with DNA samples in 2001. In 1980, an 8-year-old boy found three bundles containing $5,800 of the ransom money on the bank of the Columbia River. The FBI provided a map and asked if any hydrologists could trace the route of the $5,800 ransom money down the river. The court forced the child to split the money with the insurance company who put up the money.

Sandy and Shirlee Ann had studied the D. B. Cooper hijacking to learn the mistakes he made so they could avoid them. The Cooper episode shows the disadvantages of asking for money as ransom. Likewise, the toughest part of a ransom or kidnapping was obtaining the payoff. Shirlee Ann knew that serial numbers on any ransom bills are sent to all of the FBI field offices for distribution to commercial enterprises, such as banks, hotels, and airlines. She knew that the FBI might eventually find the $100 bills that she had spent in and around Kannapolis.

* * * * *

After the killings at the Rockets' game, Douglass consulted with Caleb Pehrson, and they decided that the next attack might be at the next Lakers' game. So on December 25, Douglass, two other FBI agents, and Caleb were sitting in the Staples Center in downtown Los Angeles. Staples Center is located next to the Los Angeles Convention Center and is the home of five professional teams: the L.A. Lakers and L.A. Clippers of the NBA, the L.A. Sparks of the WNBA, the L.A. Kings of the NHL, and the the L.A. Avengers of the AFL.

The Staples Center was financed privately at a cost of $375 million, and it is the host of nearly 4 million visitors each year. Staples paid $116 million for a 20-year naming right, or $5.8 million each year, compared to the American Airlines Center for the Dallas Mavericks at $6.5 million annually, and the FedEx Forum of the Memphis Grizzlies at $4.5 million annually.

Before the game, Douglass asked Caleb to explain the NBA salary cap.

"How many hours do we have?" Caleb joked. "The purpose of the salary cap is to keep teams, especially the ones in the larger markets, from taking their additional revenue and buying all of the best players. The cap increases each year depending upon the league's revenue numbers the previous year.

"It is extremely complicated, and I don't know all of the rules and many exceptions. We have a soft cap as opposed to the hard cap of the NFL and NHL. Basically, we have several exceptions and loopholes. With a hard cap there is little likelihood a team will exceed the salary cap, but not with a soft cap.

"We have the mid-level exception, the biannual exception, the rookie exception, the Larry Bird exception, and about five other exceptions."

Douglass asked, "The Larry Bird exception is for white players?"

Caleb laughed. "No. The Larry Bird exception allows a team to exceed the salary cap to resign its own free agents, up to the maximum salary and up to six years in length.

"Let me give you an example. In the 2007–08 season, there is a salary cap of $55.63 million and a luxury-tax base of $67.865 million. If the Dallas Mavericks have a total payroll of $79,351,704, they have to pay a luxury tax of $11,486,704 to the league. This amount is dispersed between the teams below the luxury-tax threshold," Caleb looked at Douglass. "Understand."

"No. I'm a few knives short in the salary-cap drawer. But I have another question. I saw the Florida Gators wipe out the Ohio State basketball team in the finals with freshman Greg Oden on the Buckeyes' team. The 7-footer went pro after his freshman year with a $21 million salary from the Portland Trail Blazers. His agent gets 4 percent, or around $810,000. Now he's out for his entire rookie season with a microfracture right-knee injury."

"Yeah, he had microfracture surgery, which takes about 8 months to heal. He apparently has gained at least 30 pounds of upper-body weight, which is not helpful. The Trail Blazers had MRIs on both of his knees before they drafted him, and they said they were 'pristine.' In his pre-draft physicals, some teams worried about several parts of his body and his long-term durability. The draft is a crap shoot," Caleb said.

Douglass handed Caleb a copy of an article entitled "Greg Oden Wondering If Trail Blazers Can Pay Him As Much As Ohio State." "Notice what Oden says in the article, 'Man, I was pulling in mad cash . . . bling.' 'And the first two semesters I didn't have any classes. It should be less work, too. In college they made you play defense and run the floor. Plus I can use as many pivot feet as I want.'"

"I didn't think college boosters could pay college athletes," Douglass said.

Caleb did not answer. Finally, he said, "We better find the real bad guy and let the NCAA deal with the booster problem."

Douglass and Caleb actually watched some of the battle between the Lakers and the Phoenix Suns. The Lakers beat the Suns, who were leading the Pacific Division, 122-115. Kobe Bryant had 38 points, and center Andrew Bynum had a career-high 28 points, shooting 11 for 13 from the floor with 12 rebounds. There were no attacks at the Staples Center.

* * * * *

Shirlee Ann was not at the Lakers game on Christmas day. She was watching the Miami Heat play the Cleveland Cavaliers at the Quicken Loans Arena. Their scoreboard has the DIFF, which is the difference between the two teams' scores. In 2007, the Cavaliers opened a new state-of-the-art practice facility, Cleveland Clinic Courts, at Independence, Ohio. Featuring two playing courts, a team meeting room, front offices, and a kitchen, the facility is considered the best in the league.

Shirlee Ann had read a story in the *Boston Globe* by Bruce Mohl that event owners were beginning to use a paperless ticketing system. Event owners lose control of paper tickets because around 15 percent of paper tickets are resold and 40 percent are transferred to someone else. The Cavs have a Flash Seats system that allows fans to buy electronic tickets. Just like with the airlines, a fan enters an arena by swiping a credit card or driver's license. The system issues them a paper guide to their seats. Thus, the arena owner can track the ownership of a ticket as it changes hands. This approach allows the arena owner to manage ticket resales and reclaim some of the money now going to third-party vendors, such as eBay or Ace Ticket.com.

The Heat's coach Pat Riley did not get a winning Christmas present this game, as he was seen rubbing his eyes at his team's bad playing. Cavs' small forward LeBron James was elbowed by Shaq in the face. "I could have lost two front teeth, which is not a good thing," he said. James scored 25 points in the Cavaliers 96 to 82 win over the slumping Heat. Cavs' center Zydrunas Iigauska, or Big Z, at 7'3", scored 13 points. Big Z is from Kaunas, Lithuania. The Cavaliers' power forward Drew Gooden had 9 rebounds and 18 points, more than Big Z.

Shaq received his fifth foul with 6:55 left, and Pat Riley pulled him from the game. Shaq had fouled out his past five games. O'Neal said, "We were very careless with the ball. Our defense loosened up a little bit, and they were able to score a lot in the paint."

Cavs' coach Mike Brown got the Christmas win, and professional basketball received a small Christmas present from Shirlee Ann. At the last moment she decided not to put out any poisoned basketball cards. "Not on Christmas," she said. "But as the Brooklyn Dodgers fans would say, 'Wait until next year.'"

Maybe it was Moondog, the official mascot of the Cavaliers, that kept her from dropping any deadly basketball cards, or maybe it was the beautiful Cavaliers' Girls dance team. She had previously viewed a YouTube video of the mascot making unbelievable shots into trash baskets around Cleveland. Moondog was the name that Cleveland radio disc jockey Alan Freed called himself. Freed coined the phrase "rock-n-roll."

The Cavs' small forward LeBron James has received more than an elbow in the face in the past. His Nike video, called "Chamber of Fear," has been banned in China and pulled from television because it is seen as being blasphemous. The advertisement shows James battling a martial-arts expert and a pair of dragons in a video game–style setting. The video on YouTube shows him facing demons called Hype, Temptation, Haters, Complacency, and Self-Doubt. There is Chinese language on the video, and the Chinese said that the ad breached rules about upholding national dignity. Marketing people have to be careful about the use of Chinese cultural symbols.

* * * * *

The good news for Douglass was that the extortionist had not struck in Los Angeles or another city within the past several days. Basketball ticket revenues were decreasing daily, however. She or he had spent some of the $100 bills in North Carolina, Houston, and Cleveland. There were no killings in Cleveland, so maybe the killer was headquartered in or around Cleveland. Douglass had first felt that he or she was a southerner. Maybe he was wrong.

He went back and reviewed the path of the marked cash spent from the baseball drop two years ago. Some of it was spent around the Denver area and along almost a direct line from Denver to Florida, especially around Homestead, Florida. Some of the $100s had been spent in New Orleans.

There were two hairs matted to two of the basketball cards found in the Toyota Center. They were from an African-American male. Elvin Hayes had not gone to the Rockets' game. On the surface, he did not appear to be involved. Arresting a suspect on less than probable cause just to obtain DNA evidence raises the question of a Fourth Amendment violation against unreasonable search and seizure. In the United Kingdom, all suspects can be forced to provide a DNA sample. The odds of two unrelated people having identical DNA profiles are approximately one in a trillion. Douglass did not have probable cause.

Howard Safir, NYC police commissioner in 1999, gave these benefits for DNA data-banking arrestees:

- Most major crimes involve people who have committed minor offenses.
- People are currently in prison who are innocent; if samples had been

taken at the time of arrest, these people would have been excluded early in the process.
- Moving the point of testing from conviction to arrest would result in the saving of much money and time.
- Investigators would be able to compare other cases against the arrested person's DNA profile, just as with fingerprints.

There is currently a huge backlog of DNA samples waiting to be entered into the CODIS system. DNA can provide insight into such things as legitimacy of birth, susceptibility to certain physical diseases and mental disorders, and possibly even predisposition to certain behavior and sexual orientation. The FBI prefers to get DNA from blood samples taken from fingertips, but the preferred method on CSI television shows is swabbing the inside of the mouth. The FBI has robotic technology to speed up DNA processing.

A January 2006 amendment to the Violence Against Women Act permits DNA collection from anyone under criminal arrest by federal authorities, and also from federally detained illegal immigrants. The notorious Angel Resendix, a Mexican immigrant, committed many rapes in the U.S. He was deported 17 times, and if any DNA samples had been taken, many of his murders and rapes might have been prevented.

Without probable cause, Douglass had two approaches to get DNA from Elvin Hayes. The first was to visit with him and ask for a sample DNA. After all, Hayes was now a reserve police officer in Liberty, Texas.

The other approach was to gather evidence from the suspect from traces of saliva from a glass, a cigarette, or discarded tissue. Collecting DNA from abandoned cigarette butts, empty water bottles, or chewing gum is not illegal seizure. Some experts believe that such creative investigative techniques are unethical or possibly illegal.

* * * * *

Douglass decided to take the honest, upfront approach. Two days later Douglass was sitting in Elvin Hayes's Liberty office, speaking to him. He explained the situation to Hayes.

Hayes said after the explanation, "I sometimes go to see the Houston Astros play, but I do not believe I have seen the Rockets play in recent years, except maybe a few moments on TV. How do you want to take a sample? My hair? My blood? A swab from my mouth?"

"How about a couple of hairs and some blood from a finger."

"Not a problem," Hayes said.

Back at the FBI headquarters, Douglass asked for a rush on Hayes's DNA analysis.

He had an anonymous recommendation from one of the FBI agents who participated in the brainstorming section:

Due to the seriousness of these murders and the difficulty of catching the monster, I suggest we take severe action. Assuming the next drop is in water, a package-type explosive device (IED) should be placed into the suitcase. When he or she opens the suitcase, the explosion will eliminate the extortionist. As an alternative, I suggest you drop a hand grenade on the perp, which should cause less damage to the surroundings. The sound under the water at a minimum will stun the individual.

I understand that there will be Monday morning quarterbacks who will attack the FBI, similar to the waterboarding problem with the CIA. If we eliminate this individual by death, the PR will be less severe than if we allow more and more murders. Also, such a radical approach should dampen any future copycats.

You need to consult with our lawyers with respect to any legal liabilities. I would toss the grenade.

Douglass sent a copy of the suggestion to the legal department for advice. He liked the idea. The device could be detonated with a telephone signal if he or she did not have a portable jamming device.

Sponsorship objectives vary as widely as the companies that engage in sports sponsorship activities. Some of the more common objectives are improved company and product awareness, increased sales, better community relations, entertainment for clients, or even a favorite interest of a top executive.

—JAMES ZARICK
—JAMES GRANT
—KATHRYN DOBIE

Caleb Pehrson was in the courtroom to testify as an expert witness in an ambush marketing dispute. A person may have to testify as a fact witness in a legal dispute. A fact witness tells the court about the facts involving a dispute. A fact witness cannot offer an opinion. In contrast, an expert witness may offer his or her opinion about the issues in dispute as a result of special skills, education, experience, and training. The judge, however, determines whether someone will be admitted as an expert witness.

Federal court judges and many state court judges use five factors to determine whether an expert is allowed to testify. These five *Daubert* factors that determine acceptability are:

- Whether the theory or technique used by the marketing expert can be or has been tested
- Whether the theory or technique has been subjected to peer review and publication
- The known or potential rate of error of the method used
- The degree to which the method or conclusion has been accepted within the relevant community
- Whether the theory existed before litigation began

Courts, in general, will not exclude testimony on the basis of one factor alone.

Caleb had been an expert witness in several other court battles. He was an expert for the plaintiff, and he had previously gone through a deposition. During a deposition the opposing lawyer asks you a bunch of questions, and you must answer them under oath. The other side is attempting to learn your position and trip you up. They are trying to get you to make mistakes or be untruthful.

Caleb was so lost in going through his possible testimony that the cab ride to the courthouse seemed to take no time. After paying the cabbie, he walked quickly up the courthouse steps. He had spent some time with his attorney the previous day, going over his possible testimony and reviewing his written report. In a federal court trial, an expert witness must prepare an expert report that is studied carefully by the other side. Caleb waited outside the courtroom for about one hour, but eventually he was on the witness stand.

"Do you swear to tell the truth, the whole truth, and nothing but the truth, so help you God?" the bailiff asked.

"I do," Caleb said loudly looking at the jurors. He moved his chair so he was facing the jurors. He wanted to talk and look at the jurors rather than the attorneys.

The function of an expert witness is to assist the trier of the facts, whether it is the jurors or the judge (in the case of a bench trial). Caleb knew that most trials boil down to credibility. He knew that the other side's attorney would try to present evidence and ask questions to show that he was biased. An expert witness should be an advocate for the truth, however.

An expert witness who keeps his or her cool and conveys concise, cogent information—whether in depositions or under an opposing attorney's attempts to discredit their testimonies—can have a pivotal impact on a conflict's resolution as well as the satisfaction of helping a client win.

Caleb knew that during the deposition and the "no-holds-barred" cross-examination process, the opposing counsel would try to destroy his testimony and credibility.

His friendly attorney began the direct examination. "Mr. Pehrson, for the court's record, please state your full name and current address."

"Caleb Jacob Pehrson, 1071 Balcony Lane, Boston, Massachusetts."

"Mr. Pehrson, I want to thank you for testifying today as an expert about certain marketing principles. First, I have several questions for you concerning your background. Where did you obtain your bachelor's degree?"

"North Carolina A&T."

"You majored in what subject?"

"Marketing." Caleb tried to appear friendly as he looked towards the jury box and the jurors. The judge was to his right.

"Where did you receive your MBA degree?"

"Harvard University."

"Are you listed in Who's Who in America?"

"Yes."

"Are you a member of the American Marketing Association?"

"Yes," Caleb answered. "Since 1989."

"Are you a member of the Sports Marketing Association?"

"Yes, I am a founding member."

"Do you have any professional certification?"

"Yes."

"What are your certificates?"

"I am a Professional Certified Marketer or PCM. I am required to have 36 continuing professional education hours every three years to keep this certificate from the PCM." Caleb paused.

"I have been a sports marketing professional for three years. One obtains this certification from the University of Kentucky Sports Marketing Academy. I have been a certified forensic consultant or CFC for five years."

"Mr. Pehrson, are you currently employed?"

"Yes, I am the Vice President of Sales for the Boston Celtics."

"Uh." The attorney shuffled several pages and then continued. "Have you ever appeared as an expert witness in the courtroom?"

"Yes. I have been an expert witness for marketing matters on five different occasions. I have been deposed and have provided written declarations and affidavits. I have worked for plaintiffs and defendants. I have provided services to law firms, agencies, and venture capitalists."

"Today you are an expert witness for the plaintiff?"

"Yes," Caleb answered. "But I am an advocate for the truth. I am paid for my time, my expertise, my experience, and my out-of-pocket expenses, but not for my opinion."

"Have you been an expert witness with respect to ambush marketing?"

"Yes. Twice."

"Mr. Pehrson, please give a definition of ambush marketing."

"I like the definition given by the International Olympic Committee. Every communication initiative that creates an unauthorized association with the Olympic image or intellectual property, or that uses any of the elements that are part of the Olympic intellectual property on products or packaging," Caleb said.

"Are you saying the Olympics do not like ambush marketing?" his attorney asked.

"Absolutely," Caleb said. "They say that ambush marketing is a dishonest, parasitic, and illegal way to do business. Companies that practice it deceive the consumer, threaten sports, and discredit themselves."

"Those are some very harsh words. What would be your definition of ambush marketing?"

"It's a marketing strategy where a competing brand associates itself with a sporting event without paying the sponsorship fees. These fees can be huge," Caleb said.

"Please give some examples of this parasitic practice."

"In 2005, security guards at Wimbledon thwarted an ambush marketing stunt by Colgate-Palmolive when piles of bootleg water bottles began to accumulate outside the All-England Club in southwest London.

"Nike has been an aggressive ambush marketer. In 1996, this athletic shoe and apparel maker leased a parking garage near Centennial Park to promote its athletes and peddle its products during the Olympic Games, according to the *New York Times*.

"Nike did not pay the $500 million sponsorship fee, but plastered billboards in Atlanta, handed out free banners to spectators, and erected a huge Nike center overlooking the stadium."

"What do you mean by a sponsorship fee, Mr. Pehrson?" the lawyer asked.

"In early 2007, Promo Sourcebook estimated that North American marketers would spend about $15 billion on sponsorship rights fees. That's billion, not million. A company pays an event owner or a sports player a certain amount of money to obtain certain marketing rights. For example, Sprint/Nextel paid NASCAR $700 million to rename NASCAR's premier series of races, formerly known as the Winston Cup. The races will now be called the Nextel Cup. Another example would be in soccer. The England soccer team in 2006 had sponsorship revenues of $91 million from Mc-Donald's, Pepsi, and Carlsberg," Caleb paused.

"If a company engages in ambush marketing, can this dishonest strategy affect a sponsor?"

"Yes. Research has shown that 72 percent of an estimated 75 million NASCAR fans consider racing sponsorships when making purchasing decisions. That's more than 53 million race-car fans."

"Does the event owner incur expenses when dealing with sponsorship rights?"

"Absolutely. As a general rule, an event owner should total up the necessary expenses and then tack on a 100 percent mark-up or margin." Caleb paused for a moment before continuing "Cleveland Cavaliers vice-president of sales Kerry Bubolz has found that the Cavaliers' sponsorship partners prefer binders. He says the presence of a thick book has a huge visual aspect and personalizes the sponsorship. The corporate partner can see how important the relationship is to the organization, and the binder allows the partner to sift through and appreciate every piece of work that was put into it."

"So an ambush marketer harms both the event owner and the sponsor."

"Yes," Caleb answered.

"In your judgment, Mr. Pehrson, is the defendant an ambush marketer?"

"Absolutely," Caleb said loudly.

"Was the plaintiff harmed?"

"Yes," Caleb responded. "By a huge amount."

* * * * *

Shirlee Ann was back at 601 Biscayne Boulevard, in the American Airlines Arena at the Miami Heat and Orlando Magic game. She was unhappy because Heat's 7'1", 325-pound center Shaquille O'Neal was not playing because of an aggravated bruised left hip. The injury had occurred on December 26 at Philadelphia. She found it interesting that Shaq wears size 23 shoes.

She had researched Shaq and found that he was recently sworn in as an honorary U.S. deputy marshal. He joined a Department of Justice Task

Force that tracks down sexual predators who target children on the Internet. While playing for the Los Angeles Lakers, Shaq went through the police academy and became a reserve officer with the Los Angeles Port Police. She knew that Elvin Hayes was also a reserve police officer. Although one of the dominant players in the NBA, Shaq had prepared a commercial for the Miami police in which he was dressed in police clothes. He was shown climbing a tree to rescue the Louisiana State University mascot Mike the Tiger. Shirlee Ann's ex-husband was a police officer, but he had dumped her for a younger woman. Shirlee Ann had read that Shaq divorced his wife before the 2007–08 season

Shaq played at and eventually graduated from Louisiana State University. Upon graduating he said, "Now I can go get a real job." In 2005, he obtained an MBA degree online through the University of Phoenix. He spent more than a year to get the MBA degree. When he graduated, he said, "It's just something to have on my resume when I go back to reality. Someday I may have to put down the basketball and have a regular 9-to-5 job like everybody else." When he stops playing, he hopes to go undercover or be a sheriff or a chief of police somewhere. Shirlee Ann doubted that Shaq could ever go undercover.

Shaq has appeared in at least six movies, the latest being *Scary Movie 4* in 2006. This movie is a farce on other slasher movies, and Shaq appears in a scene with Dr. Phil. Spoofing *Saw,* they wake up chained in a bedroom, and Shaq has to make a free throw with a large rock to get a saw to cut off their legs. Shaq is known for his poor free-throw percentage, with a lifetime average of around 53 percent. So opponents often commit intentional fouls against him, resulting in his nickname, "Hack-a-Shaq."

In the movie, Dr. Phil and Shaq have only two minutes to free themselves from the leg braces before dying from airborne poison. Shaq finally makes a basket, the saw falls, and Dr. Phil cuts off the wrong foot. Presumably they both die in the spoof.

The coach for the Orlando Magic, Stan Van Gundy, had resigned as the Heat coach in December 2005, and he had not been back to the Heat stadium until tonight. He saw Heat's popular 6'4" shooting guard Dwayne Wade match a career-high 48 points, with 20 coming in the fourth quarter. Coming from Marquette University, Wade has had the top-selling NBA jersey over a two year period.

At the end of the fourth quarter the score was tied, and Van Gundy had his team trap Wade constantly in the five-minute overtime. Wade was unable to get a shot off. After the game Van Gundy said that "right off the bat next game, we're trapping him the minute he walks out of the locker room."

Trapping refers to putting two players on one player very aggressively and trying to stop him from passing. There are a number of ways to trap, but one way is to catch the player as he crosses the center line because he cannot throw the ball back across the line. Or you trap the player in any of the four corners on the court.

Trapping might be like the bait-and-switch pricing strategy. A business tries to get a customer into the store through false or misleading advertising. Once the customer is in the store, the salesperson tries to get him or her to buy more expensive merchandise. Possibly the advertised merchandise is a piece of junk.

At the end of the overtime, the Magic were the winners, 121 to 114. Magic 6'11" center-forward Dwight Howard had 29 points and 21 rebounds. Magic 6'10" forward Hendo Turkoglu, from Turkey, had 22 points. He had hit a 3-pointer with 11 seconds left in regulation time to tie the game.

* * * * *

Shirlee Ann had not waited until the end of the regulation game, nor did she see the Magic win in overtime. Throughout the arena and especially in the restrooms, there were signs cautioning people not to pick up basketball cards. There were guards at each restroom. So she decided to follow the American Airlines' arena promise: the SMILE principle.

Service with a smile
Make a difference
Impress the guest
Listen to learn
Exceed expectations

She went outside to the North Miami Avenue parking lots and painted her poison on the door handles of the parked cars. She carried out her threat. Once her mission was accomplished, Shirlee Ann took the Metro-Rail to the Government Center Station. From there she walked to her motorcycle and calmly rode to her RV.

By noon of the next day, almost everyone in the United States knew about the six killings at the Miami basketball arena. Fox News, CNN, and MSNBC were in a feeding frenzy. In a poll taken by Fox News and the *New York Times*, 68 percent of basketball fans would not go inside a restroom in a basketball arena. Forty-two percent of the polled people were afraid to go inside *any* public bathroom.

Commissioner David Stern increased the reward for the capture of the killer or killers to $1.5 million.

The *Miami Herald* had the following headline: "Diabolical Killer Poisons Six at AA Arena." They rehashed the exploits of the female nurse Genene Jones in Kerrville, Texas. While Jones was working at a pediatrics clinic, seven different children succumbed to seizures and one died, 15-month-old Chelsea McCellan. When McCellan's body was tested, her death appeared to have been caused by a muscle relaxant called succinylcholine. A grand jury convicted Jones on two counts of murder and several counts of injury to six other children. When Jones was a nurse at Bexar County Medical Center for four years earlier, there were 47 suspicious deaths of children. The "Killer Nurse" was sentenced to 99 years in prison in 1984. She has been up for parole at least six times already

* * * * *

The DNA report came back to Douglass. It confirmed that the hairs on the baseball cards at the Houston game were those of Elvin Hayes. Douglass did not know what to do. Hayes had not left Texas during the Miami killings. Was someone setting him up for the crimes? He recalled how the baseball killers had set up Milt Pappas two years earlier.

* * * * *

Professor Murphy Cuneo was sitting in Commissioner David Stern's office to report on his research on improving the impact of the WNBA with respect to revenue inflows.

"Thank you for coming today, Professor Cuneo," Stern said. "First, I want you to tell me why TV poker is beating the socks off of my women's professional teams. Clearly, there is more action in the WNBA, and they are certainly better-looking than most of the poker players."

"The *New York Times* estimates that there are 50 million poker players in the U.S., and the televised tournaments are the third most-watched sports on cable television, behind car racing and football," Cuneo said.

"Poker playing is not a sport," Stern said. "Maybe a reality TV show."

"Revenues for online poker were estimated to be $200 million per month in 2005. Online venues are much cheaper than brick and mortar ones because of the small overhead costs. The point I am making is that there are many potential poker players. Peter King says that poker is so popular because anyone can be a poker player. A person can dream of becoming a millionaire by playing better poker, so they watch poker games to learn tips. Few basketball fans can slam dunk a basketball, and no tips they learn at a game can make them a better basketball player. They will never make the Celtics or Hornets team, but they may win a poker tournament."

Cuneo paused and turned a page. "The psychology of poker interests people. They watch to learn how to read other poker players.

"You've heard the mantra, 'You play the player, not the cards.' So if they learn to 'read' people, they can become wealthy. To a certain extent, greed has made poker popular. The American dream of working your way up from the busboy to poker pro with $2 million in winnings is there in front of anyone. Since 2002, the number of poker rooms in Nevada has doubled, and annual revenues have increased from $68 million to $168 million. Shana Hiatt, the host of the Travel Channel's *World Poker Tour*, said that 'playing poker can be a dream coming true for anyone.'

"Two developments have been important. The so-called lipstick spycams provide behind-the-scenes access to players' cards, and the proliferation of online and offline satellites offer amateurs an inexpensive, longshot bid for a tournament seat."

"Got it. Greed. Gambling. How can WNBA make more money?" Stern asked irritatingly.

"The good news is that the poker boom may be losing some of its legs, and televised poker is drawing fewer viewers," Cuneo responded. But the World Series of Poker is held every year for one month in Las Vegas. The event culminates with a $10,000 no-limit hold 'em 'Main Event,' attracting thousands of entries, with the winner receiving a multimillion-dollar prize. The total prize for the 2010 Main Event was $68,798,600.

"The WNBA teams generally play in the same arena as the men, but with a season that runs from May to August. The playoffs end in September. In December 2006, the Charlotte Bobcats stopped operating the Charlotte Sting, so there was no 2007 season. The players were drafted by the other teams. A total of six teams have folded," Cuneo continued.

"We have a new team in Atlanta, nicknamed the Dream, that started playing in May, 2008. We have a total of 12 teams," Stern said. "Seven now independently owned."

"Attendance has gone up and down, but generally around 8,000 per game from around 10,000 in earlier years," Cuneo interjected.

"Yes. Yes. How do we radically improve attendance?" Stern asked.

"Two economics professors, R. W. Brown and R. T. Jewell, published an article in *Industrial Relations* (January 2006) that estimated the marginal revenue product of an elite woman college basketball player to be worth nearly $250,000 annually for her name. The key word is elite. Players from less-successful programs generate little revenue for their teams.

"The problem is that the WNBA generates less than break-even income even with a carefully controlled salary structure, forcing the NBA to subsidize the WNBA. The team must split $700,000 among its players. Rookies get $30,000 and three-year veterans get $43,000, with a maximum of $100,000 to any one player.

"You have been quoted as saying that the NBA values the WNBA as an ambassador that draws new fans—especially women—to the sport, so that it is worth the financial losses the NBA has incurred over its 14-year history. How much longer will the NBA subsidize the WNBA?"

Stern did not answer.

"I have one off-the-wall suggestion. Have the men play the women once a year. Rather than the sophomores playing the rookies, have the rookies play the winner of the WNBA All-Stars game. The sophomores have beaten the rookies five years in a row. Hopefully, the women can win as often as the rookies."

"Not a bad idea," Stern said.

"Another suggestion is to start a Slam Dunk Challenge at your WNBA All-Star game. The Dribble, Dish, & Swish Skills Challenge does not sound exciting.

"Also, you need to develop some superstars like Michael Jordan. Look what he did for the NBA. For example, when Tennessee's Candace Parker, at 6'4", and LSU's Sylvia Fowles, at 6'6", were drafted, you should have pushed them as superstars. Advertise them. Make them or someone else your

Kobe Bryant or Shaquille O'Neal. Maybe Seattle Storm's Lauren Jackson or Sue Bird, Mercury's Diana Taurasi, Cappie Pondexter, or Penny Taylor. Any way to get them into movies? Can you encourage a WNBA movie?

"Candace Parker was the first woman to dunk in an NCAA tournament. Sylvia Fowles was the sixth woman to dunk in a college basketball game. You need some broken backboards at your WNBA game. Just a little humor," Cuneo said.

Stern did not smile.

"My overall suggestion involves segmentation, or developing a target market. As you know, the purpose of market segmentation is to enable you to tailor marketing mixes to meet the needs of one or more of specific segments. Segmentation will help you more accurately define your marketing objectives and better allocate precious resources.

"Which fans make up your best target market? With the ticket prices low, you need to advertise for families to come to women's games. I would zero in on African-American women with children, especially former high-school and college athletes. Encourage a family atmosphere. Mothers can bring their children to a game and spend quality time with them. Tailor your advertising and promotions to this group.

"One NBA owner said he would rather have customers than fans. Customers spend money at games, while fans sit around and listen to sports radio all day. Once you develop this wholesome atmosphere at games, the women's teams will have a better chance of finding sponsors. Sponsors are what the WNBA teams need.

"You have my full written report. If you need more clarification, don't hesitate to contact me."

"Thanks, Professor Cuneo. I will read and consider your report. I strongly believe that there is compelling logic to have 20-plus dates in an NBA arena in the summertime, to have additional programming for regional sports network, and to have goodwill ambassadors in the community promoting the sport of basketball among girls and boys and fans of all ages," Stern said. "In October 2002, we changed the business model from a centrally operated league to individual franchises that are owned and operated by NBA owners. As you know, under this model WNBA teams can be sold to non-NBA owners and moved to non-NBA cities. Three examples are the Chicago Sky, Connecticut Sun, and Washington Mystics."

15

A successful identity-oriented strategy like Nike's consists of three critical links, including the consumer, the identity and the brand. If these links are forged, then they create self-conceptual connections that can lead to advantageous marketing outcomes for companies that are savvy enough to incorporate identity into their marketing strategy.

—AMERICUS REED, II

Douglass was sitting at his desk filling out the forms to obtain fixed-wing surveillance at the next basketball murder extortion drop. He was expecting a call from her after the horrendous killings outside the American Airlines Arena in Miami. What he needed was an unmanned military predator.

Fat chance of that. Maybe the President would authorize the FBI to use a pilotless predator. He knew she would request the drop to be over water. But where?

The Posse Comitatus Act was passed in the nineteenth century after the Civil War, with the intent to remove the military from domestic law enforcement. There were exceptions to the act, and the courts have generally held that providing supplies, equipment, training, facilities, and intelligence information to law agencies was permissible. Passive, rather than active, participation is fine. Certainly the act can be sidestepped by Presidential proclamation.

The phone rang. He was expecting a call from his wife, because his son had a soccer match tonight.

"Hello, Douglass. How are you?"

Female voice. It was not his wife. "Woke up on the right side of the flower bed this morning."

"You should be sad and depressed. You are responsible for all of those deaths outside of the Miami Heat's Arena. I wanted real diamonds, not fake. But thanks for the cash. How is your wife, Jenny?"

"She's out of town."

"Sure she is. I assume you are taping me. 409 Southeast First Avenue, Florida City Travelodge. Four stars. Two evenings from today have Elvin Hayes in the Travelodge with $4 million in diamonds. Silver suitcase. Not locked. No tracers. Diamonds are to be in soft cloth pouches. I repeat, no tracer. And it's $4 million now, not $3 million."

"Why Elvin Hayes?" Douglass interrupted.

"I do not want an FBI agent. Besides, he's my partner." She added, "He should have a four-door blue Ford with a full tank of gas in the parking lot at the Florida City Travelodge. I will call you one more time and get all of his cell phone numbers. Give him three cell phones and $4 million in diamonds."

"What if Hayes cannot or will not come?" Douglass asked.

"No problem. Use Caleb Pehrson or Shaquille O'Neal. I must be able to recognize the person in the car. No one else should be in the car or in the trunk. Understand? Do not follow the car."

"Yes," Douglass answered.

"Do you know what happened in the Tokyo subway system by the Aleph group in 1995?"

"Yes." She was gone.

* * * * *

Douglass started thinking again about the military's flying assassin called the Predator. He knew that at 15,000 feet you cannot see or hear the small, slender unmanned aircraft with two Hellfire missiles. Its high-precision cameras and sensors can spot a sniper in a window.

Cruising around 80 miles an hour, this killing machine can fly for 20 hours within a range of 450 miles on 100 gallons of gas. With a wingspan of only 48.7 feet, this snowmobile engine strapped to a glider is controlled from Nellis Air Force Base in Nevada. Of course, the cost of one Predator is $4 million, exactly what the madwoman was asking in diamonds. If he could not get the Predator, maybe he would include a bomb in the drop suitcase. He knew he would be prosecuted, however. Was it worth it?

Douglass called Commissioner David Stern and told him about the new

$4 million demand. Stern said there was no reason to hold another meeting of the owners. The NBA would not pay. "If we did, we'll have extortion demands every week."

Stern told him that attendance at NBA games was down by almost 40 percent. "This crazy person is killing us. We needed to catch them yesterday. I'm putting pressure on the President to give you as many resources as you need."

"Tell him I need a Predator. We'll get them," Douglass said, "but we do need some luck."

Douglass called Elvin Hayes and explained the demand that he deliver the diamonds. He also told Hayes that the hair on one of the basketball cards was his hair.

"Someone is setting me up. Why?" Hayes asked.

"I was going to ask you the same question. Who would be mad enough to plant your hairs?"

"Maybe I've sold a lemon car or two. But we have lemon laws now. Surely no one would do this to me because of a bad car. I will send photographs of all of my employees to you. No employees have been out of work long enough to do these killings. But maybe someone went into my office and picked up some of my hairs. I'll ask around."

"Will you do the drop?" Douglass asked.

"Absolutely. I wouldn't miss it. Can I carry my gun?"

"You bet."

When he hung up, Douglass searched the Internet and found that Texas lemon laws and the federal lemon law allow compensation to Texas consumers for defective automobiles and trucks. To qualify, the consumer must suffer multiple repair attempts under the manufacturer's factory warranty. Lemon-law compensation can include a refund, replacement, or cash compensation.

Since she had mentioned Shaquille O'Neal, he searched the Internet and found that O'Neal played for the Miami Heat. "Interesting," Douglass thought. "Both Hayes and O'Neal are reserve officers. Also, Hayes was born in Louisiana, and Shaq played for Louisiana State University. Is there any connection?"

* * * * *

Elvin Hayes was at the Florida City Travelodge on Southeast First Avenue with a blue four-door Ford sitting in the parking lot. There were FBI agents everywhere, and Douglass was in the hotel room with Hayes waiting for the phone call. They were playing blackjack.

At 12:30 in the morning Douglass left Hayes and went to his room. He told Hayes that there would be an FBI agent in a car both ahead and behind him. "We cannot get too close. I believe she will send you towards Key West, so the drop will be over water. We will have aircraft following you. The silver suitcase is in the trunk. We are watching the car, and we have a tracer on the car. Good luck, and be cautious. I wouldn't wear your pistol outside the car. She told me at the last drop that a sniper was watching me. I don't believe it, but we can't be sure how many people are involved. After the drop we will stop and search every car near you."

At 1:15 in the morning Elvin Hayes received the anticipated phone call.

"Hello, Mr. Hayes."

Elvin had just fallen asleep. "Hello to you. Can you give me a name?" Hayes asked.

"A name is not important," she said.

"But we need to know if you are the one attacking basketball," Hayes argued.

"Well, I believe that your hair was found in a particular suitcase."

"How?"

"I want you to go to the blue, four-door Ford now. Take the three cell phones. Please repeat the numbers to me."

He did.

"Are the diamonds in the car?" she asked.

"Yes, the silver suitcase is in the trunk."

"Have you seen the diamonds?"

"No," Hayes answered.

"Is the car blue?"

"Yes," he said.

"Go to the car now. Keep your cell phones on, but leave your gun with Douglass. Take Route 1 south toward Key Largo. No one else should be in the car. Do not speed. Drive around 55 miles per hour. Wait for my phone call. Tell Douglass hello."

She was gone as Douglass walked into the room.

"It was her. She knew that my hair was in the suitcase," Elvin said. "I'm to take Route 1 south toward Key Largo."

Douglass handed him a map. "So the drop will be over the Keys. We'll have some boats around you."

Florida City is several miles south of Homestead (population, 32,000) and 25 miles north of Key Largo. Florida City has a population of only 7,900, and much of the city consists of hotels and other tourist facilities. Florida City is the southernmost city in the U.S. that is not on an island, and 30 percent of its population speaks Spanish.

Elvin took 994 south and swung onto Route 1 toward Key Largo. One of the cell phones rang, and he picked it up.

"Hello, Elvin. May I call you Elvin?" she asked.

"Sure."

"Welcome to the Keys. I want you to start watching the mile markers. They are the little green signs every mile from here to Key West. Key Largo has a 100-mile marker, and Key West has a 1-mile marker. Please drive between 55 and 60 miles per hour. Did you leave your gun with Douglass?"

"Yes." Elvin had not.

"Did you leave your back-up gun with Douglass?"

"I don't carry a back-up," Elvin said.

"When we search you, you better not have your pistol." She paused before asking, "Do you love your wife, Erna?"

"Absolutely," Elvin almost shouted.

"Good. Did you know that Key Largo has an operational nuclear power plant?"

"No, I did not."

"O.K., see you soon." She hung up.

Elvin drove for about 54 miles past Key Largo when a phone rang again. There was little traffic on the road. The car clock showed 2:43. He picked up the wrong phone, but finally found the ringing one.

"I'm back, Elvin. Are you sleepy?"

"I am," Elvin answered.

"What mile marker are you passing?" she asked.

"I don't know. Wait a second, and I'll tell you." About 30 seconds passed, and then Elvin said, "I'm passing marker 55."

"I want you to keep the phone on and talk to me. At mile marker 57, I want you to turn on your emergency lights. Look for the button now."

"O.K., I found the button."

"Great. Are there any cars behind you?"

"Not close."

They chatted for about three minutes about Elvin's life, but each time he asked her a question about her life, she would not answer his question.

"I'm turning on my emergency lights now," Elvin said. He did not turn them on.

"Good for you, Elvin. I see them."

In about 30 more seconds Elvin turned the emergency lights on.

"Elvin, at mile marker 60 I want you to stop, open the trunk, get the silver suitcase, and put it in the front seat. Leave the trunk open. Then open both doors on the right side of the car. Go to the other side and open both doors. Pretend that you are having car trouble. Keep the car doors open for at least 15 seconds. We want to see if there is anyone else with you. Once you get back into the car, leave the trunk open. Keep listening to me on the phone, but start counting from 1 to 100 when you exit the car."

At mile marker 60 Elvin did as he was told. When he got back into the car she said, "O.K., starting counting from one again."

He started counting. At 30, she said, "Elvin, stop at mile marker 61, take the suitcase and go to the front of the car, to the right side of the road, and stand there."

At mile marker 61 Elvin stopped, took the suitcase, and went to the side of the road.

"We are doing well, Elvin. Do you see the wires that are attached to the railing at mile marker 61?" Elvin could only hear the female voice.

"Yes."

"Good. Pull up the wires, open the suitcase, tie the cloth pouches to the wires, and drop them over the side of the road. I don't want to lose any diamonds."

Elvin did not move or say anything.

"Elvin, are we having problems? Is the suitcase locked?"

"No it's not locked."

"Then open it," she shouted for the first time.

"I can't," Elvin said.

"Why not?"

"Douglass told me not to open it."

"Why not?" she asked.

"There's a bomb in it," Elvin said softly.

"How lovely of Douglass. O.K., take three or four of the wires and attach the wires firmly to the handle and lower the suitcase slowly to the water."

Before Elvin had tied one wire to the handle, Shirlee Ann was under the water heading for safety. Using the diving scooter, she headed toward the cave that she had prepared. Her device emitted a sonar request pulse to her base stations, which allowed her to pinpoint her exact location. She had practiced the run so often that she could have done it with her computer compass. The GPS device gave her confidence and allowed her to get to the underwater cave quickly. She was able to salvage two of the base stations.

As she entered the cave she pulled a large limb across the entrance. In the small, underground cavern she changed into some comfortable and warm clothes. She had enough food and water to last a week. She had installed two grey PVC pipes through the ceiling to the outside. She could now get air from outside. She climbed onto the cot, pulled a blanket over herself, and went to sleep. She had been surprised that the FBI would put an explosive device into the suitcase. Could she sue the FBI if she got hurt? Maybe the third time would be the charm.

* * * * *

Douglass had been in a car about two miles behind Elvin. When he reached Elvin's car, Elvin was waiting beside the road. The suitcase was dangling near the water. Two boats had their spotlights on it. There were already scuba divers in the water searching for the killer. A water plane had landed nearby.

"She didn't take the suitcase," Elvin said.

"Did you tell her there was a bomb in it?" Douglass asked.

"I had to. She asked me to open it and attach the diamonds to the wires. You told me not to open it because there was a bomb in it."

Douglass walked over, pulled the suitcase up, cut off the wires, dumped it into his trunk, and slammed the trunk lid.

"Was there a bomb in the suitcase?" Elvin asked.

"Nope. Just a way to try to force her to take the suitcase with the tracking devices. She's too smart for that."

Douglass checked the map and noticed that they were at Duck Key. He, Elvin, and several of the agents drove over to the Hawk Cay Resort and rented some rooms. The next day Elvin went back to Texas, but Douglass and the agents checked out Duck Key. They found nothing, and the scuba divers found nothing but several sonar base stations. One diver said that based upon the sonar base stations, the killer might have gone to the Everglades National Park or one of the small islands in the Florida Bay. Air surveillance found nothing. The woman had disappeared into the night. Douglass wondered if the FBI was dealing with another D. B. Cooper. Douglass bet she would strike again.

Copernicus, a marketing consulting firm, has given a 50-question marketing IQ test to a national sample of more than 1,000 CEOs, and they found the average marketing IQ of senior executives is just 79, where 100 is average and 160 is the top score.

—COPERNICUS

ouglass called Caleb Pehrson and told him that the extortionist had mentioned his name as a potential person to make the previous drop. "She knows about you," Douglass said.

"Well, if I were her, I would attack during the All-Star Game to get the biggest bang for her buck. The East players battle the West players. The voting is almost over. "

"What day is it?"

"Dates. February 15 through the 17th. The Rookie Day is February 15, the three-point and slam dunk contests are February 16, and the All-Star Game is February 17. By the way, Orlando's center Dwight Howard's proposal to raise the rim to 12 feet during the dunk contest has been rejected by the NBA. Also, the 2008 dunk contest will be the first in league history that gives the final say-so on who wins to fans who vote on NBA.com."

"So she has three days to choose from," Douglass said.

"Exactly. That's why it may be the most opportune time for her to hit again for maximum damage."

"Why three days?" Douglass asked.

"Last year at the University of Las Vegas, the West beat the East 153 to 132, with Kobe Bryant scoring 31 points and winning his second All-Star MVP award."

Caleb said something and then came back. "Sorry. Two days before that, the Sophomore NBAs beat the Rookie NBAs in the T-Mobile Rookie

Challenge. On the second day, the Celtics' Gerald Green beat last year's champion, Nate Robinson, in the Sprite Slam Dunk Contest. On the same day, Jason Kapono won the Footlocker Three-Point Shootout."

"So you have sponsors everywhere," Douglass said.

"You bet. You're learning so much about basketball, you'll have to come to work with a team."

"Thanks. I may need a job if I don't catch this madwoman soon. Where will the 2008 All-Star Game be played?"

"New Orleans. By the way, the first five players on each side are chosen by fan ballots, so a player may start out at a different position. The reserves are chosen by a vote among the head coaches of each squad's particular conference. Coaches are not allowed to vote for their own players. The two coaches who lead the team with the most wins in their conference coach their respective team. The same coach cannot coach the team in consecutive years."

* * * * *

Two days later Caleb emailed Douglass information about the players voted into the upcoming All-Star Game in New Orleans. The Boston Celtics' Kevin Garnett received the most votes, with 2,399,148, followed by Cleveland Cavaliers' forward LeBron James, with 2,108,831. Other Eastern Conference players elected were Orlando Magic center Dwight Howard, Miami Heat guard Dwayne Wade, and New Jersey Nets guard Jason Kidd.

In the Western Conference, Los Angeles Lakers guard Kobe Bryant received the most votes, with 2,004,940, followed by Denver Nuggets forward Carmelo Anthony, with 1,723,701. Also voted as Western Conference All-Star starters were Houston Rockets center Yao Ming, San Antonio forward Tim Duncan, and Denver Nuggets guard Allen Iverson.

Caleb Pehrson was partially wrong. Shirlee Ann did not wait to strike at the All-Star Game. She waited four and a half days inside the underwater cave, came out, and used the underwater scooter to travel back to her RV in Marathon, Florida. Aside from reading several novels while she was in the cave, she developed her future strategy. She still felt that there was a way to get the diamonds and not get caught. Once her supplies were packed, she headed to New Orleans.

The New Orleans Hornets were having a fantastic season so far. They were atop the Western Conference. A story by Bob Licht headlined "Best Hornets Team Yet?" The Hornets were ahead of the pace set by the most-winning team in the 20-year history of the franchise. The night before Shirlee Ann arrived in New Orleans, the Hornets had crushed the defending champions San Antonio Spurs, 102 to 78, in San Antonio. They had won their eighth straight game.

The success of the New Orleans team, which had a valuation second from the bottom and a salary ranked 25 out of 30, seemed to mirror some of the academic research that says restrictive agreements such as limited player spending, player mobility, roster sizes, and the right to trade players make it less likely that team owners can use their financial acumen to buy success in basketball and other sports.

A new Republican governor, Bobby Jindal, was recently installed in Baton Rouge with the major goal of ethics reform. He was the first non-white governor elected in the state of Louisiana since Reconstruction. Mardi Gras was just around the corner, with as many as 50 parades and much king cake awaiting the citizens. And LSU had recently sprinted past Ohio State University, 38–24, in the Allstate BCS National Championship Game in the Superdome in New Orleans. LSU was No. 1. Almost everyone was happy in Louisiana, except Shirlee Ann.

The New Orleans Arena is at 1501 Girod Street, in the shadow of the Superdome. Opened in 1999 at a cost of $84 million, the New Orleans Arena is the home of the Hornets, the Voodoo (Arena Football League), and Tulane University basketball. Owned by the state of Louisiana, the arena holds 18,000 fans for basketball. Both the arena and the Superdome sustained flood and wind damage from Hurricane Katrina, and the Superdome was heavily damaged from housing about 20,000 evacuees who used the structure as a shelter after the storm. The hurricane flooded about 80 percent of the city when almost all of the levees were breached.

The New Orleans Hornets moved to Oklahoma City following the August 2005 hurricane and changed their name to the New Orleans–Oklahoma City Hornets. The Hornets played their first game in the New Orleans Arena on March 8, 2006, to a sell-out group of 17,744. Their renegotiated agreement allows them to leave in 2009 if the team does not draw more than 14,735 fans per game. They have not come close to that figure this year or in their two pre-hurricane seasons.

Tonight the Hornets were first in the Western Conference, with an eight-game winning streak. The Nuggets' newly elected All-Star Carmelo Anthony, #15, was missing his fourth game with a sprained left ankle, but their All-Star guard Allen Iverson was playing. Anthony had been snubbed last year in the All-Star match-up even though he was then leading the NBA in scoring.

Melo, as he is known, has used some of his millions earned playing hoops to open the Carmelo Anthony Youth Development Center in his poverty-torn neighborhood in Baltimore. He has also donated $1.5 million to the nonprofit Living Classroom Foundation, which is involved with education, job training, and other social programs in the same Baltimore neighborhood. Entering his fifth season in the NBA, he recently pledged $3 million to his alma mater, Syracuse University, to help fund a new practice facility for the men's and women's basketball programs.

Throughout this game, however, the 15,601 fans repeatedly shouted superlatives to the Hornets' third-year point guard, Chris Paul. There was a chance that he might be selected as one of the reserves for the All-Star Game. At the half, the Hornets were up by 20 points. They ended up shooting 51 percent for the game and out-rebounded the Nuggets, 52–23. Chris Paul had 23 points, 17 assists, and 9 rebounds, one rebound shy of a triple-double. The Hornets won their ninth straight game, 117 to 93. The game lasted 2 hours and 15 minutes.

Shirlee Ann did not go inside to see the Hornets play the Nuggets. She knew there would be warnings throughout the arena about basketball cards and guards at all of the restrooms and concession stands. Instead, she took a tour of many of the parking lots around the arena. She painted her deadly poison on many door handles. She was dressed as an old man. She looked like someone who lived on the street. She was gone before the 911 calls began and the ambulances, police, FBI agents, and fire trucks arrived on the scene. For every action, there's an equal and opposite reaction.

The headline in the *Times-Picayune* was "The Devil Went Down to the Hornets' Arena: 26 Dead." Under the headline was a story by Dan Troncale.

> Which was worse, Hurricane Katrina or the basketball mass murderer who struck last night in the parking lots around the Hornets' Arena? The hurricane was Mother Nature, but as the fans were shouting "MVP, MVP"

for point guard Chris Paul in the arena, someone or some group painted a deadly poison on car door handles around the arena while the Hornets were routing the Denver Nuggets, 117 to 93.

While the Hornets were stinging the Nuggets and extending their streak to nine games, the FBI was unable to capture or determine who is killing people at basketball arenas throughout the U.S. One is mindful of the southern rock song played by Charlie Daniels Band, "The Devil Went Down to Georgia." A boy named Johnny is challenged by the devil himself to a battle of fiddle-playing. Over the past several months, the Devil in the form of a mass murderer has been challenging the FBI and other law-enforcement organizations as he or she murders innocent bystanders in and around professional basketball arenas. Right now, the Devil is winning.

Of course, the story was big on the news. Bigger than the O. J. episode. Bigger than the alleged Kobe Bryant rape or the disappearance of Natalee Holloway in Aruba. Bigger than even the Duke lacrosse alleged rape case. The murders triggered a media frenzy.

* * * * *

From New Orleans, Shirlee Ann traveled to Baton Rouge to plan her next move. On the Saturday before Mardi Gras she attended the Spanish Town Mardi Gras parade. Spanish Town is the oldest neighborhood in Baton Rouge, which was settled by people from the Canary Island. The architecture is post–Civil War, and beads hang from trees and power lines along the parade route. Strange is the nature of the entire day, with wooden pink flamingoes adorning the surrounding lakes and yards. Why pink flamingoes? Apparently the rule of the day is that "bad taste is better than no taste at all."

The parade's theme was "Flamingeaux Phil Predicts." Each year the floats tend to be raunchy and satirical, attacking local, state, and national politicians. The floats today attacked Hillary Clinton, Britney Spears, former Louisiana governor Kathleen Blanco, Congressman William Jefferson, and Nick Saban, the former LSU football coach.

After more than two hours of floats passing by as their riders threw beads, Shirlee Ann noticed that the onlookers continually shouted and begged for the krewes to throw them beads, yet few would reach down and pick up the thousands of beads on the ground. The parade watchers carried home bags and boxes of beads afterward. "What did they do with all these Mardi Gras beads? Where did they store them? A parade would have been an excellent place to lay some poison," she thought.

Several days later, the wild-card New York Giants and their quarterback Eli Manning pulled off one of the greatest upsets of the then 18–0 New England Patriots on an unbelievable pass to David Tyree in the University of Phoenix Stadium in Tempe.

Shirlee Ann read in the paper that a distraught Kurt William Havelock had driven within sight of the stadium with an AR-15 assault rifle with six 30-round magazines and 20 loose rounds. The Tempe City Council had turned down his liquor-license application for a restaurant. He had mailed a manifesto that stated, "I will test the theory that bullets speak louder than words. I will slay your children. I will shed the blood of the innocent. No one destroys my dreams. No one." When he got to Jobing.com Arena's parking lot, he decided he could not go through with the planned massacre.

Shirlee Ann wondered why anyone would commit suicide with such a mass-murder plan. "He must be crazy," she thought. "There are better and safer ways to get even." She was curious why toothpaste was not tamper-proof.

17

Doing business without advertising is like winking at a girl in the dark. You know what you are doing, but no one else does.

—STEUART HENDERSON BRITT

éjà vu, Douglass," the female voice said to Douglass as he picked up his phone. "That was not nice of you to place a bomb in the suitcase. You could have hurt me or poor Mr. Hayes.

"How can you sleep at night knowing that if you had given me the diamonds, 43 people in New Orleans would still be alive? Professional basketball has certainly lost more than $4 million in revenue, sponsorship fees, and goodwill. Are you still there, Douglass? Has the cat got your tongue?"

"I'm listening," Douglass replied curtly.

"Good. Here's the drill. Have Caleb Pehrson or Shaq O'Neal in the Hyatt Regency New Orleans the night before the start of the All-Star Game. Register him for three nights. He should have a red Explorer and three cell phones. That's a Ford product. We need to buy American products.

"I want the $4 million in diamonds in cloth pouches. Mr. Pehrson must be able to safely open the briefcase and hand them to me. No fakes. No bombs. No tracers. No helicopters or we'll shoot them down. There will be many people in New Orleans for the All-Star Game. Do not upset us again. Douglass, repeat the date and place."

"Hyatt Regency, New Orleans. Thursday, February 14," Douglass said.

"Who should be there?" she asked.

"Caleb Pehrson or Shaq O'Neal."

"He should not have a gun. No one should be with him. Have you ever played the basketball game HORSE, Douglass?"

"Yes, I have," Douglass answered politely.

"You and I have been playing HORSE. You have HORS, and I have shot from half court and made it. If you miss, you have an "E" and you are out."

She was gone.

Douglass checked out the map of the New Orleans area and saw Lake Pontchartrain to the north of New Orleans. "The drop will be over the Lake Pontchartrain Causeway," Douglass said to himself.

Lake Pontchartrain is a brackish lake located in southeastern Louisiana, north of New Orleans. Technically, it is an estuary and not a lake because it connects to the Mississippi Sound. Covering an area of 630 square miles, it is the second largest saltwater lake in the U.S., after the Great Salt Lake in Utah. The lake averages a depth of 12 to 14 feet, but some ship channels are kept deeper by dredging. New Orleans, Metairie, and Kenner are on the lake's south shore, and Mandeville, Covington, and Madisonville make up its northern shore.

While searching the Internet, Douglass read that although most of New Orleans is built below sea level, the police there do not have boats. Eastern Airline Flight 304 crashed into Lake Pontchartrain on February 25, 1964, resulting in the deaths of 51 passengers and 7 crew members. Most of the plane and passengers were not found. On May 28, 2007, New England Patriots defensive end Marquise Hill was found dead in the lake.

Douglass called Caleb Pehrson and got him on his cell phone. "You've made the All-Star team," Douglass said.

"What do you mean?" Caleb seemed puzzled.

"She wants you to make the next diamond drop during the All-Star Game," Douglass said.

"There may be no one at the All-Star Game after the Hornets game last week," Caleb said. "Why me?"

"Maybe your boss is trying to get rid of you. Who knows. Why did she pick Elvin Hayes? She doesn't want an FBI agent with a gun. I'm supposed to set you up in the Hyatt Regency New Orleans for three nights. Since it's on behalf of America, we'll foot the bill. Will you make the drop?"

"Can I become an honorary FBI agent?" Caleb joked.

"I doubt it."

"Of course I'll do it. I already had reservations."

"Do you have a bulletproof vest?" Douglass asked.

"Only a basketball-proof vest. I have a salesman vest, also."

"What size shirt do you wear?"

"A large," Caleb said.

"I'll get a vest over to you. You'll need to wear it."

"Gee, thanks. What about my head? Keep me informed."

After hanging up, Douglass made reservations at the Hyatt for Caleb, himself, and several other agents. He had his assistant start planning for a number of boats with sonar to be in Lake Pontchartrain during the potential drop.

The FBI has approximately 14 enhanced maritime SWAT teams and a separate hostage rescue team trained to respond to maritime terrorists. This hostage team can rappel from a helicopter onto a boat or approach a ship using closed-circuit diving gear that creates few bubbles. Douglass wanted to use some of the Coast Guard's small boats, which were equipped with machine guns. Sometimes there were territorial disputes between the FBI and the Coast Guard.

Douglass wanted to be in New Orleans several days before February 14. He had never been across Lake Pontchartrain.

That night David Letterman gave his audience a multiple-choice question.

> Why were FBI wiretaps stopped?
>   a. Supreme Court decision
>   b. Internal investigation to determine legitimacy
>   c. Unpaid phone bills
>   d. Presidential order
>   e. All of the above

Letterman laughed about an old inspector general audit that found telephone companies cutting off FBI wiretaps used to eavesdrop on suspected criminals and terrorists because of the Bureau's repeated failures to pay its phone bills on time. Letterman asked, "How can the FBI catch the basketball mass murderers if they can't remember to pay their phone bills?" There was a big laugh from the audience.

* * * * *

The Hyatt Regency New Orleans, at 500 Poydras Street, overlooks the French Quarter. The 32-story atrium hotel connects to the New Orleans

Center, a shopping mecca. Caleb Pehrson arrived in the Big Easy before 5:00 p.m. on February 14. He was in his room discussing the diamond drop with Douglass and another FBI agent.

The phone rang, and Caleb said "Hello."

"Good evening, Mr. Pehrson. Do you have a red Ford Explorer?"

"Yes, I do."

"I want you to give me your three cell phone numbers."

Caleb did as directed.

"I assume the diamonds are in a briefcase. Am I correct?"

"Yes," Caleb said.

"Please open it now."

"It's already open," Caleb said.

"Good. Take the briefcase with the diamonds and go to your red Explorer. Take all three cell phones, drive north to I-10, and turn left toward Baton Rouge on I-10. At Metairie, take a right onto the Pontchartrain Causeway. Be careful because there's a lot of construction, and you can miss the turn."

When she said Pontchartrain, Caleb gave a thumbs-up sign to Douglass, who was also listening to the conversation.

"There is no toll, but I want you to start on the causeway at 7:00 P.M., not before and not after. Go close to the entrance and wait until 7:00. Tell Douglass no helicopters. See you soon."

Before Caleb left, Douglass asked, "You've got your vest on, right?"

"Yes," Caleb answered.

"I believe we have her. I have at least six Coast Guard boats in the lake, but please be careful. Do not take any chances."

"You can bet on that," Caleb said. "I have back trouble."

"What do you mean?" Douglass asked.

"Oh, I have a yellow streak from the top of the shoulders to my waist." He laughed.

* * * * *

Caleb reached the entrance to the causeway with 25 minutes to spare, so he parked at a service station. In about five minutes, one of his cell phones rang.

"Hello, Mr. Pehrson. May I call you Caleb? A good biblical name," the female voice said.

"Sure," Caleb answered. "What should I call you?"

"Oh, Mary is fine. Can you open the suitcase or briefcase that has the diamonds?"

"I can."

"Great. Are you wired?"

"No, ma'am." He was.

"Are you driving a red Explorer?"

"Yes."

"Okay, start your car and head across the causeway. Do not go faster than 65 miles per hour." She laughed. "The traffic is bad. 42,000 cars pass over the lake each day."

The causeway consists of two parallel bridges with two lanes both ways, and Caleb headed north. It is the longest bridge in the U.S. to go completely over water. The first span opened in 1956 and the second one in 1969. Caleb noticed blue call boxes with flashing lights every so often. There was an antenna on top of each box. The first one was Box 4, then 8, then 12. He was behind an SUV that had a bumper sticker that said "Save a Stray."

Every so often there was a crossover. He passed crossover #7. The crossover allows a car to move off of the road onto a short road that goes to the other side of the causeway.

As Caleb passed a call box or crossover, he would announce the number so that Douglass would know his location. Douglass had said the causeway was about 24 miles long, almost the distance of a marathon. At the 16-mile marker Caleb passed the drawbridge, and one of the phones rang.

"Hey, Caleb, where are you on the bridge?" she asked.

"Just passed over the drawbridge, about at the 17-mile marker."

"Which lane are you in?" she asked.

"Right lane," Caleb answered.

"Do me a favor. Move over into the left lane when you can. Be careful. I want you to keep the phone on for now, and begin to count from 1,000."

Caleb did as directed.

As he counted, she said, "There have been about 16 boat collisions with the causeway. At least 55 people have been killed as a result of these collisions. What is your signal to Douglass when you drop the diamonds to me?"

"The Eagle has landed."

"Cute. So you are wired. Keep counting. When you get to crossover number 2, I want you to pull into the crossover. It's fairly wide. Keep counting and only answer yes or no when I ask a question. Are you close to crossover two?"

"I don't know."

"Pull in when you see it and say, 'The Eagle has landed.' On the right side of the crossover near your side of the road are several wires that you will see attached to the railing. You will also see a tiny sheet of paper with instructions to you. You are to pretend to tie the diamonds to the wires. Do not tie them to the wires. Keep them in your car. However, get the instructions."

"I'm close to crossover two now."

"Oops, say only yes or no. Turn into the crossover and do as I instructed. Do not read the instructions until you get back into the car. Keep the phone on and put it in your shirt pocket. Understand?"

"Yes."

"When you get back into the car, say, 'The Eagle has landed.'"

Caleb stopped the car, found the wires, and pretended to tie something to them. The water appeared to be about 16 feet from the bridge. The instructions said: "Continue in the same direction, north to Mandeville. Go through Mandeville and take I-12 to the west. Left. Keep the phone on, keep counting."

"Oops. The Eagle has landed," Caleb almost shouted.

As he was leaving the crossover, he heard helicopters and saw boats approaching the crossover. He kept the phone on and kept counting.

As he was about to enter I-12, the other phone rang. He had to pull over to pick up the second phone.

"Caleb, it's me, Mary. Cut off the other phone and use this one. Keep counting but start over at 1,000. You are to go west on I-12, but shortly on your right as you pass exit 21 you will see a Louisiana rest area. Turn into the rest area and park as close as you can to an older, red Chevrolet with Georgia license plates. When you get there, say, 'The Eagle has landed.'"

After turning into the rest area, he parked near the red Chevrolet and said "The Eagle has landed."

"Excellent, Caleb. Go to the red Chevrolet and get the clothes out of the front seat. The car is unlocked. Change clothes in your Explorer. Take off the wire and throw it out the window. Someone is watching you. Keep the phone on and continue to count. Start over at 1,000."

Caleb did as instructed and threw out the wire, but put back on his vest. "Done," he said.

"Take the diamonds from the Explorer and put them in the front seat of the Chevrolet. Leave your clothes in the Explorer. In the back seat, passenger side, under the floor mat, is a key. Drive the red Chevrolet back onto I-12 going west. Stay around 65 miles per hour. Keep counting and leave the phone on. Do not take the wire with you. Understand? Wave goodbye to my observer."

Caleb did as instructed. He wondered if someone had been watching him. He hated to throw away the wire. Could Douglass still track him? Where was she taking him? A new phone that had been on the passenger-side floorboard rang. He found it and answered it.

"Mary again. Throw out the window the cell phone that you brought from New Orleans. I want you to have only the two phones that I left in the Chevrolet. Do it now before you enter the interstate."

Caleb threw the phone out the window.

"Do you have the diamonds?"

"Yes, I do."

* * * * *

At crossover #2, the boats found the wires with nothing on them. Douglass told the divers to search the area and for the boats to look for a diver with their sonar. On each of the boats, a guard held a rifle with a red-dot optical sight. The divers did not stay down long, and they were constantly looking around when they came up. Douglass knew there were alligators in the lake. However, Douglass felt that the drop had not been made, especially when Caleb continued to drive toward Mandeville. They tracked his whereabouts through Mandeville and as he turned west onto I-12. Caleb was either counting from 1,000 or saying yes or no. Several times he had said, "The Eagle has landed."

Caleb's car stopped somewhere on I-12, and he got out but then came back to his car. He seemed to be moving around inside the car. Then the wire went dead.

Douglass waited about two minutes and then shouted directions. He was still about three miles from Caleb's car. "Caleb's wire is not moving.

Move in now. His telephone signals are not moving. The tracker signal is not moving. He is somewhere beyond Mandeville near I-55. Get some cars to the location. Get a helicopter there."

In a few minutes, word came back that Caleb was no longer in the red Explorer. His clothes and two cell phones were still in the car, and the other phone and the wire were outside the car. "We've lost him."

As Douglass pulled into the rest area, a helicopter was shining a spotlight onto an empty red Explorer. He told everyone to search for a body around the rest area. Almost to himself he said, "She made him change clothes and drive away in another car. She is a smart devil monster."

* * * * *

Shirlee Ann directed Caleb to continue west on I-12. He passed an exit to Robert and Hammond Municipal Airport. When I-12 crossed I-55, she told Caleb to exit and take I-55 south toward Ponchatoula. After passing Ponchatoula, Caleb drove for some time in silence, but suddenly she was back. "When you come to Manchac, I want you to slow down in the right lane. Where are the diamonds?"

"In the front seat," Caleb said.

Shirlee Ann had put a tracer in the car, so she knew he was getting close.

"Caleb, ahead you are about to see a bridge that goes over a corner of Lake Maurepas. Please stop right before you get to the bridge. A sniper is watching you. Take the diamonds and go to the right side of the bridge. You will see four wires attached to the railing. Tie the diamond bags to the wires and lower them slowly. Then get back into the car and continue south."

Caleb stopped, tied the cloth bags to the wires, and walked quickly back to the car. He got back into the Chevrolet and headed towards New Orleans. After about a mile he pulled over and called Douglass.

"Douglass, I tied the diamond bags to wires on a bridge on I-55 that goes over Lake Maurepas."

He heard Douglass give orders for cars, boats, and helicopters to descend on I-55 at Lake Maurepas ASAP. "Lake Maurepas is to the west of Lake Pontchartrain. On my map, I see a narrow strip of water between the two lakes. Get the boats over there fast. The town of Manchac is along the eastern edge of Pass Manchac."

Before the militia arrived at Lake Maurepas, Shirlee Ann was already close to the KOA campgrounds in Denham Springs. She made a promise to get back to the Camping World of Hammond near the intersection of I-12 and I-55.

Business has only two functions, marketing and innovation.

—MILAN KUNDERA

Shirlee Ann had never planned to get into Lake Pontchartrain with those alligators. Her mother had not raised a fool. Manatees occasionally appeared in both Lake Pontchartrain and Lake Maurepas. There were alligators in Lake Maurepas, also, and she would have escaped in the water if necessary. She had "borrowed" a swamp boat and placed it near the bridge. But with no helicopters and patrol cars around, she had cut the diamond pouches from the wires and made her way around the edge of Lake Maurepas to her motorcycle.

Called an airboat, the flat-bottomed swamp boat is propelled by an aircraft-type propeller powered by an automobile or aircraft engine. The propeller and engine are enclosed by a protective metal cage. The propeller produces a rearward column of air that propels the airboat forward. The air passes over vertical rudders, which allows the operator to steer the contraption. An airboat is loud, but Shirlee Ann felt that she could lose any boats or helicopters in the Maurepas swamp, especially with her night-vision goggles. She had prepared several hiding places, but she had never seen the Coast Guard boats with machine guns.

Caleb had not seen the Pass Manchac lighthouse because of the darkness. Now condemned and crumbling, at one time the sentinel stood guard over the Pontchartrain entrance into Pass Manchac. Tonight the lighthouse sits in shallow water several hundred yards offshore in the darkness. Lake Maurepas itself is only about 12 feet deep.

Shirlee Ann knew this area so well because after college she had married the wrong fellow. They had moved to Ponchatoula, Louisiana, where he became a policeman, and she had taught at the local high school. She had hunted alligators and fished for alligator gar during the summers.

Alligators are native to only two countries—China and the U.S. Within the U.S. they are mostly found in Florida and Louisiana. There are more than 30 alligator farms in Florida, which produce more than 300,000 pounds of meat and more than 15,000 skins a year. There are more than 1 million such farms in Louisiana alone. Alligator hunting in Louisiana begins on the first Wednesday in September and continues for 30 days.

Alligators have four legs and a long tail to propel them through fresh and brackish water. They can run relatively fast for a short distance. An alligator's snout is shorter and blunter than a crocodile's, and its teeth do not protrude outside its closed mouth. No matter the differences, one does not wish to meet an alligator or crocodile in the water or on land.

Shirlee Ann and her husband would fish for alligator gar with bows and arrows, which were equipped with reels that contained hundreds of feet of steel leader. She remembered setting trotlines and fishing with yo-yos. A yo-yo is a small mechanical device that is attached to a limb, dock, or a milk jug, and you cast out the baited line. It is an automatic fishing reel. When a fish hits the bait, the yo-yo pulls the line back in rapidly to hook the fish. A trotline is a long cord with a lot of hooks dangling from it.

Ponchatoula is located north of Manchac and New Orleans off of I-55. Known as the strawberry capital of the world, in recent years the city's leaders are advertising it as the antique city. Storefronts down Pine Street are decorated with merchandise and fresh flowers. The architecture dates back to the early twentieth century, with benches nestled against the storefronts. There are more than 20 antique stores, many with second-story flats with balconies filled with flowerpots and other decorations.

Ponchatoula derives its name from the Choctaw Indian language "hair to hang" because of the abundance of Spanish moss in trees surrounding the area. Shirlee Ann thought there was less Spanish moss today than when she had lived there. While living in Ponchatoula, she had taught history and English at the high school. In such a small town, the main events were the football games and to a lesser extent the basketball games. The Ponchatoula High School teams were called the Greenwave.

The city has a strawberry festival in April with both a strawberry king and queen. The strawberry is Louisiana's state fruit, and Ponchatoula has around 250,000 visitors during the festival. There was now a Strawberry

Hall of Honor, which boasted a listing of 2,652 strawberry farmers from the 1800s.

Once Shirlee Ann ascertained that the "diamonds" from the drop were not diamonds, she went to the Dixie RV Superstores on Pumpkin Center Road on Exit 35 from I-12. She spent a few enjoyable hours, especially in the 67,000-square-foot Camping World of Hammond. She purchased a Garmin e Trex Camo Handheld Personal GPS Navigator with a hunting and fishing calculator. The device offers recommended times for the best hunting and fishing conditions.

She heard over the news that 11-time All-Star Shaquille O'Neal was traded in a blockbuster deal to the Phoenix Suns for four-time All-Star Shawn Marion and Marcus Banks. Sheriff Joe Arpaio in Phoenix had already deputized the injury-plagued center. The sheriff said, "I'm glad he's coming out to my turf. Maybe we'll go after illegal immigrants and other crime." Shirlee Ann wondered if Shaq had enough gas left in his tank to help the Suns. She knew that Shaq was around 36 years of age.

She reached the conclusion that she would never get her $4 million, so she decided to head to Mexico. Maybe she could become a dive instructor. She knew that in order to be extradited from Mexico, the prosecutor had to drop the death penalty. As she started her RV, the song "Fishing in the Dark" by the Nitty Gritty Dirt Band was playing. She smiled. So the person known as Shirlee Ann disappeared into Mexico with her RV and her scuba gear.

* * * * * * *

Douglass and the FBI searched Lake Maurepas for two days. They found the swamp boat, and the K-9 unit followed footprints to a tire mark that appeared to be a motorcycle. The red Chevrolet had been stolen and was found wiped clean. Some black hairs, however, had been found in the front floorboard and trunk. The hair was found to be from Elvin Hayes. The wire at the scene was similar to the wire at the previous drop sites.

There was a note in the glove compartment which said, "Good luck, Douglass. Hope you get a nice pay raise, and try to get on David Letterman's show." Neither happened.

Nothing happened to fans during the All-Star Game weekend, either. The Cavaliers' Daniel Gibson scored eleven 3-pointers and won the MVP award as the Sophomores destroyed the Rookies on Friday night in New Orleans with a score of 136–109. This contest was the sixth straight loss for the Rookies.

On Saturday night, Orlando's Dwight Howard became the 2008 Super Slam Dunk Champion. The athletic 6'11" Howard, dressed like Superman with an S on his chest with a red cape trailing behind him, was picked by both the judges and the fans. This year was the first time that fans were able to vote. The All-Stars used a variety of props, such as ladders and even a cupcake with a single candle, to try to influence the voting.

Although he was not chosen to play in the All-Star Game, Jazz guard Deron Williams beat Hornets' Chris Paul in the Skills Challenge Competition. His time of 25.5 seconds to complete the obstacle course of shooting, passing, and dribbling set a new record. He earned $35,000 for the victory.

Toronto Raptors' 6'8" guard Jason Kapano became a back-to-back winner of the Foot Locker Three-Point Shootout with 25 points. He beat out Cavaliers' point guard Daniel Gibson with 17 points. Kobe Bryant withdrew from the shootout because of a torn ligament in the little finger of his shooting hand.

NBA commissioner David Stern announced Saturday that the Seattle SuperSonics will probably leave Seattle either this year or when their lease expires in 2010. Sonic owner Clay Bennett hopes to move the team to his hometown of Oklahoma City. Stern also said that the Hornets can opt out of its lease at the New Orleans Arena if it does not average 14,735 fans a game, but up to the All-Star game they have averaged only 12, 645 fans.

On Sunday night the weaker half of the NBA, the East, beat the West, 134–128, to reduce some of their humiliation from their 2007 loss in Las Vegas, 153–132. Celtics shooting guard Ray Allen scored 28 points, and Cavaliers' 6'8" LeBron James scored 27 points. With 9 assists and 8 rebounds, James was the MVP for the second time in three years.

In a different part of the country on the same Saturday, the 50th running of the Daytona 500 was won by Ryan Newman, driving a blue Dodge with its Alltel Wireless advertising around the car. Newman had not won a race since September 2005. In second place was Kurt Busch, in a blue Dodge with its Miller Lite advertisements. Called the Great American Race, the Chevrolets and Toyotas were supposed to win. Chevrolet has been the dominant brand, but Toyota was mounting a major offensive.

Daytona is a restrictor-plate race, where a thin aluminum plate is installed at the intake of the engine to limit its power for safety reasons. But some argue that slowing down acceleration and the overall top speed cause the drivers to race in packs with only one second separating them. These large packs reduce wind resistance, which allow the cars to run faster and draft more easily. Thus, there is more likelihood of the "Big One" or a multicar pileup during a race. Some argue that the purpose of slowing the cars down is so the sponsors of the cars can be seen.

Some believe that #88, Dale Earnhardt, Jr., is one of the best restrictor-plate drivers in NASCAR, but on this Sunday he finished ninth in his green Chevy promoting AMP Energy drink.

Douglass received no more calls from the female voice during the remainder of the basketball season.

* * * * * * *

Months later, Shirlee Ann learned that the Boston Celtics and Los Angeles Lakers had made it to the playoffs. For the fourth game between the Lakers and Celtics, she was sitting in the bar at the Hilton Villahermosa in the southeast part of Mexico. Villahermosa, known as the "Emerald of the Southeast," is an important business center of Mexico's oil industry. Shirlee Ann was working her way toward Belize. She knew that English was spoken in Belize, and a number of American retirees moved to this small country.

She watched a Lakers' 24-point lead evaporate. The Celtics were down 20 points in the third quarter, but they made one of the most remarkable comebacks in NBA history, winning the fourth game.

Earlier that day, Shirlee Ann had surfed the Internet and learned about the disgraced ex-referee Tim Donaghy's allegation that two of three referees in Game 6 of the 2002 Lakers-Kings playoff series purposely ignored fouls made by one team (Lakers) and made phantom calls on the Kings, putting the Lakers' players on the free-throw line. The Lakers had 40 free throws to the Kings' 25 in that game. The Lakers eventually won the 2002 NBA championship.

NBA Commissioner David Stern vehemently denied Donaghy's allegations.

She also learned of the firing of Knicks coach Isiah Thomas after compiling a 56–108 record as head coach. A story by Edmund Lee stated that

Thomas had cost the Knicks more than $187 million. Yet he is still owed $18 million from a long-term contract extension the previous year.

Although Thomas was hired to reduce payroll in December 2003, his team has been on top or near the top in the league on player salaries. According to Edmund Lee, his poor trades and personnel moves caused the Knicks to be hit by $137 million in luxury taxes over the past four years. In 2007, the Knicks paid $45 million in luxury taxes, which was four-and-a-half times more than the total paid by every other team.

Shirlee Ann stayed in Villahermosa and watched the Celtics on their new parquet floor win their seventeenth NBA title after 22 dry years. The Celtics won in a blowout over Kobe Bryant and the Lakers, 131 to 92. The 39-point win was the biggest margin of victory in an NBA clincher. After the game, Celtic Kevin Garnett kissed the leprechaun on the parquet floor at the center court and then embraced Celtics Hall of Famer Bill Russell. Garnett scored 26 points with 14 rebounds.

In the middle of June, after she reached Belize, Shirlee Ann was surfing the web in an Internet cafe. She ran across a story on CNN.com about the police in Charlotte, N.C., investigating a wife who had had five husbands since the 1950s, now all dead. Police had charged 76-year-old Betty Neumer with solicitation of murder. Shirlee Ann wondered why there were so many black widows in North Carolina. "Maybe the drinking water made me turn bad," she thought.

* * * * * * *

Caleb Pehrson had the opportunity to go to the Beijing Olympics with the USA Redeem team. What a remarkable marketing platform it had been. All the elements were utilized: *advertising, personal selling, sales promotion,* and *distribution*. It was the largest television event in history, surpassing World Cup soccer and NFL Super Bowls.

Coca Cola, already the most well-known brand in the world, took advantage of the venue to be a global *sponsor* of the games. With its products sold in 107 countries, it was a perfect way to reach all Coke's markets with a single message. What a difference it was when shortly thereafter Pepsi's name was promoted by virtue of its having paid for naming rights of the Pepsi Arena, where the Democratic National Convention was held. The exposures, and thus promotion value, of the two brands during this compressed timeframe did not compare. Further, Republicans might switch to Coke.

China gained *public relations* exposure through hosting the Olympics. Souvenirs were *sold* in stores and kiosks throughout China. Hotel accommodations, restaurants, and retailers made millions. They even managed to keep dog meat on some of the restaurant menus. Talk about cultural differences!

However, the big winners were NBC television and the Phelps family. NBC, which had been at the bottom of the Nielsen ratings, bounced back for at least a few weeks and the revenue from *advertising* time sold may have sustained the company for the foreseeable future.

Michael Phelps, who set a record for the most gold medals won in a single Olympics, should reap millions from endorsements and appearances in television commercials and ads. Even his mother signed a contract to become an *advertising* spokesperson.

Talk about *logistics*! Can anyone really imagine what went on behind the scenes to prepare the facilities and to carry out the opening and closing ceremonies? Everything from participants to costumes to stages and props had to be synchronized and delivered to the right place at the right time. All in all, it was a remarkable marketing performance from event sponsors and advertisers to the gold-medal winners who are sure to become future spokespersons in their home countries or even around the globe.

Caleb was there to see the Team USA's thrilling basketball win over Spain, 118–107, to earn the gold medal. The Redeem Team had crushed the opposition before this closer win over Spain. Lebron James, Carmelo Anthony, Kobe Bryant, and the other American players locked arms and stepped onto the medal podium as one. Nearly all of the players took their medals off and draped them around Coach Mike Krzyzewski's neck.

* * * * * * *

Back in the U.S., Special Agent William Douglass was quoted in a Washington, D.C., newspaper: "She is still on the run. We will get her when she answers the inevitable call to return to her North Carolina roots. Justice will prevail."

That's a wrap!

* * * * * * *

"Many people trace the beginnings of modern sports marketing to one man—Mark McCormack. In 1960, Mark McCormack, a Cleveland lawyer, signed an agreement to represent Arnold Palmer. With this star client in hand, McCormack began the International Management Group, better known as IMG. Today IMG is a multinational sports marketing organization that employs over 2,000 people, has sales of over $1 billion, and represents some of the finest professional athletes in the world."

—Source: *SPORTS MARKETING, 2nd Ed.* By Matthew D. Shank. Pearson Education, Inc./Prentice Hall, 2002.

This sample contract is for educational purposes only and is not meant for unauthorized use in any manner. All sample documents are expressly intended for educational purposes. All player/agent contracts must be obtained from the NBPA or WNBPA.

STANDARD PLAYER AGENT CONTRACT

AGREEMENT made this _____ day of _____, 20___, by and between _____ (hereinafter the "Agent") and _____ (hereinafter the "Player"). In consideration of the mutual promises hereinafter contained, the parties hereto promise and agree as follows:

1. *General Principles*
This Agreement is entered into pursuant to and in accordance with the Women's National Basketball Players Association's ("WNBPA") Regulations Governing Player Agents (the "Regulations") as promulgated effective January 1, 2000, and as may be amended thereafter from time to time. The Agent represents that in advance of executing this Agreement, he has read and familiarized himself with the Regulations and has applied for and been certified as a Player Agent by the WNBPA.

This Agreement shall apply only with respect to the Agent's performance of services described below.

2. *Contract Services*
Commencing on the date of this Agreement, the Agent agrees to represent the Player—to the extent requested by the Player—in conducting individual compensation negotiations for the performance of the Player's services as a professional basketball player with the Women's National Basketball Association ("WNBA") and/or the Player's WNBA team as well as for the performance of the Player's services in connection with any team and/or WNBA Marketing Agreements.

[If the Agent will not be "conducting individual compensation negotiations," then insert in lieu of those quoted words: "in assisting, advising, or counseling the Player in connection with individual compensation negotiations."] After a contract with the WNBA and/or the Player's team is executed, the Agent agrees to continue to assist, advise, and counsel the Player in enforcing her rights under that contract.

In performing these services the Agent is the WNBPA's delegated representative and is acting in a fiduciary capacity on behalf of *both* the Player *and the WNBPA*. In no event shall the Agent have the authority to bind or commit the Player in any manner without the express prior consent of the Player and in no event shall the Agent execute a player contract on behalf of the Player.

3. *Compensation for Services*
The Player shall pay fees to the Agent for services performed pursuant to this Agreement in accordance with the following schedule:

(A) For compensation received by the Player which represents the Player's annual base salary, the parties have agreed that the agent shall receive a *maximum* fee of *five* percent (5%) of the compensation received by the Player for each such season. The *agreed upon fee must be indicated in the space below, and signed by both parties.*

The parties hereto have agreed to the following fee:

Player's Signature _____

Agent's Signature _____

(B) For compensation received by the player resulting from an agreement between the player and the WNBA and/or the Player's WNBA team for the player to perform additional non-playing services on behalf of the WNBA and/or the Player's WNBA team, the Agent shall receive a *maximum* fee of *five* percent (5%) of the compensation received by the Player for each such year of the agreement. *The agreed-upon fee must be indicated in the space below, and signed by both parties.*

The parties hereto have agreed to the following fee:

Player's Signature _____

Agent's Signature _____

In computing the allowable fee pursuant to paragraph 3(A) or (B) above, the term "base salary compensation" shall include base salary and signing bonuses; no other benefits provided in the player contract shall be taken into account in the computing of the fee—including, but not limited to, the fact that the contract guarantees compensation to the Player for one or more seasons, the value of a personal loan, an insurance policy, an automobile, or a residence, etc.

4. *Time for Receipt of Payment of Agent's Fees*
The Agent shall not be entitled to receive any fee for the performance of her/his services pursuant to this Agreement until the Player receives the compensation upon which the fee is based. Within fifteen (15) days of the Player's receipt of each compensation payment (as defined in paragraph 3 above) during the term of this Agreement or any extension, renewal, or modification thereof, the Player shall make her fee payment to the Agent in an amount computed in accordance with paragraph 3 above.

In no case shall the Agent accept, directly or indirectly, payment of her/his fee from the WNBA or Player's team. Further, the amount of the Agent's fee shall not be discussed with the WNBA or any WNBA team with whom the Agent is negotiating on behalf of the Player, nor shall the Agent or Player secure an agreement from the WNBA or Player's team respecting the amount of the Agent's fee.

5. *Expenses*
All expenses incurred by the Agent in the performance of the services hereunder shall be solely the Agent's responsibility and shall not be reimbursable by the Player, except that with respect to each player contract negotiated under this Agreement (irrespective of the number of playing seasons covered) the Player shall (a) reimburse the Agent for reasonable travel, living, and communications expenses (e.g., telephone, postage) actually incurred by the Agent up to Two Hundred and Fifty Dollars ($250); provided, however, if the expenses exceed Two Hundred and Fifty Dollars ($250), the Player shall be obligated to reimburse the Agent for the fees and expenses of any attorney, accountant, tax consultant, or vices to the Player, but only if such services are other than in connection with the negotiation and execution of such player contracts. The Player

shall promptly pay all expenses, fees, and costs for which she is obligated under this paragraph 5 upon receipt of an itemized statement thereof.

6. *Term*

The term of this Agreement shall begin on the date hereof and shall continue in effect until terminated by either party, at any time upon providing written notice of termination to the other party; and provided, further, that if the Agent's certification is suspended or revoked by the WNBPA or the Agent is otherwise prohibited by the WNBPA from performing the services she/he has agreed to perform herein, this Agreement automatically shall terminate effective as of the date of such suspension or termination.

Upon being terminated pursuant to either of the above provisions, the Agent may be entitled to be compensated for the reasonable value of the services she/he has already performed based upon the fee schedule contained in paragraph 3 above.

7. *Arbitration: Resolution of All Disputes Arising Out of This Agreement*

Any and all disputes between the Player and the Agent involving the meaning, interpretation, application, or enforcement of this Agreement or the obligations of the parties under this Agreement shall be resolved exclusively through the Arbitration procedure set forth in the WNBPA Regulations Governing Player Agents. As provided in those Regulations, if any arbitration hearing takes place, the WNBPA may participate and present, by testimony or otherwise, any evidence relevant to the dispute. Because of the uniquely internal nature of any such dispute that may arise under this Agreement, the Player and the Agent agree that the arbitrator's award shall constitute a final and binding resolution of the dispute and neither party will seek judicial review on any ground.

8. *Notices*

All notices hereunder shall be effective if sent by certified mail, postage prepaid.

If to the Agent:

If to the Player:

If to the WNBPA: Women's National Basketball Players Association
1700 Broadway, Suite 1400
New York, New York 10019

9. *Entire Agreement*
This Agreement sets forth the entire agreement between the parties.
This Agreement cannot be amended or changed orally and any written
amendments or changes shall be effective only to the extent that they are
consistent with the Standard Form Agreement approved by the WNBPA.

This Agreement replaces and supersedes any agreement between the
parties entered into at any time on or before the effective date of this
agreement.

10. *Governing Law*
This Agreement shall be construed, interpreted, and enforced according
to the laws of the State of New York.

11. *Filing*
This contract should be signed in triplicate. *An original* must be promptly
delivered by the Agent to the WNBPA Committee on Agent Regulations
within *three* (3) days of its execution; one (1) original must be promptly
delivered by the Agent to the Player; and one (1) original should be retained by the Agent.

EXAMINE THIS CONTRACT CAREFULLY BEFORE SIGNING IT
IN WITNESS WHEREOF, the parties hereto have hereunder signed
their names.

_____
PLAYER AGENT

_____
PLAYER
PARENT or GUARDIAN (if Player is under 21 Years of Age)

_____
Date of Birth

Some Forensic Marketing Information

Forensic marketing services consist of the professional assistance marketers provide to the litigation process at the federal and state court levels. These services may involve marketing, sales, advertising, quantitative analysis, investigative, and survey research skills, coupled with an understanding of the legal process in order to provide assistance for actual, pending, or potential legal or regulatory proceedings before a trier of the facts (jurors or judge) in connection with the resolution of a dispute between parties.

These services are most commonly associated with gathering evidence that will be presented in a civil or criminal court of law as part of a marketing dispute. He or she may need a working knowledge of the legal system and excellent communication skills to carry out expert testimony in the courtroom and to aid in other litigation-support engagements. Marketers may be retained as consultants, expert witnesses, or special masters to deal with such issues as advertising, packaging, sales forecasting, franchising, the Lanham Act, lost sales, consumer behavior, antitrust matters, deceptive trade practices, consumer protection, branding, claims, damages, and intellectual-property issues.

A marketer may be hired by an attorney to gather and interpret facts, prepare analyses, help the attorney interpret evidence, advise about issues and strategies involved in a legal matter, locate other marketers to act as consultants or expert witnesses, and help expert witnesses form their opinions. Marketers acting as consultants will not be asked to testify in a judicial or regulatory proceeding, and their work usually will be protected from disclosure by the attorney work-product privilege.

A marketer may be retained by an attorney or court as an expert witness to testify in a judicial or administrative proceeding. Marketers retained as expert witnesses will be expected to give their opinion in a judicial or administrative proceeding and can expect their work for a lawyer or court to be available to others involved in the litigation.

Marketers sometimes are appointed by a court as a master to assist the court in some matter (e.g., to determine certain facts or compute damages). They also may be appointed to act as the court's representative (referred to as a *special master*) in a particular transaction.

The powers and duties of masters and special masters depend on the terms of the order making their appointment and applicable court rules. The compensation paid to a master or special master is set by the court and paid by the parties or out of any fund or subject matter of litigation.

The five major phases of litigation are:

- Pleadings
- Discovery
- Trial
- Outcome
- Possible appeal

Much of the work for forensic marketers occurs in the discovery stage. The pleadings consist of:

- Complaint—Plaintiff files
- Service of process—Served on defendant
- Answer—Defendant must admit or deny allegations
- Demurrer—No cause of action exists
- Possible cross-complaint—Defendant files

An attorney's job is ultimately to avoid trial and the resulting lost time and expenses. Thus, the goal of a forensic marketer is to help the attorney to avoid the cost and uncertainty of a trial.

There are many ways for an expert witness to be excluded from the courtroom. Both simple and complex *Daubert* and *Frye* challenges are becoming frequent as tort costs climb. Daubert on the web indicates that marketing experts are rejected about 66 percent of the time. Marketers must take the qualification process seriously in order to avoid adversely affecting clients and their personal reputation. Lack of independence, conflicts of interest, side-taking, ghostwriting, and result-oriented work are some of the situations to avoid.

In federal courts and many state courts, an expert witness must prepare a written report. Due to the practice of electronically prepared draft reports, these drafts are often not recorded on paper. Not retaining draft copies is quite common among litigation experts and consultants. Often if a consultant's report is provided to the expert, these reports are requested from opposing counsel.

Is an expert required to save all drafts? Saving a new version of every keystroke is extremely burdensome. However, since draft reports provide a glimpse into an expert's understanding of a dispute, opposing counsel want these draft reports in order to cross-examine the expert with respect to the input provided by counsel and the evolution of the final opinion. Saving drafts is no longer required in federal courts, but may be required in state courts.

Another Take on Forensic Marketing

"Forensic" is from Latin, meaning "forum" or "public." In business or commerce, forensic things are generally those items that relate to a legal forum or court. In general, "forensic" refers to items that are used in debate or argument.

The Forensic Science Society of the UK describes forensic science as the application of science to law, and the American Academy of Forensic Sciences defines forensic science as science used in public, in a court, or in the justice system.

In 1995, Gavin Barrett asserted that forensic marketing is a mnemonic designed to focus marketers on a more methodical, rational, or scientific process in developing the briefing when dealing with a professional supplier. His mnemonic is designed to "ensure that sufficient rigour goes into the briefing." A mnemonic is a technology or system of improving the memory by the use of certain formulas. In general, his forensic marketing approach is a communication strategy.

Barrett has eight steps in his communication strategy:

- Focus on the facts
- Observation
- Research
- Evaluation
- Negative indicators
- Strategy compliance
- Inertial barriers/factors
- Check and re-check

His approach is an attempt to move marketing more to being a science rather than an art. He provides this diagram to demonstrate the interaction between the stakeholders and the points where forensic approaches will make the difference between an ordinary solution and an excellent solution:

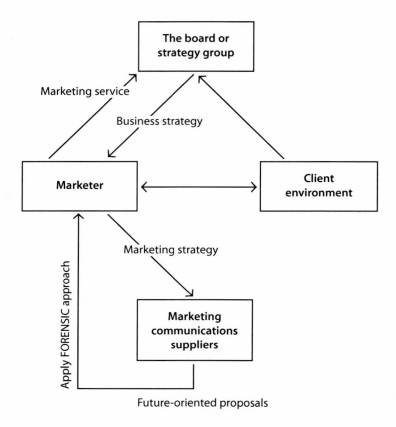

Barrett's definition of forensic has little relationship to the general concept of forensic, except that he at least attempts to get the marketer to gather evidence before making marketing decisions.

NCAA Licensing Agreement

License Agreement. A license agreement with the NCAA grants a manufacturer the right to use certain NCAA-related designations, including each year's championship logos, on specific articles of merchandise pursuant to conditions and restrictions set forth in the agreement. The agreement also grants the right to use NCAA trademarks and logos in advertising, promotion, and merchandising of these articles subject to prior approval by the NCAA.

A license agreement does not indicate the endorsement of the NCAA for a product. The NCAA does not endorse products covered in license agreements; the NCAA only permits use of its registered trademarks for products that have met strict standards of excellence and quality, and that enhance the image of the NCAA.

"Officially Licensed Product." By the terms of a license agreement, a product is "officially licensed" by the NCAA, and the NCAA urges its licensees to advertise this association.

A licensee can communicate its association with the NCAA through advertising, packaging, and promotional copy for licensed products. It may state that the merchandise is an "Officially Licensed Product of the NCAA." Products under the license must bear an approved hangtag or label stating that the product is licensed.

Protection of NCAA Registered Marks. The NCAA's marks are protected under both federal and state statutory and common-law principles, which enables the NCAA to protect against the unauthorized and/or counterfeit use of its marks by third parties.

Lanham Act. Under the Lanham Act (15 U.S.C. 1114), the unauthorized production, distribution, sale, offering for sale, or advertising of any goods or services displaying a registered mark of the NCAA may also obtain an ex parte seizure order from the court authorizing the seizure of goods displaying a counterfeit mark, the means used in the production of such goods, and any records documenting the manufacture, sale, or receipt of items as a result of the counterfeit use.

Judicial Procedures. The NCAA also utilizes state counterfeiting statutes, which provide criminal remedies against any individual or company involved in the production, distribution, sale, or offering for sale of any infringing or counterfeit goods bearing the NCAA's marks.

NCAA Trademarks and Logos. All rights to the identifying marks and symbols of the NCAA are reserved. No one may reproduce or copy them except with the permission of the NCAA and never endorse either directly or indirectly a product, service, or commercial venture without a written license. Vigorous legal action will be taken against violators.

These trademarks may NOT be used to refer to other championships (i.e., the semifinals of any championship other than Division I Men's and Women's basketball may not be referred to as "The Final Four," "final four" or "Final Four").

Local Organizing Committee Assistance.
The host institution/conference and/or local organizing committee (LOC) can be of significant assistance to the NCAA in its efforts to protect its marks. The NCAA may ask the LOC to:

1. Provide the names and addresses of retail establishments in the area of the championship and, in particular, any contact with a downtown merchants association.

2. Provide access to local media, print and electronic, for the national office staff to provide NCAA licensing guidelines and enforcement proceedings for championships.

3. Provide the NCAA with city, county, and state administrative and law enforcement personnel for purposes of organizing a trademark-enforcement effort.

4. Present the NCAA to local media to discuss the trademark-enforcement effort. This should be an ongoing dialogue between media and the NCAA staff during the 90 days before the championship and during the championship competition.

5. Present the NCAA to the chamber of commerce, downtown merchants association, and/or other comparable organizations regarding this enforcement activity.

6. Disseminate information regarding NCAA registrations and names and contacts of NCAA licensees to merchants.

7. Monitor the marketplace for infringements on merchandise or in advertising or promotion and forward information to the NCAA staff.

PANEL 16

How To Increase An Audience

The following list is a sample of what can be done to draw customers to events:

- Pre-event entertainment
- Youth games at half-time
- Special group promotions (e.g., Boy Scouts, Girl Scouts, mother and son outing, father and daughter outing)
- Special rates for groups (e.g., senior citizens, ladies' night, honor students, high-school band members and families)
- Giveaways (e.g., miniature baseball bats, baseball caps, miniature basketballs, miniature footballs, t-shirts, pins)
- Scheduling doubleheaders
- Reduced ticket fees
- Shoot-out contests at halftime
- Event buses
- Special days (e.g., hometown day, specific town day, specific school day)
- Student athletes visiting schools as role models
- Clip-out coupons
- Radio giveaways to listeners (e.g., tickets)
- Use of pep band at events
- Team color night (i.e., offer half-price admission to anyone dressed in team colors)
- Face-painting contest (i.e., encourage students to come early and face-paint each other in an area separate from the event area, judge the painting jobs, and provide prizes to the winners at halftime)

—Source: Sawyer, T.H., & Smith R. (1999). *The management of clubs, recreation, and sport: Concepts and applications.* Champaign: Sagamore Publishing, 137.

Why Sport Teams Lose Fans

There are a number of reasons why sports teams lose fans. Sports managers need to be aware of these reasons so that strategies can be developed to eliminate them. The reasons include:

- Fans did not feel as though they were important
- Cost outweighs enjoyment
- Dirty facilities
- Boring food service
- Poor seating
- Inconvenient parking
- No luxury seating
- No picnic areas
- No non-smoking areas
- No non-drinking areas
- No place to change young children's diapers
- No day-care facilities
- No playground for young children
- Too-costly souvenirs
- No other entertainment but the game itself
- Team is not exciting
- Team fails to win consistently
- No opportunities to meet the players

—Source: Sawyer, T.H., & Smith R. (1999). *The management of clubs, recreation, and sport: Concepts and applications.* Champaign: Sagamore Publishing, 137.

Cooking the Books—Symbol Technologies

- From 1998 through February 2003, Symbol used a so-called "Tango sheet" process through which fraudulent "topside" accounting entries were made to reserves and other items to conform the unadjusted quarterly results to management's projections.

- Fabrication and misuse of restructuring merger and other non-recurring charges to artificially reduce operating expenses, create "cookie jar" reserves (overstating inventory write-offs) and further manage earnings.

- Channel stuffing and other revenue recognition schemes, involving both product sales and customer services; stuffed the channel by granting resellers return rights and contingent payment terms in side agreements.

- Manipulation of inventory levels and accounts receivable data to conceal the adverse side effects of the revenue recognition schemes.

- Warehouse arrangement with a large foreign distributor that served as a vehicle for improperly recognizing several millions of dollars.

- Directed employees to refrain from scanning new components or returned goods into the automated accounting system.

- Backdated (cherry picked) stock option exercise dates.

- When "days sales outstanding' because too large because of fraudulent revenue recognition, reclassified past due trade accounts receivable into notes receivables. A growing DSO figure is often a sign that receivables are impaired due to channel stuffing, etc.

- Deferred $3.5 million of FICA insurance costs to a later year.

- Recognized revenue that was processed in one quarter, but shipped the next quarter.

A Framework for Analyzing the External Environment

1. Competition
   a. Our brand, product, generic, and total budget competitors
   b. Their characteristics: size, growth, profitability, strategies, and target markets
   c. Their key strengths and weaknesses
   d. Potential responses to our marketing efforts

2. Economic Growth and Stability
   a. Trends
   b. Customer outlook: optimistic or pessimistic
   c. Buying power in the target market

3. Political Trends
   a. Changes in political landscape
   b. Relations with legislative bodies

4. Legal and Regulatory Issues
   a. Proposed regulations: local, national, and international
   b. Recent court decisions that may affect our marketing activities
   c. Global trade agreements impact

5. Technological Advancements
   a. Impact of changing technology on our customers
   b. What changes in technology will affect the way we do business?
   c. Do technological changes threaten to make our products obsolete?

6. Sociocultural Trends
   a. Changes in demographics and values that may impact our business
   b. Challenges of diversity and inclusion
   c. General attitude of the public toward our company
   d. Ethical or social issues

—Source: O. C. Ferrell and M. D. Hartline Collection, *Marketing Data Information*. Thomson Learning, 2008, 99–106.

NASCAR Internet Microsites

From its humble beginning in the South with the souped-up autos of moonshiners outrunning authorities, NASCAR racing may be the number-one spectator sport in the U.S. today, with as many as 75 million fans. NASCAR estimates that there are roughly 30 million avid fans who consume 8 hours a week of NASCAR media. These fans spend between $1.5 to $2 billion on NASCAR-related merchandise, with at least 200 licensees selling clothes, souvenirs, die-cast cars, and other items. Females make up about 40 percent of the fan base.

Although television is still important, NASCAR and sponsors are accelerating efforts to reach these fans on the Internet. Advertising featuring drivers and their cars are proliferating on websites, digital videos, recorders, satellite TV and radio, video-game consoles, and mobile devices. NASCAR.com attracts almost 4 million unique visitors each month.

Since the rabid fans are high-tech, Sprint is sponsoring a "Speed is Beautiful" campaign on sprint.com/speed. Computer users will be able to download wallpaper, send customized email messages to friends, and design their own "burnouts." A NASCAR/ Sprint mobile application for cell phones will provide data such as lap times, speeds, and point standings. There will be in-car driver communication for all 43 cars entered in the Daytona 500, which takes place on February 17, 2008. Sponsors have special websites called microsites devoted to NASCAR, which are separate from their mainstream websites. Fans will often surf the web while they are watching the race. There microsites allow the sponsor to engage the fans in blogging, podcasting, and offering video clips.

Office Depot's online advertising campaign has a marriage-proposal theme, created by teaming up with the romance-book publisher Harlequin. The contest opens February 14, 2008, and the winner will have his or her proposal for marriage (or renewal of vows) featured on the No. 99 Ford Fusion, which is sponsored by Office Depot and driven by Carl Edwards.

Best Western International has a microsite devoted to NASCAR. Their promotion has an April Fool's day theme whereby consumers can upload funny photographs of family members and others to a section of their

Best Western website. The photo of the winner will appear on the Best Western Toyota Camry driven by David Reutimann at the NASCAR race in Phoenix on April 11, 2008.

—Source: Stuart Elliott, "Marketers Are Putting NASCAR on Different Kinds of Circuits," *New York Times*, February 15, 2008, p. C-5.